THE AMERICAN GLADIATORS

TAFT VERSUS REMUS

by

ALBERT ROSENBERG
CINDY ARMSTRONG

Aimwell Press

ISBN 0-9648784-0-2

Library of Congress Catalog Card Number 95-80892

Manufactured in the United States of America

For Family and Friends

CONTENTS

ACKNOWLEDGEMENTS

Since we regrettably failed to keep an accurate record of those who helped us during our research, we offer them our thanks and an apology. Following is a list of the institutions to which we are indebted: Library of Congress; Newberry Library; University of Cincinnati Library; University of Chicago Library; University of Redlands Library; University of California at Los Angles Library; University of California at Riverside Library; Redlands, California, Public Library; Hemet, California, Public Library; St. Louis, Missouri, Public Library; Cincinnati, Ohio, Law Library; Department of Labor; Justice Department; National Archives (Washington D.C. and Chicago, Illinois); Criminal Courts, Chicago, Illinois; Cincinnati Historical Society; Chicago Historical Society.

Albert Rosenberg, Hemet, California
Cindy Armstrong, London, U.K.

Central Police Station, Cincinnati, Ohio, the morning of October 6, 1927:

A man entered the police station and calmly stated:"I want to give myself up. I've shot my wife."

****

The following is the true story of the two Americans involved in the ensuing trial. A trial that was front page news across the nation for the next three months. To accommodate the crowd of reporters a room adjoining the trial court room was set aside and seven Western Union wires leading directly to the court room were installed, along with the special wires of the news services. An estimated 50,000 words a day were sent out by the newspapermen. The defendant, George Remus, former "King of the Bootleggers", was the son of a working class German immigrant. The Prosecuting Attorney, Charles P. Taft the 2nd, was the son of the only man to serve the country as both President and Chief Justice of the Supreme Court. They would face one another on November 14th in an unprecedented legal battle that for the former could mean life or death, for the latter national prominence with definite White House possibilities or a much less exalted career in public service.

BOOK ONE

THE GLADIATORS

The "gladiatorial combats" of big criminal trials, notably the Remus trial in Cincinnati, were assailed by Professor Felix Frankfurter. "The problem of crime," said Dr. Frankfurter, "is dealt with in America too much from the dramatic standpoint. Dramatic presentation of evidence in criminal crimes," he said, "is inimical to thought." He suggested that the trial of criminal cases should have the "the austerity of the operating room" and not the savor of "gladiatorial combats."

Speech at the 26th conference of the New Jersey State Conference of Social Work. New York *Times* (Dec. 5, 1927)

"This defendant started in life at $5 a month, and he may have contaminated his neighbors. I would gladly lay down my life today for one drop of the blood which flows in the veins of your prosecutor, son of that noble statesman, Chief Justice of the United States, and a former President, but ladies and men of the jury, we could not all be born with a golden spoon in our mouths like Charles P. Taft the Second."

George Remus (Closing argument, December 18, 1927)

"Remus has corrupted more young men than any other person in this country, and apart from being a law violator, and an undesirable alien, has become a menace and a contaminator of the morals of the communities in which he has resided, not only because of the examples which his lawlessness has established, but because of his speciality in openly flaunting the laws of this country, and in seeking to undermine and imperil the prestige of the courts and its enforcement officers by intimidating, influencing and corrupting public officials and court attaches."

Letter to Department of Labor, Immigration Services--name blocked out pursuant to 5 U.S.C. 552 (b) (7) (C) of the Freedom of Information Act.

GEORGE REMUS: NAPOLEON OF THE CHICAGO BAR

George Remus was born on November 13, 1876, in the small German village of Friedeberg, near Berlin. His father, Franz Remus, an only child, was orphaned when only a few weeks old, when his parents died in a cholera epidemic. Franz and Amelia Karg raised the infant orphan, and in time he became an apprentice in their woolen mill. Franz Remus later married the Karg's daughter Marie. George was the fourth child born to Franz and Marie Remus. He was the first to survive infancy. When George was four years old, his family, and many members of the Karg family, joined the steady flow of immigrants from Germany to the United States of America, the land of freedom and opportunity. Failing to obtain passage from Hamburg to New York on an ocean liner, they had to endure a rough passage with sub standard accomodations on the S.S. *Irthington*, a freight steamer. They first settled in Milwaukee, where George attended kindergarten; but before long they moved to a city with a large German population: "The Metropolis of the West," the most American of American cities, Chicago.

Chicago in the 1880's was a rapidly growing city still in the process of rebuilding after the disastrous fire of 1871. In Chicago, big was best, and so the new buildings rose higher and sprawled out further. As the city grew, so did its industrial base, creating a need for skilled and unskilled labor. This availability of jobs and the prospect of a better life attracted more and more immigrants to the city. By the time Frank Remus and his family settled there, immigrants constituted one third of the entire population of the city, and the majority of them were of German descent.

As the flow of immigrants continued, the city became more cosmopolitan and more segregated. Chicago may have been the epitome of the American dream, but it fell short of realizing its potential as a "melting pot." The different ethnic groups in Chicago settled in separate areas and set up essentially segregated infrastructures. Early in the history of the city, a system of private benefaction, rather than government bureaucracy, was instituted. The immigrants established their own schools, churches and social services in separate areas of the city. The majority of the German immigrants settled in the north end of the city, and by the end of the century they had set up a virtually self sufficient community. They had their own newspapers, schools, libraries, theaters, social clubs and beer gardens. The dynamic Chicago economy drew thousands of new inhabitants each year. Despite an exconomic depression and crippling strikes, Chicago still attracted people seeking to improve their lot in life by hard work.

George Remus' family lived in the predominately German North Side, and his father worked as a lumber scorer, a day laborer, " the most he ever earned was $11 a week". George, an energetic young boy who loved reading, attended a German Lutheran school from the age of six and proved himself an able student. In 1890 his father, suffering from articular rheumatism, was no longer able to work. So at the age of fourteen George left school and got a job to help support his parents, his brother and his three sisters.

George worked as a clerk in his uncle's drug store for $8.00 a week, and in his spare time he studied towards a degree at the Chicago College of Pharmacology. He never graduated. He failed one of his exams and later claimed that this was the result his leading a class walkout. Whatever the reason, he never returned to the school. However, this did not deter him. In 1895 he was licensed to practice pharmacology, and for $6,000 he bought Schroeder's Drug Store on the corner of Milwaukee and Chicago Avenues, which his uncle had sold previously. To own the property, he gave his age as twenty one. He was only nineteen.

Remus was hard working and ambitious. He took courses in opthalmology and otology at the Masonic Temple and graduated from the Mc Fatrick School of Otology, and allegedly praticed limited medicine in his community. By the age of twenty one, George Remus was so succesful that he purchased a second drug store, bought the house that his family was renting, and purchased a farm in Wisconsin. He was an independent, jovial young man who took great care and pride in his personal appearance. He enjoyed socializing, and was pleased when he was invited to join the Blue Lodge of the Masons. Remus also enjoyed physical activity, especially swimming. He was a member of the water polo team at the Illinois Athletics club and sometimes competed in the marathon swimming events held on the Mississippi River. He was fond of reading good books and eating good food, but he never touched alcohol or tobacco.

Remus' financial standing, sense of humor and self confidence made him a popular young man, and it was not long before he was courting a young woman, Lillian Hansen, a customer at one of his drug stores. They were married in 1895, when Remus was twenty two; nine years later Mrs. Remus gave birth to a daughter, Romola, their only child.

Still eager to better himself, Remus started studying law, taking night classes at the Illinois School of Law.. The course normally took three years to complete, but he managed to finish it under two; and in 1904 the twenty-four year old George Remus was admitted to the Illinois Bar. Remus' practice started small, but in time he became known as a competent criminal and labor union lawyer, and clients flocked to his office in the Chicago loop. His flamboyant manner and his dramatic presentations were effective in the courtroom, but they were objectionable to some of his colleagues, who referred to him as "the weeping, crying Remus." Whatever his methods, he was a very successful lawyer. In 1901 he represented eighteen defendants in murder cases.

In one sensational murder trial Remus defended a man accused of poisoning his wife. The evidence was stacked against the defendant, and his conviction seemed certain until Remus made his final statement to the jury. While discussing various aspects of the case, Remus calmly picked up the bottle containing the remainder of the poison the defendant had given to his wife, and after making sure that the jurors saw the black skull and cross bones on the label, he declared: "There has been a lot of talk about poison in this case, but it is a lot of piffle. Look." Then he lifted the bottle to his lips and drank the rest of its contents. He calmly continued his speech as the astonished jurors expected him to collapse and die at any moment. What they didn't know was that, having studied pharmacology, Remus knew the antidote for the poison and had taken a dose of it just before entering the courtroom. It took the amazed jury only 15 minutes to bring in a verdict of not guilty. .

In 1914, Remus once again employed an unusual strategy in defending an accused murderer. On the 16th of October, 1913, employees of a Chicago hotel discovered William Cheney Ellis and his wife lying entwined in a pool of blood. Mrs. Ellis had been shot four times, and her throat was cut. She was dead. Mr. Ellis had also been shot and had deep cuts on his neck and wrists. However, he was alive, although barely conscious. Ellis told the doctor who attended to him that he and his wife had made a suicide pact. His wife had shot herself and then slashed her own throat. Ellis had attempted to follow suit. Later, at the coroner's inquest, he changed his story and stated, "I want to say that I shot my wife. I suppose that my mind must have been affected."

Remus, using the writings of Dr. R. von Kraft-Ebing, Professor of Psychiatry at the University of Vienna, as the basis for the defense, claimed that Ellis was not guilty becuase he was suffering from "transitory insanity."

He informed the jury: "We will prove that Mrs. Ellis was infatuated with a man by the name of Caldwell, who lives in Canada. She had confessed to Ellis her love for this man. She had told Ellis that she had only one desire and that was to obtain a divorce from him and marry Caldwell. This produced a 'brainstorm' or transitory insanity, in Ellis." Remus went on to define transitory insanity as "a condition in which a man may commit an act and then fall asleep, and when he wakes up he will have no knowledge of what he has done, but will be perfectly sane. This is the influence under which Mr. Ellis killed his wife." Therefore, Remus argued, Ellis was not responsible for his actions at the time.

During the trial, the defense called prominent residents of Cincinnati to testify that Ellis had been insane for some time before the tragedy. The prosecution brought into evidence letters that Ellis had written prior to the killing which clearly incriminated him. He had written to his brother-in-law: "May God forgive me for what I am about to do. I love Elanor and the children more than life, but cannot live withour her love. Destroy this and blame everything on business reverses."

Ellis was on trial for murder, and the prosecution asked for the death sentence. The evidence against Ellis was overwhelming. Moreover, the father of the slain woman arose in the crowded courtroom and shouted at Ellis: "I'll kill you! I'll kill you! I'll kill you!" and the mother insisted that her daughter "was a good woman. She was the victim of a whisky-crazed man." Ellis' chances of escaping the death penalty seeemed slim. After deliberating for three and a half hours and taking ten ballots, the jury found Ellis guilty; however, because four men believed he was insane and would not vote for the death penalty or even for a twenty five year sentence, a compromise verdict was reached, and Ellis was sentenced to only fifteen years in prison, the minimum he could receive without being acquitted. The verdict was hailed as a victory for the defense; Ellis escaped from the death penalty and served only seven years and three months. Remus never forgot the Ellis case.

Although Remus was a very successful lawyer, he was not always well liked. His flamboyant and often unorthodox histrionics in the courtroom outraged some of his conservative colleagues. Several times Remus appeared before the Chicago Bar Association's ethics committee, but he managed to escape without being disbarred. Despite his problems with his colleagues,

Remus prospered. By 1920 he was reputed to be earning $50,000 a year and was often called the "Napoleon of the Chicago bar."[1]*

Although he had an impressive record regarding acquittals and reduced sentences gained for his clients, he did see a few go to the gallows, and this motivated him to become an active member in the Anti-Capital Punishment Society. Through this society, and through his work with the labor unions, Remus made the acquaintance of Clarence Darrow. Occasionally Remus and Darrow would represent the same labor union, with Remus handling the local affairs and Darrow the national concerns.

Remus' popularity as a lawyer and his involvement in community affairs encouraged him to run for political office. After serving as district leader for the Republican party for a few years, he became a candidate for alderman in the 24th ward. However, his hopes for a political career were dashed when he failed to be elected. Remus' successes in court room battles also led to some attractive offers of positions in the Prosecutor"s office, but he turned them down. Favoring the underdog, he chose to remain a defense lawyer.

Remus was more successful as a lawyer than as a husband. In March, 1915, his wife sued for a divorce on grounds of cruelty, accusing him of making her life a misery with his obscene and violent language, his physical abuse and threats against her life. A month later she changed her mind and withdrew her petition.

In February, 1919, Remus' name became linked with that of a young divorcee from Evanston. A plumber charged Remus with assault after being forcibly ejected from the residence of Imogene Holmes. Remus was supposedly visiting friends in the apartment above that of Mrs. Holmes, an attractive divorcee who was employed in his office. However, it was later established that he had been with her at the time. Mrs. Remus had suspected her husband of having an affair for the past five years, and this report confirmed her suspicions. She confronted Imogene, who admitted her guilt and offered to end the affair. However, Mrs. Remus declined her offer; this

---

[1]Typical prices in the 1920's: 5 passenger Buick sedan-$2095; First class postage-2 cents; 3 bedroom house-$4,500; Florsheim shoes-$10; Thanksgiving dinner-$1.50; Campbell soups 12 cents a can; Suite at hotel with private bath-$4; 10 pounds of sugar-50 cents; Typists usually started at $10 a week; Ex-President William H. Taft received $6,000 a year as a professor at Yale University; Federal Judge Keesahw Mountain Landis received $7,500 a year.

was the chance to get rid of the man who she claimed "hasn't supported, me to speak of for five years."

Later that month she re-instituted divorce proceedings citing the grounds of adultery as well as cruelty. She claimed that over the last five years Remus had given her not even $20 a week for her and her daughter to live on,preferring to spend all his money "on that Holmes woman." She testified that she had first found out about his affair in 1916 and that she had questioned him about it, but he vehemently denied everything and threw her out of his office. As to Remus' character, she stated that "he doesn't drink but he..he's just sporty." Remus argued his own case, but he still ended up paying a lump sum of $50,000 to his wife and $30,000 to his daughter, Romola, as well as $25 a week alimony.

REMUS: KING OF THE BOOTLEGGERS

The 18th Amendment to the Constitution:

After one year from the ratification of this article the manufacture, sale, or transportation of intoxicating liquors within, the importation thereof into, or the exportation thereof for beverage purposes is hereby prohibited.

"A national prohibition amendment to the Federal Constitution will be adopted against the views and practice of a majority of the people in many of the large cities and in one-fourth or less of the States.

The business of manufacturing alcohol, liquor and beer will go out of the hands of the law-abiding members of the community, and will be transferred to the quasi-criminal class."

William Howard Taft (Quoted in the report of the Wickersham Commission-Vol V, p. 201.}

"No serious difficulty is expected in the enforcement of the law."

John F. Kramer, Prohibition Commissioner (Chicago Tribune January 16, 1920}

Chicago, January 16, 1920:

Hicks' Buffet on Madison Avenue displayed in its front window a flower bedecked coffin containing a large bottle of whiskey. The inscription read: "John Barleycorn: Born Almost with the first man--Died Jan. 16, 1920."

The Green Mill, Marigold Room, Sheridan Inn, and Rainbow, famous German beer gardens, were closed.

Alderman Michael Kenna, known as "Hinkey Dink," owned two bars. One was closed; the other was converted to a candy store.

The Celtic bar in the Sherman House was deserted.

Righemer's was closed and was being converted to a drug store.

Stillson's, a hangout for newspapermen, was opening as a coffee shop.

Moran's on Randolph Street was transformed into a lunch room.

Prohibition had come to Chicago.

As expected, opposition surfaced almost immediately. A few hours after the dry law went into effect, a gang of armed, masked men overpowered the guards protecting freight cars loaded with whiskey and made off with whiskey "for medicinal purposes" valued at about $100,000. The war had started.

The Treasury Department and The Department of Justice were jointly involved in enforcing the 18th Amendment. Congress appointed only 1,500 agents and appropriated only two million dollars for enforcement. The agents were political appointees paid about $35 a week. Assistant Attorney General Mabel Willebrant admitted that "The force of prohibition agents created under the Volstead Act was untrained, incompetent, and sometimes dishonest." She admitted "that there were scores of prohibition agents no more to be trusted with a commission to enforce the laws of the United States and to carry a gun than the notorious bandit Jesse James."

People could still legally purchase liquor and store it in their own homes. Only those who sold the liquor were breaking the law. Enforcement of the new amendment was provided for by the Volstead Act, a 73 section long act with a plethora of legal technicalities. It prohibited the manufacture, sale, barter, transport, import, export, delivery and illegal possession of intoxicating beverages. Intoxicating was defined as one half of one percent of alcohol by volume. There were exceptions: alcohol for industrial, medicinal and religious purposes was allowed, and permits were issued which made the possession of such liquor legal.

With the new laws came new criminals, and Remus found himself frequently defending small time bootleggers. By mid-June the Federal Courts were swamped by prohibition cases with a backlog of some six hundred pending trials. Remus was amazed by how easily men with no brains were able to succeed in the liquor business, and he believed that with his intelligence and knowledge of the law he could make a fortune.

So Remus carefully studied the Volstead Act and discovered loopholes concerning the sale of medicinal whiskey through government bonded warehouses. He then did some research and discovered that almost 80 percent of the bonded whiskey in the United States was situated within 300 miles of Cincinnati, despite the fact that Ohio was the operational center of the Anti-Saloon League. He also learned that some of the owners of these distilleries were unaware of, or unwilling to take advantage of, the potential market for their medicinal whiskey, and therefore these distilleries could be bought at bargain prices.

Remus was financially secure, but he foresaw the opportunity to become very wealthy and to move up on the social ladder. He also thought that bootlegging could offer him a new and exciting challenge in life. "I went into it mostly for the thrill and excitement," he later admitted. He did not drink, but he had no moral aversion towards the consumption of alcohol. Moreover, he believed that the new laws were unconstitutional, maintaing that the customers were just as culpable as the bootleggers. He was also aware of the relatively slight penalties for violationrs of the Volstead Act, the maximum sentence being two years in a federal penitentiary. However, he lacked experience in the bootlegging business and he could use some additional financing, so he formed a partnership with John Marcus and another New York gangster, men who for years had run liquor from Mexico into the dry southern states in the pre-national prohibition days. So in late 1919, Remus, motivated by an insatiable desire for wealth and publicity, closed up his law office and moved to Cincinnati.

Remus arrived in Cincinnati with about $100,000 and a plan. He invested $10,000 in the purchase of his first distillery with his partners, whom he referred to simply as "the two Jews." The rest he deposited in the Lincoln National Bank. By the end of the following year he owned more than a dozen distilleries and warehouses in five states. Since he no longer needed his partners' bootlegging expertise, and he feared they would double-cross him, he bought them out, paying them $900,000 each and seeing to it personally that they boarded a train for New York.

Because of the nature of his business, Remus did not have an accurate bookkeeping system, but it is estimated that within a five year period he banked over five million dollars. In one eighteen month period his deposits averaged $30,000 a day, and one year he deposited over $2,800,000 in the Lincoln National Bank. He also had accounts at other banks with fictitous names such as George Ryerson or George Reiner. He once boasted to the Vice President of the Lincoln National, Mr. W.C. Wachs, that "If I want to I can put $2,000,000 in this bank tomorrow."

When Remus moved from Chicago to Cincinnati in 1919, he was accompanied by Imogene Holmes and Ruth, her daughter from a previous marriage. George and Imogene married on June 25th in Newport, Kentucky. They resided for a while in a hotel in Cincinnati. Remus spent most of his time travelling to his various distilleries or conducting business from his office in a downtown Cincinnati building locaterd on the corner of Pearl and Race streets, which he purchased and named the Remus Building.

When he wasn't working he usually could be found at a local athletics club where he swam and worked out. A short man with a powerful build, he was always conscious of his appearance and dressed in expensive black or gray suits. His balding head distressed him, and he tended to wear a hat in the company of strangers. He was known to be rich and socially ambitious. He sought to socialize with prominent Cincinnati families such as the Tafts, Hollisters, and Seasongoods. To do this, he felt he needed an majestic estate where he could entertain guests he wished to impress.

So in December, 1921, he purchased a mansion that had once been the home of the Lackman family, famous Cincinnati brewers. Situated on the corner of Hermosa Avenue and 8th Street in Cincinnati's exclusive Price Hill neighborhood, this gray stone 20 room palatial mansion stood in the grounds of a ten acre estate surrounded by a wrought-iron fence and guarded at either side of the entrance by two stone lions which cost a reported $4,000 each. The grounds were planted with thirty three different varieties of trees and shrubs, many of them rare and exotic species. $100,000 worth of marble statuary and ornaments completed the landscaping.

Remus also disregarded cost in furnishing the inside of the house. Oriental rugs valued at over $50,000 were scattered on the floors, and marble statuary and ornaments were prominently displayed. Claiming that he loved the fine and beautiful things of life, Remus bought entire collections of rare books and manuscripts. He even owned an autograph of George Washington for which he reputedly paid $3,800. Remus even bought a gold leaf plated piano for Imogene's daughter, Ruth, whom he had adopted. Ruth was studying at the Cincinnati Conservatory of Music and was known for the piano which she alone was allowed to touch and for the expensive trinkets which she was wont to bestow on friends and fellow students.

The Remus' loved to entertain, and they frequently hosted elaborate dinner parties. At these parties guests often found a 100 dollar bill under their plates. Naturally, there was always plenty of liquor at these parties, but smoking was restricted to the grounds of the house or the smoking room inside. Remus was nauseated by the smell of smoke.

On New Years Eve 1921, George and Imogene Remus invited some 200 guests to a party featuring the dedication of their new 60 by 20 foot indoor swimming pool, recently finished at a cost of $100,000. Made of marble with mosaic inlays resembling a Roman bath, the swimming pool was the center piece of the evening's entertainment.

The front of the house was decked with cut flowers from door to attic. The Remus' guests reclined on Roman style lounges while being served vintage champagne and rare wines by glamorous chorus girls dressed in white tights. Musicians, dancers and aquatic performers brought from Chicago provided the entertainment. One enthusiastic guest likened the party to a page from "The Arabian Nights."

Remus made an eloquent speech dedicating the pool and then dove into the pool fully clothed. At one end of a marble columned room an orchestra played popular tunes. While some of his guests danced to the strains of "Avalon," "My Man," and "The Shiek of Araby," Remus sat in his library with a bowl of ice cream reading a biography of Abraham Lincoln. Imogene Remus, who had once wowed a courtroom by displaying her ankles, was dressed in a white one piece bathing suit that was extremely daring for the time. Towards the end of the evening she displayed her prowess and figure on the diving board, executing various dives accompanied by the four hired "nymphs."

The climax of the evening came with the presentation of gifts to the guests. The men were presented with $25,000 worth of jewelry which Remus obtained by purchasing the entire inventory of a local jeweler. Then the women were astonished and delighted as each was presented with a small card which entitled the bearer to a brand new Pontiac automobile! The estimated cost of this event was well into five digit figures. Remus felt that such a grand party was undoubtedly newsworthy. At Christmas he had given gold watches to fourteen members of the local press, and he was confident that the society editors of the Cincinnati newspapers whom he had invited would attend. However, they declined his invitation, and there was no mention of the party in the next day's papers.

Remus' bootlegging business was established around the sale of legal, government bonded whiskey. In June, 1920, there were 53,406,552 gallons of taxable distilled spirits stored in privately owned bonded warehouses. The amount of whiskey in a warehouse was attested to by a corresponding number of certificates. No whiskey could be added to the supply without the release of a corresponding number of government issued certificates, and no whiskey could be removed without a government controlled permit.

The Volstead Act stipulated that "nothing in this act shall prohibit the purchase and sale of warehouse receipts covering distilled spirits on deposit in government bonded warehouses." The owner of the liquor was protected from seizure of his property, and he could sell it even though it was illegal to move it without a government permit. When prescribed by a physician, permits for liquor for medicinal purposes could be purchased from the Commissioner of Internal Revenues. Consequently, Remus purchased distilleries and drug stores, becoming the wholesaler as well as the retailer. Thirsty citizens soon discovered that the drug store had replaced the saloon. Mabel Willebrant, the Justice Department's chief enforcer of the prohibition laws, called permit alcohol "the big leak" and identfied it as the "greatest single source of liquor supply."

The whiskey in government bonded warehouses was guarded by a guager, who had the only key. Remus' first step in gaining control of this whiskey was to buy the distillery and warehouse and then purchase the certificates. In this way he would become the sole owner of the whiskey, and his transactions were perfecftly legal. Remus reportedly expended between $50,000 and $325,000 in purchasing distilleries. Payment for the certificates was calculated over and above that.

The next step was to remove the whiskey from the warehouse. One way was to arrange to have it stolen. Sometimes the whiskey was siphoned out through hoses attached to a pump in a neighboring building. The whiskey was pumped straight into barrels which would be trucked to a safe hiding place. The empty barrels were then filled with water and alcohol, or just enough barrels would be left full so as not to rouse the suspicions of the gauger. More whiskey would then be distilled without the knowledge of the gauger and would be stamped with stolen or forged "Bottled in Bond" stamps, certifying the whiskey was legally produced under the auspices of the government gauger.

Other times whiskey would be loaded onto the trucks legally, using legitimate certificates, but Remus' own men would "hijack" the trucks on the way to their destination. The hijacking would be reported to the authorities, but they were given false and misleading information about the crime.

Another way to remove the whiskey was through legal channels to wholesale drug companies. These companies were not restricted on the amount of whiskey they could buy as long as they had the necessary permits; and so Remus set up a number of wholesale drug companies and bought his own whiskey on both legal and forged certificates. When this whiskey was shipped to a fictitious drug store, it would end up in one of Remus' many hiding places.

Some of Remus' drug companies were legitimate companies with complete stocks and employees. However, most of the drug companies existed in name only. Whiskey was sent out from Remus controlled distilleries to companies such as the Alpine Drug Company and the Imperial Wholesale Drug company, both of New York. Neither of these companies existed, and yet permits were made out and receipts were signed for large consignments of whiskey to them. When shipments to a particular company became too large, and Remus believed the authorities were suspicious, he would simply close down the company and open another.

Various means were used to get hold of the permits needed for the release of liquor from the warehouses. Some would be legal permits; others would be obtained through bribery, or the figures would be changed so that one case of whiskey would become ninety one cases. Other permits were forged. These could be bought for about $6 a case.

In 1921 the Treasury Department limited the amount of whiskey any drug company could withdraw to ten percent of its gross business income; so the books were rigged. Also merchandise would be sent to non-existing addresses and would usually end up being sold as unclaimed freight. The permit to purchase more whiskey thus obtained more than compensated for any such losses. Remus himself often wondered what became of these consignments, which amounted to thousands of dollars worth of goods.

Remus' operation started off small, with the one distillery, but it expanded at a rapid pace. He paid between $50,000 and $325,000 for each plant . Eventually he owned about a dozen distilleries. His trusted right hand man, George Conners, was a former Internal Revenue Service agent. Together they built up an impressive organization, employing over 3,000 men and running a fleet of eighteen vehicles. By the latter part of 1921 the whiskey trucks were removing whiskey from one of Remus' distilleries more than twice a week; and at times these trucks returned to the distillery more than once in one day. "The Napoleon of the Chicago Bar" had become "The King of the Bootleggers."

In one four month period about 7,4000 gallons of whiskey were removed from the W.P. Squibb distillery that Remus owned. The need to protect his whiskey shipments became apparent to Remus when he was nearly killed and was scarred for life while thwarting a hi-jacking attempt. To obtain adequate security, Remus hired an ex-nightclub owner, Ernest "Buck" Brady. Brady was given a commission of two dollars for every case of whiskey that made the journey from distillery to destination, and within one year it is estimated that he earned a total of $208,000. Brady was essentially an anti-hijacker. His armed men would ride in the whiskey trucks and in high powered armored cars ahead and behind the convoys. On occasion Remus would ride with his men.When attacked on deserted roads they would not hesitate to return fire, and major gun battles would be fought. Fatalities would later be listed by the County Coroner as died at the hands of persons unknown, and hardly any inquiries were ever made into these deaths.

A farm just outside of Cheviot (Lick Run Road Rural Box 11 1/2) was the nerve center of Remus' operation. Situated outside the Cincinnati city limits but close enough to be accessible, it was viable as a retail outlet and also conveniently near to Remus' distilleries in Indiana and Kentucky. Most of the whiskey was brought to the farm after being released by permits or stolen by Remus' own men from his distilleries. Here barreled liquor was bottled and labelled by means of a fully operational bottling plant that was set up in one of the sheds. The whiskey then was ready for sale to the public or to other bootleggers. Cincinnati citizens would make trips out to the farm to buy their bottle or case of liquor while prominent citizens would order their whiskey over the telephone and have it delivered to them.

However, most of the whiskey was sold to independent dealers, called "rum runners" who, in order to supply their thirsty customers, came from cities throughout the Mid West, and even occasionally from as far as Texas and California. Often this whiskey would end up in the so called "cutting houses" where water and pure alcohol would be added, although Remus was always proud that he never sold anything but pure, good whiskey.

The farm was nicknamed "Death Valley" or "Hole in the Ground" because of the high mortality rate among those hi-jackers foolish enough to attack it. Its excellent security made it an impregnable fortress Nevertheless Remus and his men feared rival bootleggers more than prohibition agents. The farm consisted of a large, two story frame farmhouse with several barns and other buildings scattered around it. The lofts of these barns provided excellent lookouts and were manned night and day by men carrying powerful deer rifles. A road that passed through a clearing in the woods before arriving at the farm compound was the only entrance to the farm. Guards were posted as lookouts over this clearing, and every movement in and out was monitored.

An electric buzzer system gave instant warning to the main building if any unexpected visitors arrived, and powerful electric floodlights were available to illuminate the entire farm yard. To make it look less suspicious to people or agents who might happen across it, the farm had a number of pigs and chickens in highly visible pens. As a precaution, a secret cellar capable of storing ten thousand barrels of whiskey was constructed in the barn.

The side road that led from Queen City Avenue to the farm was well hidden and could be easily missed by anyone not knowing what to look for. A tar line that curved out from the main road in towards the farm road was the marker that guided whiskey trucks and customers to the farm. Because it was managed by two of Remus' lieutenants, Johnny Gehrum and George Dater, the farm was also referred to as "John's Place" or "Dater farm." Smaller whiskey depots were established at Hamilton, Glendale, and Reading in Ohio, across the river in Covington, Kentucky, and in Buffalo and New York City.

A large operation such as Remus ran with his lieutenants could not have existed without the collusion of heavily bribed officials. Nearly a quarter of Remus' entire gross profit was channeled into payoffs. For example, railroad officials were bribed so that rail cars transporting illegal whiskey could be shunted into deserted sidings for unobserved loading or unloading. Once Remus was able to send eighteen freight cars full of barrels of illegal whiskey across the state line from Kentucky to Cincinnati, where they were loaded onto his trucks for removal to Death Valley.

Whenever possible gaugers were bribed so that whiskey could be removed from the distilleries with a minimum of subterfuge. Local law enforcement agents were also bribed; and Remus actually boasted that he would always know ahead of time if a raid was scheduled. The manager of the local prohibition office, B.E. Kelley, could be counted on to alert the people at the farm whenever a raid was planned. On one occasion he actually procured a warrant to search the premises and then reported that there was no liquor there. When he was questioned and it was suggested that "if reports are true you missed something." Kelley described the farm, mentioning men in overalls and sheds and barns, just like an ordinary farm.. This incriminating information was forwarded to prohibition officials, Captain Flora and Captain Dickerson, but no action was taken because of it.

On another occasion a pair of agents looking for a local still wandered into Death Valley by mistake. They were each given a thousand dollars and a bottle of whiskey and sent happily on their way. In time Remus became known as the "star corrupter" of the bootlegging business.

As early as 1920, the Treasury Department became suspicious of him. They hired William Mellin, who worked for various government agencies as a wiretapper, to plant a bug in a hotel room which Remus occupied. Mellin took an adjoining room, and by use of a duplicate key, he was able to enter Remus' room and plant a microphone there.Then by drilling a hole in the wall he was able to run the wires from the microphone through into his own room. He also located the appropriate terminals for Remus' telephone extension and connected those to his telephone. Thus whenever the telephone rang in Remus' room, it would also ring in his, and in this way he could listen to both incoming and outgoing calls. Two government stenographers monitored the wiretap and recorded every word. They learned that Remus was bringing eighteen freight cars full of illegal whiskey to Cincinnati from Covington, Kentucky. They also heard Remus paying out bribes averaging a thousand dollars apiece to 44 people. Federal agents, deputy marshals, and politicians were among those bribed.

Mellin presented this information to a prominent federal official in Cincinnati who insisted that it be hushed up because of its potential political damage. Some of the prominent men involved were political appointees, and this was an election year. In fact, Mellin was told bluntly to "go back to New York and forget it." The information was never used. In later years when Remus was told of the wiretap, he was not surprised and claimed that he was "very, very active" in the business of issuing bribes.

Remus' web of corruption was not confined to Cincinnati. It reached as far as Washington D.C. by way of Jess Smith, right hand man and close friend of the Attorney General, Harry Daugherty. Smith and Daugherty had actively campaigned for Warren Harding in the 1920 Presidential campaign, and during his administration they were frequent guests at the White House and often played poker with the President, whom Smith usually addressed as "Warren." Jess Smith shared a house with Daugherty and even had his own office in the Department of Justice, although he never held an official position and was not on the payroll. However, he was known as Daugherty's right hand man, and to see Daugherty, you had to go through Smith's office.

Remus' attorney, Elijah N. Zoline, introduced him to Smith in New York in early 1921. They met at the Commodore Hotel and discussed the possibility of protection for Remus in exchange for large payoffs. A "gentleman's agreement" was reached by which Smith gave his word that Remus and his associates would never be knowingly harassed by the Justice Department, and if the unforseen happened, there would never be a conviction. Remus and his men would never see the inside of a jail cell. For this assurance Remus paid heavily. His first payment to Smith was fifty one thousand dollar bills. The total amount that he ended up paying Smith for protection alone in the next year and a half was approximately $250,000 to $300,000. Remus made all the payments personally at various hotels in Washington, New York, Indianapolis and Cleveland, and all were made in the form of cash or checks made out to cash. Remus kept track of some of these payments by penciling in the initials "J.S." on some of the checks.

No one has ever proved that any of this money ended up in the hands of the Attorney General, but Remus did testify, at a later date, that he saw Daugherty with Smith on a number of occasions and once, at the Union

Station in Indianapolis, Remus claimed that Jess Smith excused himself from the company of the Attorney General in order to walk over to where he was standing and that the Attorney General must have known exactly who he was.

Remus also had a separate deal with Smith for the procurement of legal whiskey certificates. Smith was paid between $1.50 and $2.50 per case of whiskey released on certificates obtained by him. It is estimated that Smith made between $400,000 and $500,000 on this commission alone. In all Remus ended up paying about $19 to $21 on bribes per each case of whiskey he sold. He reportedly sold the whiskey for between $75 and $91 a case, so his profit margin was still considerable. In his first year he sold approximately 700,000 cases of whiskey. Remus himself claimed, at a later date, that although the amount paid on bribes "may seem a large sum here, to the whiskey world it is not so large."

For one and a half years Remus' bribery payments paid off. He was so well protected that he was able to carry on his business with virtually no interference. Interviewed years later he stated: "I now felt that no matter what happened, I was safe. I believed that I had the Department of Justice 'fixed' and regardless of any attempts that might be made to prosecute me, I would never go to prison. When you have Washington 'fixed' you don't need to worry about 'fixing' anybody else. I had my man in the Department of Justice, right next door to the Attorney General's private office. That was enough for me. I had plenty of permits, and I began operating more openly than ever." When the neighborhood children followed his trucks shouting, "there go the whiskey trucks," he could smile and not worry. He had paid for the privilege. In fact, he felt so well protected that on one occasion his trucks were loaded with whiskey from one of his distilleries at 2 o'clock in the morning. This was obviously not a legitimate transfer of legal whiskey. He also boasted that through the influence of Jess Smith he could "tear the heart out of Washington if he was crowded too far."

Remus soon found out, though, that not everybody could be bribed, and even he could not bribe everybody. There simply was not "enough money in the world to buy up all the public officials who demanded a share." The first person he encountered who could not be bribed was Sam Collins, Kentucky Federal Prohibition Director, earning $4,600 a year. Collins foresaw how difficult it would be to regulate the legal shipment of whiskey from Kentucky across the state line by truck, so he ruled that any whiskey leaving Kentucky had to be shipped by rail. This ruling did not stop the illegal removal of whiskey from Kentucky, but it did make it more difficult and expensive for the bootleggers who now had to pay out more on bribes and take more chances than before.

Remus and his men offered Collins $200,000 to allow them to ship their whiskey by truck, but their bribe was refused. They then offered Collins half a million dollars to quit his job. When he refused, Remus gave up, and he was forced to drastically scale down his operations in Kentucky. When Collins was asked if he was ever tempted to take this bribe money, he replied: "Why not at all. It doesn't cost me any particular effort to be honest. We folks down in this country--the Black Pine Mountain Country, near the Virginia border--are not used to much, and what we ain't got we get along very comfortably without."

THE RAID

In the summer of 1921 Remus was discussing the purchase of at least three more distillery warehouses in Kentucky and Cincinnati which would have given him control over one third of the entire store of bonded whiskey in the United States. He was also planning to increase the size of his operation at Death Valley, with the construction of more storage buildings.

However, before any of these plans could be implemented, things began to go wrong. The ever increasing complaints of citizens about the failure to enforce the prohibiton laws put pressure on the law enforcement officials. Sephen Mc Grath, Cincinnati's Internal Revenue Commissioner, lashed out at his critics: "I am tired of hearing insinuations against this office. I want the people of Cincnnati and this district to know that the slimy trail of the whisky ring does not lead here." He explained that he was not authorized to enforce the prohibition laws. He blamed the officials in Washington for failing to arrest and prosecute "the 'King of the Bootleggers' and his 'Princes' and 'Princesses'." He blamed them for not breaking up " a gang which had been operating in this section in defiance of all law and in the very teeth of the Government." He asked "Why is it that such utter disregard for law and open defiance of the greatest Government on earth is permitted? Why hasn't the 'King of the Bootleggers' and his assistants been apprehended? There is a Governmental department charged directly with the enforcement of the prohibition law. Why have activities been directed seemingly only against the little fellow who has a small still in his celler or attic?" His sentiments were echoed by J.S. Porter, former Chief Inspector of the Federal Prohibition Service, who declared that the enforcement of the Volstead Act was a joke, and he blamed political influence in Washingrton for the deplorable situation.

National Prohibition Commissioner Roy Haynes quickly denied that his office was aware of the existence of the whiskey ring in Cincinnati. He declared that it was the responsibility of the Ohio officials to investigate "if there is any truth in the report."

However, in late October Remus' luck ran out. When William Gallagher was arrested in Indiana for the shipment of illegal whiskey. he panicked and confessed that this whiskey came from Death Valley and that the farm was the distribution center for sixty Indiana towns and cities. Acting on this information, and armed with a statement made by one Howard Hughes, a group of Indiana agents, led by Federal Prohibition agent Gus Simon, approached Cincinnati officials to get a search warrant. In his statement Hughes claimed to have gone to the farm, which he called "John's Place," where he purchased one case of whiskey (12 bottles) for $100 from a man by the name of John.

On the 23rd of October, Commissioner Thomas M. Gregory issued a search warrant for the investigation of the alleged activities at "the premises of John Gehrum, situated in the county of Hamilton and state of Ohio." The following day a combined team of prohibition agents from Indiana and Cincinnati descended on Death Valley. They arrested ten men including John Gehrum and George Dater, and confiscated thirteen barrels of whiskey, 500 gallons of gin, 12 quarts of champagne and over 50 bottles of imported Scotch whisky. In addition to the seizure of this liquor valued at approximately $40,000, they also confiscated a large number of firearms, ranging from revolvers to machine guns and sawn off shotguns. Some of these firearms had notches cut into the stocks, assumed to be a record of the number of hijackers or rival bootleggers the owner had shot.

George Remus and John Conners were not at the farm when the raid occurred. When he was informed, Remus was furious and wanted to gather a gang of his men and capture the governement agents and remove all the incriminating evidence. He was forcibly restrained by Conners and some friends.

While the Federal agents were at the farm, a number of people drove up seeking to buy liquor. Their names were taken for future reference. Agents also took telephone calls from people asking for liquor to be delivered. These names and addresses were also recorded. Inside the farmhouse the agents discovered books listing the names of clients, including many distinguished Cincinnati businessmen; some of them were publicly identified with the dry movement. Also listed were directors of exclusive clubs, as well as members of the city police force. Some of the transaction recorded amounted to thousands of dollars. District Attorney James R. Clark claimed that when he saw the list he "realized for the first time why government officers have had so much difficulty in rounding up dry law violators."

Over the following weeks Clark interviewed the people whose names were on the list. Clark gave these people an ultimatum: either they cooperated with him and told all they knew about the farm and its owners or they would be arrested and charged with conspiracy to violate the prohibition laws. Clark referred to this process as "separating the sheep from the goats." Most of the people questioned were reluctant to help, forcing Clark to make a public appeal to "all good citizens" to "come forward and lend their assistance now." One good citizen who did not come forward was a multi-millionaire manufacturer prominent in Republican politics. His name was reportedly on the list when it was first seized, but it had disappeared by the time the list was given to Clark.

While Clark was interviewing the citizens on the list, the Cincinnati police, under Chief Copelan, were conducting their own investigations of those police officers and detectives on the list. The only public report made about the alleged police involvement was a statement regarding one officer, and even he was exonerated because he claimed that his name had been used fraudulently and he had never been to Death Valley farm or bought any whiskey from there. It was a complete whitewash.[2]

The raid on Death Valley was seen as a significant breakthrough for prohibition enforcement. The government officials believed that this was the largest distribution center in the central United States, and they were confident that the records seized there would enable them to strike a fatal blow at bootlegging in the Mid-West.

Among the records seized at the farm were books showing payments to George Connors and Harry Brown along with a bank statement and deposit slip for $5,000 from the Lincoln National Bank. The name on the deposit slip was never revealed, but it was widely believed that it was an alias used by George Remus. The officials at the bank denied having any knowledge of the transaction. However, George Remus was mentioned in some of the records seized, and the Federal agents believed he was the leader of the bootlegging gang. They launched an all out effort to build an airtight case against him. A work force of twenty Internal Revenue Department deputies watched his every move. They were determined to "draw the net tight about him."

Eventually, Clark was able to get some strong affidavits, among them a statement by Edward Kunkle, a watchman at the farm. He stated that he helped unload the whiskey from the trucks and that he had seen Remus there often. He also claimed that some of the whiskey had been removed prior to the raid because of a warning from Remus. Another watchman, Elijah H. Hubbard, identified Remus as the proprietor of the farm. Then two truck

---

[2]In April, 1925 59 Cincinnati police officers and neighboring "dry" area agents pleaded guilty in Federal Court to receiving bribes for protection and were fined and sent to prison for up to eighteen months.

drivers, Sam Koby and James Truck, signed statements that they had driven the whiskey trucks on occasion and had helped unload the whiskey at the farm.

One hindrance to the collection of evidence was the feeling of bad blood between the Attorney General's office and the local prohibition forces. The prohibition agent for the Cincinnati area, Robert E. Flora, had played a significant part in the raid on Death Valley and was now involved in the collection of evidence and the surveillance of Remus. The main case, though, had been worked up under the auspices of the Justice Department. This incensed the National Prohibition Director, Roy Haynes, who first heard of the raid when he stopped in Cincinnati on his way to Kentucky to inspect some distilleries there. He was at the railway station when he heard the newspaper boys calling out the headlines "all about that big whiskey raid!"

He complained that Indiana agents, instead of ones from Ohio, had controlled the raid and subsequent arrests, but when he was shown evidence of alleged bribery of Cincinnati officials, he changed his tune, and he subsequently announced that irregularities within the prohibition department would be investigated and arrests would be made. "No stone will be left unturned to uncover wrongdoing," he announced. That he did not once contact Clark while he was in Cincinnati did not affect the investigation, but it did call attention to the fragile relationship between the two Government agencies.

While gathering evidence for the forthcoming trial, the government officials realized there might be a connection between Death Valley and the Squibb distillery in Lawrenceburg, Indiana. In June, 1921, Remus bought this distillery and its stock of 3,200 barrels of whiskey for a reputed $450,000. He did so through a third party, one H.S. Paterson and his attorney, Thomas Cravens, who handled the negotiations. Remus paid $50,000 in cash and the rest in checks from the Lincoln National Bank in Cincinnati. He then installed his brother-in-law, Harry Brown, as president and Harry Gardewing as manager.

Federal agents became suspicious when Cravens visited the office of the I.R.S. collector in Indianapolis and attempted to purchase a permit to ship the liquor out of the warehouse. He did not get the permit, but during September and October 18,000 cases were shipped to non-existent drug wholesalers in New York and Pennsylvania on forged or fraudulent permits. When Gallagher was arrested, almost all of the liquor he was carrying was from the Squibb distillery. While the raid was taking place at Death Valley, officials were on stand by in Lawrenceburg. Once it was established that a large amount of the liquor seized in the raid was Squibb Whiskey, these officials moved in on the distillery. Armed with search warrants, they searched the premises and found only 925 cases left of government bonded liquor in the warehouse. They seized them and closed down the distillery, posting guards around the property. Agent Flora was given all the permits relating to the distillery, and warehouse and he duly placed them in the safe in his office. Not long afterwards, though, they disappeared and were never found again.

Soon after the raid on Death Valley, federal agents watching Remus' house reported that he and two men had left Cincinnati in a powerful touring car. Soon after that report a car pulled up at the Squibb warehouse. Three men got out and walked towards the main entrance. They were challenged by the guards, who asked them what they wanted there. The three men quickly turned around and ran for their car. The guards opened fire on the car as it sped away, but no fire was returned. There was no hard evidence that Remus was involved, but if he were, he would have learned that the government officials had him under surveillance and linked him to both the Squibb distillery and the Death Valley farm.

It was time for Remus to see his protector. However, Jess Smith either did not know about the raid on Death Valley, or found that in this situation he could do nothing to help Remus. Naturally, Remus was livid. He wanted to know what his money could do to get him out of trouble. Smith had assured him that he would not even be indicted, but if he were, he would never be convicted. Remus assumed that these assurances came with the backing of Attorney General Daugherty, but he was unaware that soon after the indictment, District Attorney Clark met with Daugherty to discuss the case. Clark was instructed by Daugherty, who was troubled by persistent rumors that he was connected to Remus, to go ahead with the prosecution. Later, during the Senate Investigation of Daugherty, Remus testified :"Mr. James Clarke, the former district attorney of Cincinnati, told me after my conviction that he had talked with the Attorney General in Columbus in reference to my case, at which time the general told him that he had to prosecute my case, as there was some talk in Columbus that he was one of my partners."

While Remus was discussing the matter with Jess Smith in New York, George Conners was trying to find out whether there would be any more raids on the farm because not all the liquor there had been discovered during the raid. The day after the raid took place, Conners met with Commissioner Gregory and learned that there were no other warrants pending. Conners then attempted to influence Gregory by offering him a case of whiskey as a "gift," and when this was refused, Conners tried, in vain, to have it delivered to Gregory's home.

. This offer of liquor was an obvious attempt by Conners to bribe the Commissioner, or at least to discredit any testimony he might give later. Conners would have witnesses, in any subsequent court action, to the fact that he had delivered whiskey to the Commissioner's house, and he would be able to claim that he had been ordered to make the delivery. Commissioner Gregory gave all the information about his dealings with Conners to the Prosecuting Attorney's office. The prosecution believed it would actually strengthen their case.

THE "DRY LAW" TRIALS

On October the 31st, 1921, George Remus appeared before Commissioner Thomas Gregory for arraignment on a charge of conspiracy to violate the Volstead Act. Remus seemed to be in a good mood and not visibly worried when he arrived at the Courthouse with his wife and his attorneys, J.J. Kilgarriff and James Linton. Hundreds of people were already lining up for seats in the courthouse, eager to see the infamous "whiskey king;" and newspaper reporters thronged the doorways waiting to ask Remus about the alleged millions he had made through the sale of illegal whiskey. Laughing, he answered, "I only wish that were true, I have not sold a gallon of whiskey for bootlegging purposes." He went on to say that he suspected the Anti-Saloon League of being somehow involved in his arrest.

As expected Remus pleaded not guilty. The prosecution then requested a bond of $50,000, contending that Remus was the head of one of the largest whiskey rings in the country. The defence lawyers protested against the unusually high bond, asserting that Remus was a prominent resident and landowner in Cincinnati and that it was incomprehensible that he would skip town. They also reminded the Court that Remus had appeared on his own volition, not waiting for a warrant to be served. Commissioner Gregory, unmoved by the defence's pleading, ruled that in view of the magnitude of the alleged transactions in the case, the bond would be set at $50,000.

This was the highest bond ever set by a Federal Court in the district, and an incensed Remus jumped up from his seat exclaiming: "That amount is excessive. As an officer of the Court I protest. It is outrageous!" He continued his protest until he was forcibly restrained. Then Mrs. Remus signed as surety on the bond. She testified that she was worth $200,000 with the Remus mansion in Price Hill and another piece of property at 1039 Overlook Avenue, both in her name. She gave the value of the mansion as $185,000 although it was considered to be worth considerably more. The bond was signed, and Court was recessed.

When Judge Peck dismissed the Grand Jury later that month, District Attorney Clark requested that they remain on standby in case he felt it necessary to return an early indictment against Remus and his cohorts. Judge Peck did as requested, but Clark did not call on the jury, choosing to wait until the next Grand Jury was sequestered in April of the following year. This gave Clark and his assistant prosecutors four to five months to work on their case against the defendants, but it also gave Remus time to continue his bootlegging as well as to work on his defense.

He set up an account at the Lincoln National Bank under the name of J.P. Alexander, and he continued doing business using this alias. An indignant citizen wrote an excoriating letter to the Attorney General stating: "It is inconceivable that you are not fully advised of the operations of the Whiskey Ring in Cincinnati, and particularly of the head of the conspiracy against law and order, one Remus, who, notwithstanding his recent indictment and the restraint of a $50,000 bond, is now flagrantly, notoriously and fearlessly violating the very law under which he was indicted and boasts that he is protected by men holding high official positions. I am advised that the wife of this same Remus declares that your own office is not without taint. Isn't it about time for you to rise in wrath and sweepingly annihilate this nest of animals?"

Remus also met with Jess Smith at least four times between December and April. At some of these meetings his chief counsel, Elijah Zoline, was present, and together they discussed what they could expect from the Justice Department. Smith continued to assure Remus that if he did have to go on trial, the prosecution would put up a plausible fight, but there would be little chance of an ultimate conviction; moreoer, if a jury somehow did convict him, the decision would most certainly be reversed on appeal. Remus paid Smith about $10,000 at each of these meetings. Meanwhile, John Gehrum was using Remus' money in various attempts to influence the federal agents involved in the prosecution.

On November the 26th, Gehrum and Remus travelled to Indianapolis to bribe Prohibition agents, George Winkler and William Holman. When they found these men unwilling to be bribed, they arranged a meeting with the Prohibition Director, Bert Morgan, and one of his agents, Daniel Moore. Once again they were unsuccessful. Morgan could not be bribed. On March 24,1922, Gehrum made one last attempt at bribing George Winkler, but to no avail.

The new Grand Jury, impaneled in April, 1922, returned four indictments against Remus and thirteen associates. The first and most important was that of Conspiracy to Violate the Prohibition Laws of the United States of America. On May 8,1922, Remus and thirteen others entered the United States District Court in Cincinnati for the hearing of the first case against them, with Judge John Weld Peck presiding. Remus sat at a table with the six defense lawyers, including Elijah N. Zoline from New York, the author of several law books and generally regarded as the best lawyer money could hire; Michael Igoe from Chicago, a former Assistant United States Attorney; and James Linton from Columbus, Ohio, who had been retained by Remus in October of the previous year, but had since been appointed special Assistant Attorney General to Harry Daughterty. Linton remained counsel to Remus and the other defendants throughout the Federal trial in spite of a possible conflict of interest. Behind Remus and his lawyers, sat his alleged co-conspirators; and behind them, in the public seats, sat his wife Imogene, who had offered him her total support. Opposite him sat the Prosecuting Attorney, Thomas Morrow, who had succeeded James Clark, and his assistants, Dickerson and Reynolds.

Before Court went into session James Killgarriff presented a motion for the return of all property seized at Death Valley and for the inadmission of any testimony based on the use of these items as evidence. The motion contented that the search warrant through which these goods had been seized was illegal. Kilgarriff cited various sections of the Search Warrant Act of June, 1917, which stated that a search warrant could not be issued unless it was supported by an "affidavit, naming or describing the person and particularly describing the property and the place to be searched." Killgarriff claimed that the search warrant used in this case failed to meet this requirement because the description of the property did not accurately describe the Death Valley farm, and could have referred to a number of farms in the area, two of which were knowingly occupied by men named John.

Killgarriff also cited sections four and five of the act, which stated that it was the duty of the Commissioner who signed the warrant to examine on oath the complainant and that said complainant had to present facts showing that the property was being used for illegal purposes. The complainant cited on the Death Valley search warrant was G.J. Simons, who was acting on a signed affidavit from one Howard Henry Hughes. This affidavit was sworn before Simons, who, as a Federal Prohibition Agent, did not have the authority to take the affidavit under oath. The resulting complaint put forward by Simons was thus legally based on hearsay, and neither he nor Hughes were examined by Commissioner Gregory, under oath or otherwise. On these grounds the defense motioned to have the warrant declared illegal.

Judge Peck immediately rejected the motion. He asserted that the evidence discovered at the farm was proof enough that the basis of the warrant was correct, but he did allow the information in the motion to be entered as part of the court record. He also rejected a further defense motion to conduct a preliminary hearing for the determination of evidence and information that may have been obtained through the result of the search warrant. If Judge Peck had accepted either of these motions, the prosecution would have suffered a serious set back.

Although the defense had received its first defeat, Remus was still confident that there would be no conviction. The evidence might be there, but none of his men had actually been caught selling any liquor. Remus did not realize that the prosecution did not need to prove that Remus and his men had actually violated the prohibition act. They had been charged with conspiracy to violate the act, and the prosecution merely had establish that a conspiracy had existed.

The prosecution now struck a telling blow. The doors of the courtroom were held wide open as men carried in barrels of whiskey, cases of gin and champagne, and even 50 bottles of highly prized, imported Scotch whisky along with an assortment of firearms and placed them in the open space in front of the jury. Remus' lawyers protested vehemently, but in vain.

Assistant Prosecuting Attorney Dickerson now related how Remus arrived in Cincinnati in late 1919 with a modest sum of money, and forged an organization through which he had amassed a fortune and brought so many people under his command that it amounted to a "near army." He promised the prosecution would reveal how Remus hid his illegal dealings by using middlemen and placing his own employees in top positions. "But," he noted, "we expect the evidence to yank the gentleman into the limelight and bring him so clearly before you in many of these transactions."

The defense reserved their opening speech until the conclusion of the prosecution's case. The first prosecution witness, Gus Simons, related how Howard Hughes had made a sworn statement before him on the 20th of October, 1921, at the police station in Hammond, Indiana, claiming that on the 18th of October he had made inquiries into the possibilities of purchasing a case of liquor and had been directed to a farm in Cheviot called "John's place."

He had followed the directions and was led into a small shed next to the barn by a man named John, who then sold him one case consisting of twelve one quart bottles of Old Dearborn Whiskey manufactured by the W.P.Squibb distillery. He paid $100 for the case of whiskey. With this affidavit Simons applied for a search warrant.

The following day the prosecution put their star witness on the stand. Mrs. Mary Hubbard was the widow of one of the night watchmen at the farm. Her husband had been willing to testify against Remus and his alleged co-

conspirators and had signed a written affidavit prior to the trial, but he had died of poisoning before the trial began. Her testimony was motivated by her belief, shared by many, that her husband had been murdered to seal his lips. Mrs. Hubbard's testimony was very specific. She stated that she and her late husband lived in a small house which overlooked the farm where her husband worked. Claiming that "a great many men here were at the farm often," she stepped down from the witness box and pointed out those of the defendants that she had seen. When she reached Remus, she called him by his full name and declared that he "came to the farm every day or every other day." She testified to seeing the trucks drive up to the farm where the boxes and barrels would be unloaded. When asked by the Prosecuting Attorney whether she recognized any of the labels or markings on these containers, she replied "Yes" and proceeded to name the brands of various distilleries owned by Remus, such as Fleischman and Squibb.

The entire time Mrs. Hubbard was on the stand, and for the duration of the trial, she was guarded by a secret service man specially appointed by Assistant Attorney General Mabel Willebrandt. At least one known attempt had been made to kidnap Mrs. Hubbard. A few days before the trial a man tried unsuccessfully to get her into his car under the pretense of showing her a house that was for sale. In addition, the authorities, fearing that attempts would be made to tamper with the jury, added additional security: three men were assigned to watch the jury, and others were strategically placed around the courtroom..

The prosecution next presented witnesses who testified that they bought liquor, ranging from between $78 and $91 per case, from a number of the defendants at the Death Valley farm. Then Mrs. Hubbard was recalled to identify some of these witnesses as people she had seen visiting the farm. Nathan Goldman, a junk dealer from Indianapolis, testified that he visited the farm on a number of occasions and had seen George Conners, Harry Brown and George Remus at different times. In his written affidavit he claimed to have dealt directly with Remus and even to have slept at the farm when Remus was present, but when he was asked to identify Remus, he was unable to do so. On cross examination defense attorney Bensinger discredited this witness by forcing him to admit that he had been arrested in September, 1921, in Marion County, Indiana, for violation of the Prohibition Act.

Then witnesses testified to the sale of a number of distilleries and their warehouses and pointed out those of the defendants who were present at the various stages of transaction. By this time all the defendants were so used to being identified that instead of sitting quietly while they were pointed out, they rose up each time their names were called, and smiled at the witness. Remus was the only one who remained seated. Much of the testimony concerned the transactions involved in the purchase of the Squibb Distillery in Lawrenceburg, Indiana, with Harry Patterson testifying to the transfer of funds in the presence of George Remus and George Conners.

Robert Squibb, one of the previous owners of the distillery, testified that he continued to work out of an office near the distillery and from there he was able to observe the activities at the distillery. He noted that a large amount of bottling was done in June and July of 1921, and that trucks were transporting liquor out of the warehouses a number of times a week. He noted that these truck were always accompanied by an armed guard, but was unable to identify any of the men that he saw carrying rifles.

Under cross examination he admitted that a number of armed hi-jackings had occurred in the area and that the armed guard might have been necessary. Then the government gauger at the Squibb distillery testified to having seen Remus at the bottling works "five or six times." Through the testimony of various witnesses it was ascertained that over two thirds of the entire stock of the Squibb distillery was removed in the period between the sale transaction and the closure. Eight of the fourteen defendants were named and identified as being connected with the distillery.

Next Bert Morgan and George Winkler testified that they were offered bribes before the trial began. Both claimed that the conversations they had with the defendants concerned possible bribes for future enterprises. Both had been approached with the possibility of cooperating in the re-opening the Squibb warehouse, which had been sealed by government agents the previous year, and Morgan testified that he was asked to approve unsigned but legal permits that would allow the removal of liquor from certain warehouses.

Then proof that legal but unsigned documents were readily available was revealed by the testimony of Miss Olga Clemens, a clerk in the office of the Prohibition Officer at Pittsburgh, who stated that thousands of permits to remove liquor from bonded warehouses were missing from her office, but they "didn't mean anything without the stamp and signature of the proper officials." She also admitted that permits calling for less than five cases of liquor were authorized by junior clerks, with no higher authorization necessary.

Commissioner Gregory, who took the stand next, testified about the conversations he had with Conners after the Death Valley raid. During cross examination the defense attempted to show that he had asked Conners to supply him with whiskey and had conspired with him by not acting on the information he had received during the conversation. Gregory denied asking Conners to supply the liquor and, in answer to the second charge, claimed that it was not within his jurisdiction to investigate crimes unless someone presented him with evidence of a violation and swore out a warrant. He stated that he fulfilled his duty by filling out a report on the matter.

On the fifth day of the trial the defense scored an important victory. Judge Peck changed his mind and ruled that the liquor and other evidence seized in the October, 1921, raid was inadmissable due to irregularities in the search warrant. He advised the jury that they were to omit this evidence from their consideration when it came to the weighing of evidence. Testimony given by witnesses pertaining to the raid and what was found there was stricken from the record.

The prosecution, in desperation, offered to drop all charges against John Gehrum, legal owner of the property, as long as the evidence would still be admissible against the other defendants. The deal was refused, and the evidence was removed. Although the decision came as the prosecution was virtually winding down its case, it was hailed as a victory for the defense, but it was a hollow one. The physical evidence had been sitting in the courtroom in full view of the jury for four days and had been described by witness after witness throughout the trial. In spite of the Judge's instruction to the jury to omit this evidence from their consideration, it would be exceedingly difficult, if not impossible, for them to do so.

The prosecution concluded their case Monday the 16th of May, and the defense called Harry Gardewing as their first witness. Gardewing, the former manager of the Squibb distillery and warehouse, had also managed the Edgewood Company for approximately ten days. He testified to keeping the government records required by law, and to paying the due taxes on whiskey withdrawn. The Squibb compamy taxes amounted to more than $190,000 paid between June and October 1921. He claimed to have known Clem Herbes and Elmer Roth for many years, but had not met any of the other defendants before their appearance in the courtroom.

Prosecuting Attorney Dickerson's cross examination of Gardewing thoroughly discredited his testimony and was damaging to the defense. Gardewing, obviously ill at ease, was unable to explain how companies that were only allowed 100 gallons every quarter of a year were sent consignments of up to 1,500 quarts in one shipment, or how gin was shipped on permits for whiskey. When asked why he had never received receipts for the 16,900 gallons of liquor shipped from the Edgewood distillery when he was there, he answered that he "didn't know it was necessary." He was handed a pile of permits pertaining to the Edgewood Company, which showed that before the liquor was even shipped out the receipts had already been signed. He figited for awhile before answering that this was the first time he had seen those signatures, and when asked whether the signatures for two different companies didn't look familiar, he hesitated and meekly replied that he couldn't tell. He claimed that it was not part of his job to enquire whether any of the shipments ever arrived at their destinations.

Gardewing did admit to being a bit suspicious at one point when the trucks which were transporting the liquor returned for more in one day. He allegedly asked the driver, Charles Wissman, about this, but was satisfied with the answer that the previous shipment had been transferred to another truck. He admitted that he never received any receipts from the truck drivers for these shipments, and again claimed that he was not aware that he needed to have any. When asked why the company preferred to ship the liquor by road rather than rail, he intimated that whiskey shipped by rail often went missing.

The following day the defense team put four more witnesses on the stand, none of whom contradicted any of the statements made by the prosecution witnesses, and then, at approximately 10.30 a.m., the defense surprised the Court by announcing that its case was closed. The main witness for the defense had been Harry Gardewing, who had proved, under cross examination, to be an extremely vulnerable witnesses. The defense attorneys obviously felt that their strongest point was the illegality of the search warrant and the inadmissibility of the testimony obtained by its use. In their opinion this left only Mrs. Hubbard's testimony that could prove the charge of conspiracy.

In his closing argument, Attorney Igoe, hoarse of voice and perspiring freely in the warm courtroom, referred to the inadmissible evidence and testimony. He argued that Judge Peck's order for the jurors to omit it from their decisions was preposterous. "All you saw, you did not see," he told them, "and all you heard, you did not hear and all you were told you were not told, because by one motion all of this was removed from the case." He then challenged them to decide whether they could realistically forget this evidence and surrounding testimony, and if they could not, if they had any doubts, then they should find in favor of the defendants. He went on to discuss the relevancy of Mrs. Hubbard's testimony, claiming that the entire government case relied on the accuracy and truth of her statements. "This was the one link between these two places - the distillery and the farm."

Bensinger, making the final statement for the defense, sought to raise doubts concerning the accuracy of Mrs Hubbard's testimony. He reminded the jury that she and her husband had been accomplices in the alleged activities at the farm, and insinuated that she may have become a little nervous and cut a deal with the prosecution. "I wonder," he said, "what percent of her testimony is gathered from fact, what percent from newspaper reading and what percent from guessing." Attorney Linton then reminded the jury that the morals surrounding the prohibition laws were not on trial here and that they should put aside their personal feelings on this subject. The question to be answered was whether the defendants had actually conspired to break the law. He pointed out that his clients had done everything they did openly, "in the blazing light of the sun. Hardly the way of the criminal."

Assistant District Attorney Dickerson opened the government summation by stating that "Whatever else you might think of these men you cannot help but admire their nerve, admire their resourcefulness, admire their recklessness," but he went on the show that their defense attorneys had failed to prove any of the accusations that they had made against Mrs. Hubbard and had actually demonstrated that she was telling the truth.

Captain Morrow delivered the final speech. "We have just scratched the surface of this tremendous conspiracy," he said, claiming that this was a national conspiracy which stretched from Kentucky to New York. This is not a little case where a man is accused of having a bottle of liquor in his hip pocket, or a case where a man is accused of having a little still in his house, or transporting a case in an automobile. No; there are millions involved here. I say it tests the very foundation of this country of ours." He pointed out that the defense had failed to produce one single witness who could refute the testimony of the government's witnesses. "They did not bring a single purchaser of liquor from any of these plants here to say, 'I got a gallon of whiskey on this permit or that permit'." "I say that our testimony," he continued, "with a very small exception, has been absolutely uncontradicted."

Then Morrow referred to the various attempts at bribery as seriously contravening the laws and constitution of the United States. Then In an emotional voice he identified one juror as having fought gallantly for our country in the recent World War and asked the jurors whether they considered a country run by armed men in trucks, disregarding the laws and terrorizing the people, a country worth fighting for. The defense lawyers stongly objected to this type of argument, but they were overruled. Morrow concluded by stresssing that the prosecution had proved that Remus was "the financial head of a large organization of which these men are a small part and that a conspiracy was formed to violate the law."

Judge Peck then reminded the jury that the indictment consisted of four counts against the defendants: that they conspired to acquire, transport, possess and finally to sell liquor contrary to the laws of the United States of America, "but," he continued, "I say to you that it is only necessary that one be proved, and in order to prove this one, it is necessary to prove only one overt act looking toward the accomplishment of that thing." The jury took just two hours to deliberate before returning a verdict of guilty in the case of each defendant.

Remus appeared to take the news calmly and even turned to smile at the other defendants, but when he was asked whether he had anything to say prior to sentencing, he answered in a wavering voice, "No, Your Honor." He was probably aware that had he entered a guilty plea and taken the blame, the conspiracy might not have been proven and some of his men might have been acquitted. But he had put his faith in Jess Smith, whom he had paid large sums of money for the promise that they would not be convicted.

The sentences imposed on the fourteen men ranged from one year and one day imprisonment in Atlanta Penitentiary and a $1,000 fine to two years in the Atlanta Penitentiary and a fine of $10,000, the maximum penalty allowed under the Prohibition Act. Remus received the maximum sentence.

Judge Peck now fixed new bonds on the defendants, who still faced other charges connected to the conspiracy. The new bonds were slightly lower than the previous ones with Remus being bailed on $25,000, Brown and Conners on $10,000, and the rest on $5,000. Imogene Remus, dressed in bright red, signed surety for her husband and then co-signed twelve others with him. During the signing, the defendants were in remarkably good spirits, with Remus doing the rounds, shaking their hands and joking about the amount of time they would spend in jail.

After the bond signing, Remus and Imogene left the courtroom, stopping only long enough for him to make a statement to the press: "I have been engaged in many business transactions during the last few years, but in none of them have I been conscious of violating the laws of the United States. We will, of course, file our appeal, and I hope for better results if we can obtain a new trial." He was hoping to get better results from the judicial system, and he was depending on Jess Smith to exert his powerful influence on his behalf.

Federal officials believed that the verdict in this case sent a clear message to bootleggers that their business was a dangerous one, and if they were caught, the government was not going to let them off lightly. Consequently the price of bootleg whiskey rose dramatically as bootleggers weighed their potential profits against the threat of imprisonment. One court spectator, who claimed not to have missed a day of the trial, declared that the very air seemed "a little dryer," and reflected, "The way of the transgressor is hard, but the way of the thirsty citizen is harder." Roy Haynes, the Federal Prohibition Director, confidently predicted that the verdict in this trial would stimulate the enforcement of the Prohibition Laws. He noted that the trial had followed federal policy in apprehending the leaders of the bootlegging gangs, as well as the immediate offenders. "It is encouraging," he remarked, "to have the efforts of the enforcement agencies sustained by juries and courts."

Two other charges against Remus were ruled by Judge Peck to involve double jeopardy and were consequently dismissed. However, Remus still faced charges the he, along with seven others, "unlawfully, knowingly and willingly" maintained a nuisance at the Death Valley farm. The defense attorneys pleaded that double jeopardy was also applicable in this case; but Judge Peck ruled that the first trial involved charges against the conspiracy act, whereas the charges in this case related to the prohibition act.

Hardly any new testimony was presented in the new trial. Witnesses who had testified in the first trial repeated their testimony. The only sensational testimony came from Bert Morgan, who revealed the exact amount of the bribe he had been offered prior to the trial. He told how he was offered $500,000! Morgan testified Herbes and Gehrum showed me a book in which they said were the names of men high in the government-including Senators and Congressmen. They said "These men were getting theirs and I ought to get mine."

The defense attorneys routinely objected to the testimony of every witness on the grounds of double jeopardy. Judge Peck finally put a stop to their constant objections by ruling that evidence introduced in the first trial to prove a conspiracy could also be introduced in the same form to establish that the act actually took place and thus constituted a nuisance.

The jury deliberated for less than two hours before bringing in a guilty verdict. Remus received the maximum sentence: one year in the Montgomery County jail and a fine of $1,000. The Justice Department was extremely pleased with the results of the trials. Assistant Attorney General Mabel Willebrandt immediately sent a telegram to Morrow congratulating him on the splendid manner in which he and Dickerson had handled the case. Morrow also was pleased with the cooperation he received from the prohibition department, and asserted that the government's victory was in a great measure to be attributed to this harmony.

While the government officials were congratulating one another, Remus's lawyers were busy filing Writs of Error and preparing their case for the Court of Appeals. Most of their objections concerned the first trial and the evidence which, in their opinion, should never have been introduced. They also argued that their clients did not face an impartial jury. They named four jurors who had direct connections with organizations favoring prohibition. Juror Wymer was a member of the Law and Order League; juror Marlett's wife was a member of the Anti-Saloon League; juror Thomas knew the Prohibition Director; and juror Higgins was a member of an organization devoted to the enforcement of the prohibition act. These jurors were apparently allowed on the jury because the defense had exhausted their preemptory challenges when they were called. That these jurors could hardly be classed as unbiased should be, they claimed, reason enough to reverse the jury's decision and permit a re trial.

Three days later Remus and Elijah Zoline, his attorney, met Jess Smith in the Washington Hotel in Washington D.C. Remus was furious with Smith around whose promises Remus had conducted the entire strategy of his trial. "The conviction is there," he told Smith, "what assistance will you give now?" Smith assured him that the Court of Appeals would reverse the decision, and Zoline agreed with him. Smith, wanting to cover himself completely, went on to say that, should the unthinkable happen and the decision be upheld by the Court of Appeals, then the matter would be taken to the Supreme Court and would either be reversed or a commutation would be entered. "There is no likelihood," he assured Remus, "of you ever going (to jail) at anytime, or any of your men." Smith claimed that he had the Attorney General's word on this. The last meeting Remus had with Smith was in early 1923. Remus paid him another $30,000 to ensure a favorable verdict from the Court of Appeals who would hear his case in June.

Smith did not live to hear the Court of Appeal's decision. He died on May 30th at the apartment he shared with Harry Daugherty in Wardman Park. No autopsy was done, but at the coroner's inquest it was announced that Smith had placed his head in a wastebasket and shot himself. No documents or files pertaining to his alleged criminal activities were ever found.

Remus' case went before the United States Court of Appeals on June 6th, 1923. He sat quietly, listening to his case being argued, and he showed no emotion when the convictions and sentences imposed in Cincinnati were upheld. The final hope was a reversal by the Supreme Court. The appeal was denied on January 7th, 1924.

The situation was now really desperate. Senator James A. Reed of Missouri was persuaded to visit the White House and plead with President Coolidge to grant Remus a stay during which his entire case could be reviewed .The Senator claimed that "Remus had been improperly treated and too drastically prosecuted." He also wrote a letter to that effect. However, President Coolidge forwarded the letter to the Justice Department and a strong personal protest by Assistant Atorney General Mabel Willebrant blocked the Senator's effort, and now Remus and his co-conspirators would have to spend some time in prison.

THE FEDERAL PENITENTIARY

Two weeks later a train bearing a special, private car pulled out of the station at Cincinnati. On it were Remus, his wife and the eleven men who had stood beside him in Court and were now facing their sentences together. They were on their way to Atlanta Penitentiary where one of their number, Clem Herbes, had already served most of his sentence and was due for parole. The atmosphere on the train was rather festive. Remus visited with his men, cheering them up and sharing in the fine meal that was served by a staff of private waiters. Remus' love of fine food was legendary, and he joked about the sort of fare he could expect in prison, declaring that at least he should be able to shed some of his 225 pounds. When he tired of socializing, he passed the time reading Dante's *Inferno*, which he described as being the only bad place he knew of.

When the train arrived in Atlanta a large, cheering crowd was already assembled on the platform. Reporters from the Cincinnati and Atlanta newspapers waited impatiently after having had their cameras confiscated by the authorities who were attempting to play down the whole event. Remus, though, was intent on making this a day which the public would long remember. He wanted to be thought of as the man who supplied the public with the pure whiskey that they wanted and which their government refused to allow them. He stepped down from the train wearing a pearl gray suit with a diamond studded tie, lamenting the fact that he had not been able to bring his valet along and thus would have to appear before the warden unshaven. He then made a great show of handing over a bag full of diamonds to his wife for safekeeping; then he turned to the porter and handed him a silk monogrammed shirt, before entering the gates of the penitentiary.

George Remus had not been incarcerated in the Atlanta Penitentiary very long before information started to reach Assistant Attorney General Mabel Willebrandt regarding special privileges he was receiving from Warden Sartain. Congressman W, D, Upshaw of Georgia charged that Remus "is being treated like a kingly visitor in the penitentiary where he was sent in punishment of his crime against society and the Constitution of our country." Remus was reported to be sleeping in private quarters in the isolation building and taking his meals with the prison Chaplain. He was assigned to duties in the library, which was considered soft work, but Warden Sartain, in a letter to Mrs Willebrandt, claimed that Remus had been given this job because of his educated status and because he was a lawyer. He felt that Remus was best utilized here where he could help the other inmates with their legal documents and applications for parole. He flatly denied that Remus received any special privileges.

The rumors persisted, though, and Remus himself added fuel to them when, in May, 1924, he sent a request to Mrs. Willebrandt asking to serve his pending one year sentence in the Atlanta Penitentiary instead of the Montgomery County jail. He argued that this would save the government money and it would aid in the preservation of his health. Mrs. Willebrandt denied this request on the grounds that such a transfer would involve a change of sentence for which she did not have the authority. Obviously Remus wished to serve out his sentence in an institution where privileges were provided for wealthy inmates.

When ordinary prisoners started asking why they could not receive these privileges, only to be answered, "If you have the money you can," government officials could no longer ignore the rumors. A thorough investigation was eventually launched, and Warden Sartain, his assistant, Fletcher and the Chaplain, Father Hayden, were indicted for solicitation and acceptance of bribes. During the ensuing trial it was revealed that Remus, and three other wealthy bootleggers had paid $7,000, which had been divided between Sartain, Fletcher and Hayden, for certain comforts and privileges such as their private cells with baths and maids. Remus reportedly paid an extra $2,000 to Hayden for the privilege of eating his meals with him, and another payment of $2,000 ensured him his job in the library.

In December, 1924, Remus and six other prisoners were moved from Atlanta to the Clark County Jail at Athens, Ga., dining at a restaurant on the way. The officials claimed that they had been moved because of the accusations of bribery, but it was rumored that they had been moved because of threats on their lives. Six months later all these prisoners were back at Atlanta. An envious fellow prisoner revealed that their cells were decorated with comfortable chairs, desks and radios, and their meals were served by a personal waiter. Their privileges were somewhat curtailed once they returned to Atlanta; however, they remained in cells located away from the rest of the inmates in an area referred to as "millionaire's row." Finally Warden Sartain was found guilty of accepting bribes, and he ended up as a prisoner in his own penitentiary.

Desperately seeking to get out of prison as soon as possible, Remus provided information to Franklin L. Dodge, a special agent of the Bureau of

Investigation. In a letter to his boss, J. Edgar Hoover, Dodge enclosed receipts establishing that large shipments of whiskey from the Hayner Distillery at Troy, Ohio. were consigned to fictitious drug concerns owned by Remus. Dodge wrote: "Remus further told me that he secured these withdrawls papers through former Prohibition Director J.E. Russell's office, with the assistance of one Fred Schwenck, ... and that Mr. Schwenck advised Mr. Remus that Mr. M.B. Copeland, an employee in the Prohibition Director's office, cooperated with him in securing the Prohibition Director's approval of these permits for the withdrawl of the whiskey at the Hayner Distillery."[3] Remus also asked his wife to try and influence Dodge on his behalf.

[3]On June 20, 1925, Russell and Copeland, along with nine other men, were fined and sentenced to two years imprisoment in the Atlanta Penitentiary for the illegal withdrawal of whiskey from the Troy distillery.

THE SENATE INVESTIGATION

The disclosure of widespread corruption in the federal prison system led to increased criticism of Attorney General Daugherty. Congressman Oscar Keller of Minnesota called for Daugherty to be impeached for failing to prosecute war profiteers and bootleggers and employing corrupt people in his department. Largely through the efforts of Congressman Volstead, the charges were dismissed, but Daugherty's troubles were far from over.

He was troubled by the continuing controvesy concerning Jess Smith's death. Despite the coroner's verdict of suicide, there was widespread belief that he had been killed because his corrupt activities were about to be made public and some important politicians, including Daugherty, would be implicated. Senator Thomas L. Heflin of Alabama charged that Jess Smith was murdered. In a fiery speech in the Senate Chambers he declared: "Jess Smith knew so much that it was desired to get rid of him. We were conducting a general investigation of the whole thing. It was rumored, also, that Jess Smith grew exceedingly nervous over it and that he had made up his mind to make a clean breast of it all, but Jess never lived to make that clean breast. He died. He was murdered."

Whether Jess Smith committed suicide or not, his mysterious death led many people to believe that there was widespread corruption in the Department of Justice. President Harding, loyal to his close frined, continued to publicly support Daugherty, but the harrassed Attorney General lost a friend and ally when Harding died in August, 1923.

Despite repeated attacks, the Attorney General refused to resign and denied all rumors of corruption in his department. However, President Coolidge had little faith in the Attorney General. Early in the new administrtion, February 19, 1924, Senator Wheeler introduced a resolution in the Senate calling for an investigation into the activities of the Justice Department and, in particular, those of the Attorney General. In March the Senate adopted the resolution, and an investigating committee was set up with Senator Brookhart as Chairman and Senator Wheeler as Prosecutor.

The hearings began on March 12th with Roxy Stinson, Jess Smith's ex-wife, taking the stand as the first witness. She testified to Smith's involvement with the Ohio Gang, and his subsequent corrupt dealings. She implicated Daugherty in a number of these deals, claiming that not only did he know about them, but he was often involved and given a share of the payoff. She also told of Smith's fears before his death and told how he would not even walk out in the street at night alone because he feared for his life. She too believed that he had been killed because he knew too much.

Harry Daugherty denied every allegation made by Ms Stinson, claiming that she detested him because he had never thought her a fit wife for his friend, and that this was her way of getting back at him. Whether her testimony was completely true or not, it was certainly damaging and increased the pressure on Daugherty to resign. On March 27th, after a number of other witnesses had also linked his name to the various deals carried out by Jess Smith, President Coolidge asked Daugherty to resign. He did so the following day, complaining that he had not been given a chance to prove his innocence.

The Senate Investigation continued, and in May, George Remus was brought from Atlanta to testify. He took the stand claiming that the short period he had spent in the penitentiary had already begun to take its toll on his nervous system, and as a result he was not "in the best mental condition." Nevertheless, he managed to give a fairly detailed account of his dealing with Jess Smith, who he had every reason to believe was representing the Attorney General and offering help that only the Attorney General could provide. He further claimed that he had not desired to appear at the hearings because he believed that Harry Daugherty still had significant influence within the Justice Department, and he feared that he would be prosecuted further if he testified.

Remus was questioned thoroughly about his activities as a bootlegger. When asked about his dealing in medicinal whiskey, he referred to the provision in the Volstead Act that allowed the sale of medicinal whiskey for medicinal purposes as a farce, calling it "the greatest comedy, the greatest perversion of justice that I have ever known of any civilized country in the world." It was his belief that there was not one "scruple of liquor ever prescribed by physicians that is used absolutely for medicinal purposes."

Remus then told of checks on which he had written the initials of Jess Smith and the others he had bribed for favors in Washington. Ordinarily they would have been destroyed, but his wife had saved them for income tax evidence. He offered to fetch them from their hiding places, and Mabel Willebrandt at the Justice Department was rquested to grant him leave to do so. She adamantly refused, declaring: "We do not feel justified in allowing a man who, during the past two and one half years we have been prosecuting him, has brought to bear upon every public official he could approach in an effort to secure favors, to be absent from prison walls for a trip around the country in the informal manner suggested." This was seen by some as an attempt by the Justice Department to block the evidence Remus alleged he could produce. However, Mrs. Willebrandt's refusal was overturned by the Federal Courts, and Remus was eventually allowed to fetch the checks, which were introduced as evidence in June of that year.

Mrs. Willebrandt then took the stand and defended her former boss, Harry Daugherty, claiming that he had never tried to influence her decisions in any way and had always supported her, even when she came under pressure from influential politicians to postpone cases and thereby facilitate their eventual dismissal. She also defended the Justice Department against accusations from Senator Wheeler that its agents "pass whiskey saloons every day and make no attempt to stop the violations." She reminded him that the Treasury Department, and not the Justice Department, was responsible for prohibition enforcement.

Senator Wheeler's answer that "Prohibition is a football" with the Justice and Treasury Departments passing it backwards and forwards was indicative of the general lack of co-operation which seriously weakened prohibition enforcement.

Then Mrs. Willebrandt denied that Jess Smith was a powerful influence within the Justice Department. She said that she had always regarded Smith as a valet, a sort of "glorified personal servant", and she never took too much notice of what he had to say. Senator Wheeler challenged her characterization of Jess Smith by informing her that Smith had been a frequent visitor to the White House and had taken yacht trips with the President. When she was questioned about Remus' political influence, she admitted that he had political influence that extended from local Ohio politicians almost to the White House. She then mentioned the letter written by Senator Reed of Missouri to the President. The letter was forwarded to the Justice Department, where the request for a 60 day stay prior to the incarceration of Remus and his associates in the Atlanta Penitentiary was denied. She said that the request was not a very strong one, and she felt that it was simply another desperate attempt by Remus and his lawyers to overturn his conviction. She denied that any real pressure was placed on her to have Remus' conviction reversed.

In spite of the testimony of Remus and other witnesses with equally damaging revelations, the Senate Investigation did not uncover enough evidence to justify prosecuting Harry Daugherty. However, Daugherty's reputation suffered irreparable damage. Moreover. he still faced further investigations, and few people believed his claim that he was unaware of Jess Smith's corrupt activities.

On August 29th, Remus surprisingly retracted his testimony. He claimed that an attorney, Harry Stern, who was working for the Senate Committee, had offered him the complete support of Senators Wheeler and Brookhart if he would agree to help them implicate Harry Daugherty. He said that he was promised early release if he would implicate Daugherty in instances of bribery. Remus denied that he had bribed any Justice Department officials. He suggested that the rumors of corruption in the Department might have been started by an offer Gaston Means made to him regarding the possible reversion of his sentence at Supreme Court level in exchange for $250,000.

Claiming that he had agreed to give the perjured testimony because he "craved liberty and caught at every chance that suggested a possibility of any relief from imprisonment," Remus denied having any dealings with Harry Daugherty or Jess Smith. He also asserted that when he was giving his perjured testimony he was stopped whenever it became apparent that he was about to say something favorable to the Justice Department, and that he was told by Senator Wheeler that he would be recalled to give further testimony, which did not happen.

Senator Wheeler asserted that Remus himself requested the chance to testify as a witness, and had sent the Committee telegrams to that effect. He dismissed Remus' allegations that he and Senator Brookhart had promised him early release if he testified. "The assertion," he said, "that either Chairman Brookhart or myself had any influence that would enable us to offer pardon, considering our attitude toward the executive branch of government is and was highly amusing." Senator Wheeler added that Remus had not been recalled to testify again because while he was on the stand for the first time they had received information which led them to be cautious in their dealings with him. He did not reveal what this information was.

On his release from Atlanta, Remus once again surprised everybody by announcing that his repudiation a year before had been false and that he had not perjured himself during the Senate Inquiry. "I am ready," he announced, "to stand by my testimony before the Committee because that was the truth." His claim this time was that the repudiation had been signed under duress and with the promise of an early parole. He claimed that James N. Linton, who had been one of his attorneys at his trial and was now Warden Sartain's attorney, had repeatedly badgered him to sign the affidavit, which Linton knew was untrue. Attorney Linton naturally denied these charges.

Both repudiations indicated that Remus was prepared to do just about anything to obtain his release from jail. However, the testimony he made at the Inquiry is generally accepted as the truth. The check stubs bear out his testimony of payments to Jess Smith. Moreover, witnesses at the Senate Inquiry testified that Remus carried out his operations so openly that it became obvious that he had purchased important political protection. Thus it can be assumed that the first repudiation was generally false.

Remus must have been aware that in September of 1924, he would be eligible for parole. It was standard practice for most Federal prisoners to become eligible for parole after serving one third of their sentences. Indeed Remus may have offered to testify knowing that this would favorably impress the Parole Board. What he did not realise was that parole was denied to prisoners who had pending indictments or other sentences facing them. Remus had both. He had another one year term to serve in a County jail on the nuisance charge, and he had two indictments hanging over him in Indiana and Missouri. The one in Indiana was for almost exactly the same conspiracy charge that he had already been tried for in Cincinnati. The charges against his co-defendants had been dropped by Assistant Attorney General, Mabel Willebrandt, but she had opted not to drop those against him as insurance that he would not obtain early parole.

The other indictment was for being involved in a conspiracy to violate the Prohibition Laws through the diversion of liquor from the Jack Daniels Distillery on St Louis. There were also a number of counts still standing on which he and his co-conspirators had been charged under the Conspiracy Act, but which Judge Peck had ruled against because, in his opinion, they related to violations of the old Internal Revenue laws which had been superseded by the Volstead Act. Attorney General Morrow had taken these to the Court of Appeals and the decision had been reversed, but the defendants had never been tried on these particular counts.

A month after Remus' repudiation of his testimony, in September, 1924, Mrs Willebrandt came under verbal fire when she dismissed these counts against Remus and his co-defendants. She claimed that she had quashed them because she felt that the defendants had been given adequate sentencing. Her opponents pointed out that Remus had testified that he felt that former Attorney General Daugherty still had a lot of influence in the Justice Department, and they believed this influence had been brought to bear with her quashing of these counts after Remus repudiated his testimony.

Mrs. Willebrandt denied these accusations claiming that the letter authorizing Cincinnati officials to drop these charges was written in July, one month before Remus repudiated his testimony and she further claimed that even Senators Wheeler and Brookhart would acknowledge that to try even

Remus on these two counts would be unfair persecution. So Remus did not get his early parole in spite of all his efforts.

In August, 1925, Remus had one month of his two year sentence left to serve in the Atlanta Penitentiary, but he still faced the one year sentence to be served in the Montgomery County Jail in Dayton, Ohio. He was confident that he would not have to serve this sentence, though, because his co-defendants in the Nuisance trial, Brown, Gehrum, Conners, Dater and Weismann, had all applied for and been granted a dismissal of this second sentence by means of a Writ of Habeas Corpus.

They had argued that as neither of the sentences actually mentioned when they were to be served, or in what order, they had in fact been served concurrently. They also cited the right of the defendant to be aware at all times which sentence he was serving. The defendants claimed that this right had been violated. The application cited various cases of precedence which the Attorney General's office maintained did not apply in this case, Their argument was that the two charges for which the defendants had been convicted carried completely different classes of sentences. A sentence under the conspiracy charge could only be served in a Federal Penitentiary because it was a Federal crime, while the sentence under the nuisance charge, which was a State offense, had to be served in a County jail. Thus the distinction between the two was obvious, and the defendants would have been constantly aware of which sentence they were serving. However, Judge Hickenlooper, who heard the petition, granted the writ to the defendants maintaining that the defendants had been sufficiently punished for their crimes.

The District Attorney, Haveth Mau, did not appeal because he and assistant Attorney General Willebrandt both agreed with the Judge's opinion and felt that these men had been mere employees of Remus and since they had paid the fines for both sentences; and since they only faced a few months in the County Jail, they should be given some leniency. A year later the Justice Department was attacked in Congress for their handling of this case. It was charged that the Justice Department should have appealed against Judge Hickenlooper's verdict in the first instance if they intended to appeal in the second. The fact that Remus, the ring leader, was not involved should not have been taken into consideration as it was a matter of law, and the initial decision set a legal precedent.

Knowing of Judge Hickenlooper's precedent setting decision, Remus wrote to Mrs Willebrandt in August requesting that she cancel his one year sentence and make it unneccesary for him to petition for a Writ of Habeas Corpus. He called her attention to the dismissal of his co-defendant's sentences and requested that he would be given the same consideration. By granting him an outright dismissal, he argued, she would save both him and the government money, and it would also save him the embarrassment of being escorted by a United States Marshall to Cincinnati to file the petition.

Mrs. Willebrandt denied him his request and made it plain that, should the District Court find in his favor, she would most certainly instruct the District Attorney to appeal the verdict. In her opinion Remus was the ring-leader in the conspiracy and deserved to serve every minute of his sentence.

Undaunted, Remus continued his efforts to gain his release from Atlanta. Once again he encouraged his wife to seek Franklin Dodge's influence on his behalf. A tall, handsome man with a reputation of being attractive to women, a real "ladies man," Franklin L. Dodge worked under Mrs. Mabel Willebrandt, and Remus hoped that he would prove corruptible.

Imogene Remus stood by her husband when he was convicted and and moved to Atlanta to be near him. She visited him frequently in the penitentiary and even helped to keep his cell clean and tidy. She also had power of attorney over her husband's finances and, with his business still operating, this amounted to control over money enough for her to offer generous bribes. Although Dodge refused to even support Remus' application for parole, Mrs. Remus continued to be seen with him.

Rumors of his wife's involvement with Dodge reached Remus, but he assumed she was only doing his bidding. He eagerly awaited the day of his release, expecting his wife to be waiting for him at the penitentiary gate with a Pierce Arrow automobile. He even contemplated skipping bond to avoid the year in jail he was still facing. He declared: "Damn 'em, $5,000 won't hold me and $55,000 won't hold me; when I get out I am gone." He told his wife to get things ready so they could make their "get-a-way." He was shocked when shortly before his release from prison, she sent him a note penciled on a Western Union blank informing him that she was going to file for divorce and implying that he had suggested she do so: "You told me to go ahead and file, I think I will follow your advice." He denied that he ever suggested divorce and in a long, eloquent letter he pleaded for a reconciliation: "Never have such matters arisen between us, that we cannot agreeably, mutually and beneficially adjust to our utter satisfaction." But it was a futile attempt. On August 31st, his wife served him with divorce papers. In her petition she charged her husband with cruelty, maintaining that he had humiliated and embarrassed her and her daughter, Ruth. In addition, she claimed that Remus had struck her on several occasions, and "he will, if not restrained. do her severe bodily harm." She asked that he be kept away from her. Remus declared that the allegations were nonsense. ""My wife must have been misled and ill-advised. I have showered luxuries upon her and she has stood by me through my imprisonment here. We have been devoted to each other." Still just before leaving the penitentiary, Remus filed a counter suit naming Franklin L. Dodge as the correspondent and asserting that Dodge and Imogene had conspired to frame him to ensure his confinement so that they could steal his property. He also charged that the couple were guilty of misconduct.

Remus was released from Atlanta on September 2nd 1925, but he remained in the custody of United States Marshall Stanley Borthwick, who escorted him to Cincinnati where he visited the office of the United States Immigration Bureau and deposited documents challenging the allegation that he was an illegal alien. He later accused his wife and Franklin Dodge of instigating these proceedings against him. He also filed a petition for a Writ of Habeus Corpus on grounds of double jeopardy, seeking to avoid the year in jail on the Nusiance conviction.

Before boarding the train to Dayton, Remus announced that he would make a lecture tour on his release from prison. The topic would be "Crime does not pay." "It has been terrible," he said alluding to his two years in Atlanta, "a day seems like a year and a year seems like eternity while you are in prison." He pledged that he was through with his criminal activities and claimed that his life henceforth would be lived within the confines of the law.

When reporters asked him about the divorce his wife sought, Remus answered that he would contest it. Noting that the suit came as a complete surprise, "like a bolt from the blue," leaving him dazed and astounded," Remus told them what a loving, considerate wife she had been and what a wonderful marriage they had. He expressed his belief that their marriage could still be saved, and he yearned for the day when they would be united again in "the best and most lovable family in the world."

Remus was later released from the County jail in Dayton when Judge Hickenlooper found in his favor on the double jeopardy motion. The Justice Department immediately appealed against the findings, but for the time being Remus was free to leave the jail. However. he was almost immediately re-arrested on charges of conspiracy in the theft of almost 31,000 gallons of whiskey from the Jack Daniels Distillery in St. Louis, Missouri. for which he had been indicted in May, 1924. It had taken federal prohibition agents over two years to obtain sufficient evidence to indict over thirty men, mostly influential St. Louisans, in the conspiracy.

Remus was taken to St. Louis where he agreed to testify for the Government. Nevertheless, his bail was set at $50,000 because of rumors that he intended to skip bail. No actual agreement was drawn up between Remus and the Prosecutor's office, but Remus knew, as a lawyer, that his co-operation would result in the charges against him being dropped. Remus' testimony proved to be so valuable to the prosecution that a grateful John Marshsall, the chief prosecutor, pleaded with the Attorney General's office for a dismissal of its appeal on Remus' one year nuisance sentence. However, all the efforts on Remus' behalf were in vain. Remus could not escape spending more time in jail.

MILKING JACK DANIELS DISTILLERY

Remus had first heard of plans to "milk" the Jack Daniels whiskey in May, 1923, from his former partner, John Marcus, who suggested that Remus' expertise might be needed by the conspirators who were politically powerful, but knew little about the bootlegging business. Since his conviction in Cincinnati the previous year, and while his case was being appealed in the higher Courts, Remus had continued to operate in the whiskey business and had even invested in a number of small distilleries, but he was wary about getting involved in any large scale operations.

Nevertheless, he agreed to go to St. Louis with Marcus to at least hear about the proposed operation. There he met Fred Essen, who introduced him to Nat Goldstein, a Circuit Court Judge and an influential Republican politician. Nat Goldstein in turn introduced him to Jack Kratz, who was to be responsible for the paying of bribes for protection and influence. Goldstein then explained to Remus how he had used his influence to have Arnold Hellmich, a co-conspirator, appointed as Collector of Internal Revenue. This was a pivotal placement in the conspiracy because the Collector was the ultimate supervisor of bonded whiskey in the County.

Remus did not commit himself to the project immediately. He had several more meetings with Goldstein and Kratz, and he met with many of the others involved, including influential people like Michael Whalen, a bondsman and member of the Democratic City Committee, Morris Multin, a large whiskey dealer and William Kinney, the brother of State Senator Michael Kinney. Although the Senator was never present at any of these meetings, Remus was led to believe that the Senator's influence would be available whenever needed. Although he was still a bit hesitant, believing that "there was too much of the element of personal friendship and political association in it," Remus finally agreed to join the conspiracy.

The Jack Daniels Distillery and Warehouse, which occupied almost an entire block on Duncan Avenue in St Louis, was owned in 1923, by Jack Daniel's nephew, Lem Motlow and five lesser shareholders. Their original asking price for the distillery and whiskey certificates on 31,0000 gallons was $300,000, which Remus and his partners refused to even consider. They finally agreed on a price of $125,000 and $200 a month rental on the actual warehouse building. A dummy corporation was created, and a contract was drawn up on June 19th, and signed at a meeting held in the office of a St Louis Attorney, Vance Higgs, on June 26th. At the same meeting Whalen signed a $90,000 bond with the Southern Surety Company as protection for Lem Motlow should the government confiscate the warehouse for violation of the prohibition laws. Lem Motlow was no fool when it came to the whiskey business.

Of the $125,000 purchase price, Remus was to pay $50,000 with Multin, Whalen and Mrs Remus contributing the rest. In return Remus was to get 60 percent of the profits or 60 percent of the whiskey. He chose the profit option. He also paid $6,000 for the required pure alcohol. In addition he had to contribute his share to the bribe money, roughly $15 a case. Of this, $12 a case would go to Hellmich, who would keep a portion and use the rest wherever necessary within the Collector's Office. William Kinney, who was appointed deputy Revenue Collector and later storeman gauger at the warehouse, received between $1 and $3 per barrel. Other bribes would be distributed when necessary. Remus and Multin decided that $30 a case would be a reasonable price for the whiskey. Unfortunately, when the whiskey was tested, it was discovered that some of it had been diluted by the previous owners. As a result, the whiskey did not sell as fast as they expected, and they had to drop the price to $27 a case, which was low for bootlegged whiskey at that time.

However, before the conspirators could sell the whiskey, they had to get it out of the warehouse. Remus devised a plan that would bring steady profits with minimum risks. There were 896 barrels in the warehouse; each contained 40 gallons of whiskey. Remus' plan was to remove approximately six gallons from each barrel, which would give them about 5,000 gallons and a guaranteed profitable return on their investment. The barrels would then be filled up with water and enough alcohol to bring the liquor up to proof. These barrels of diluted whiskey would remain in the warehouse until they were tested in December, after which the process would be repeated. This way the partners would get an early return on their investment, and the risk of discovery would be negligible. Moreover, the profit margin on the second and third siphonings would be greater than the first because they would be selling diluted whiskey.

The St. Louis men argued against this plan, claiming it would take too long. They wanted to remove as much whiskey as soon as possible while they had both Hellmich and Kinney on their payroll. Remus violently opposed their plan. He warned them that they would never get away with it, and he threatened to withdraw his men if they proceeded.

No final decision was made at that stage, and Remus returned to Cincinnati to arrange for a pump which he had used at the Fleishmann distillery to be taken to St. Louis. In July, 1923, John Marcus travelled to St Louis with the pump, guarded by two of Remus' men, Edward Meininger and Harry Boyd. Meininger was installed as manager at the distillery on a salary of between $60 and $70 a week and a further 50 cents per gallon to be paid once the operation went into effect. Boyd, hired as a cooper and delivery man, spent most of that month delivering whiskey to various drug stores in the St Louis area. Since the government gauger at the time of the transfer, C.H. Schuerman, was due to go on vacation on August 1st, the conspirators decided to wait until then to replace him with their man, William Kinney. When, for some unknown reason, Schuerman did not go on vacation, Hellmich was forced to have him transferred to another distillery. He was replaced by William Kinney, who had absolutely no prior experience as a gauger.

With all the conspirators' men in place by August 1st, the operation began on a large scale. The St. Louis men rejected Remus' cautious plan and informed Boyd that they wanted all of the whiskey out by August 15th. Remus found this out when he returned to St. Louis, and he was extremely nervous and unhappy about the decision. Mrs. Remus was also upset, and she made sure everyone was aware of the consequences should they get caught. "After it is all over, keep quiet," she warned Harry Boyd, "It means ten years if we are caught."

Working between the hours of 7.30 a.m. and 4.30 p.m., which were Kinney's normal working hours, Boyd and Meininger set out to remove the whiskey from the barrels. The warehouse, situated on the second floor of the building, could only be reached by means of an outside elevator from Duncan Road. Outside the door was a platform where Kinney stood guard while Boyd drilled holes through the concrete of both the first and second floors. He then ran a thick hose through from the warehouse to the boiler room in the basement. From there the hose passed out of the building through the basement windows and ran to a garage type building 150 feet away which was only approachable through an alley. Trucks loaded with empty barrels would drive up the alley and into the garage where their activities were supervised by John Marcus. He would press a buzzer connected to the distillery to indicate that they were ready to start pumping the whiskey. Boyd, with the help of John Conners, would then start siphoning the whiskey from the barrels. The buzzer sounding twice signified that the barrels on the truck were full, and the pump would be shut off. During this process, Meininger would either be in his office, or standing guard outside with Kinney It was very unlikely that anyone's suspicion would be aroused by this activity..

At first they would put the hose directly into the barrels, but the charcoal in the bottom would clog the hose. Their solution was to build a large copper plated trough into which they poured the whiskey before pumping it out. As fast as they siphoned out the whiskey, they replaced it with water and alcohol to bring it up to proof. If the alcohol level were tested at this stage, without the liquor being tasted, the deception would not be discovered. Boyd and Meininger were under a lot of pressure to finish the job by August 15th, but they never put themselves at risk by working at night. Everyday before 4.30, when Kinney finished work, they would pack up the hose and the pump and clean up the warehouse so that the night watchman would know nothing of the daytime operations.

The stolen whiskey was taken from the distillery to either a farm on the outskirts of St. Louis owned by an ex-convict named Foley, or to the storage rooms of one of Whalen's illegal saloons. There the whiskey was diluted and poured into five gallon drums before being delivered to the Walker White Bill Posting company. Rum runners, most of them Remus' men, picked up their loads here.

The business side of the operation was run from a this downtown office, owned by a fronting company. Remus had an office in this building from which he tried to keep an eye on his investment. He had a feeling that he was being cheated and was intent on proving it. However, he was not the only one watching the office. Federal Prohibition agents were suspicious of the activities within this office, and although they could not link it to anything specifically, they decided to watch it. Two agents rented a room from a photography shop across the road. Because the room was on the same level as the Rex Realty office, through binoculars they could watch what went on, and they were able to identify known bootleggers such as Marcus and Remus. They also gained entry to the office and were able to plant a bug there, but they did not hear anything incriminating.

After they finished their work at the warehouse, Harry Boyd and John Marcus would, on occasion, drive one of Remus' trucks. Boyd testified later that he made four trips between St. Louis and Cincinnati and one to Chicago, and on a couple of occasions Remus accompanied his trucks in a touring car filled with armed guards. Remus went along on these trips not only for the thrill of it, but also to personally protect his investment.

Long before the federal agents were aware of the conspiracy a St. Louis gang known as "Egan's Rats," learned about it.[4] When the conspirators were asked to accept "Egans's Rats" as partners, they were in a bind. They could not call in the police, and if they refused the gangsters' request, they had good reason to fear for their lives. They decided to buy them off by giving them a small percentage of the profits. This angered Remus; it cut into his share and it forced him to implicate one of the most vicious gangs in the country when he testified for the government.

By mid August almost the entire stock of the Jack Daniels distillery had been removed. Only one barrel of unadulterated whiskey remained. It was a tradition in liquor warehouses for the government gauger to be allowed an occasional drink from one of the barrels. Therefore, the barrel of good whiskey was left near the doorway in the Jack Daniels warehouse for the refreshment of the new gauger, Charles Barlow, who had just replaced Kinney. As long as the gauger received his drink, and was satisfied with the whiskey in that barrel, he would have no reason to investigate any of the other barrels.

Unfortunately for the conspirators, one evening in September Barlow became thirsty while he was patroling the warehouse with the night watchman, Fink. Because they were on the other side of the warehouse, Fink suggested they open one of the closer barrels, and Barlow did just that. What he tasted was sour whiskey that was rapidly turning into vinegar. (The government would later sell this "vinegar" for a reported $1,200). Alarmed, he rushed around the warehouse, knocking out the bungs of fifteen more barrels and tasting the contents. Every one he tried was the same. He then alerted the local prohibition officials who opened every single barrel and discovered they all contained water and alcohol. Some arrests were made, but the federal agents knew that this was an extensive operation, and they were determined to get the men at the top, the financial backers of the scheme.

On December 15, 1923, the Sheriff of Marion County, George Snider went to check out a report about a possible still on a farm. He found nothing, but on his way back he noticed a truck with Missouri plates travelling at about

---

[4]Organized in St Louis about 1900 by "Jellyroll" Egan, it served as "legbreakers" for anti-union companies. About 1920 its new leader, Dinty Colbeck, expanded the gang's activities to include bootlegging, safe-cracking and armed robbery. As a sideline they handled contract killings for other gangs. Two of their members, Frederick R. Burke and James Ray were implicated in the St Valentines Day massacre, and gang memberr Leo Brothers was sentenced to 14 years in jail for the murder of newspaperman Jake Lingle.

40 miles an hour behind a large touring car. He followed the truck and forced it to pull over near a bridge on a federal highway in Indiana. It was carrying Jack Daniels whiskey from St. Louis to Cincinnati. He drew his gun and ordered the driver to get out of the truck. Meanwhile the touring car in front stopped and a man, later identified as John Marcus, got out and started walking towards the Sheriff. He had a gun in his overcoat pocket, and he was ready to use it. Fortunately for the Sheriff, a backup car with a number of police deputies arrived on the scene, and both Marcus and Ben Doncaster, the driver, were arrested. The bulletproof truck was carrying four barrels of Jack Daniels whiskey valued at approximately $16,000. This incident was an important factor two years later when the Justice Department officials sought to have the trial of the Jack Daniels conspirators moved from St. Louis to Indianapolis.

In May, 1924, approximately 28 people, from more than four states, were charged with a conspiracy to violate the Prohibition Act. This was the culmination of a year of investigative work by the prohibition agents, and it would take another year before all the alleged conspirators would finally be indicted. The Jack Daniels case was regarded by the government as one of the most important liquor conspiracy cases. The Justice Department was determined to see all those indicted convicted, especially the influential men at the top. Moreover, Justice Department agents were instructed to investigate any instances of bribery or perjury. However, making a case in St. Louis proved to be difficult. Because many of the local men indicted were politically powerfull, many witnesses were reluctant to testify.

Therefore the Justice Department tried to have the trial moved to Cincinnati on the grounds that the conspiracy originated in Ohio, but they did not have enough convincing evidence. Their other option was to try the case in Indiana, reputedly the driest state in the Union. The lawyers for the alleged conspirators fought every effort of the Justice Department to change the venue of the trial. However, the Justice Department won the battle when it was ruled that there was enough evidence to prove that whiskey from the Jack Daniels distillery and the pump used to remove it had been transported through the state of Indiana.

On October 28th, a special session of the Federal Grand Jury was called in Indianapolis. John Marshall presented the government's case. Various federal investigators testified at the hearing, but Geoge Remus was the star government witness. He agreed to testify because he believed that he had been double crossed. The Grand Jury indited 39 people on charges of conspiracy, citing seven overt acts as the basis of the conspiracy. Six of the acts dealt with the transportation of the liquor and the pump, and one with the raising of the $50,000 Remus was alleged to have paid for his share in the plot, and which had been transported through Indiana.

The District Attorney requested that the case go to trial as soon as possible because Judge Robert Baltzell, a harsh sentencer of bootleggers, was due in another district in January.

THE CASE OF JACK DANIELS

The Jack Daniels trial started at noon on the 14th of December with 31 of the 39 defendants in attendance. The defence suffered an early set back when three of the defendant, all rum runners for Remus, entered guilty pleas. They were removed from the courtroom, and rumors began to circulate that three others might plead guilty and testify for the government if granted immunity.

The Courtroom was full throughout the trial, but there was little room for spectators. The thirty one defendants had fifteen lawyers, and, for security reasons, many Federal secret service men were stationed around the room. There were also detectives from the local police department who checked credentials and searched people as they entered the room.

John Marshall opened the government's case maintaining that it would prove that a conspiracy existed and that every one of the defendants was involved. The first witntess, Harry Boyd, described how the whiskey was removed from the barrels in the warehouse and pumped out to the waiting trucks in the garage.While on the stand he implicated many of the defendants. He told his story slowly and steadily as though he were describing a legitimate business transaction. At times he even seemed slightly bored by the proceedings. The defense lawyers' cross examination of Boyd was so vigorous that Judge Baltzell was forced to rebuke them several times. However, Boyd was unshaken and did not change his testimony.

George Remus was not in the courtroom on the first day; he was reported to be sick. His wife, Imogene, one of the defendants, claimed that it was simply some plot of Remus' to either avoid testifying or to gain some sympathy. "You don't know George Remus as well as I do," she said, "He has a scheming and conniving mind." Shortly afterwards, for no apparent reason, she burst into tears and ran out into the corridor. She was followed by her attorney, Joseph Breitenstein, who managed to ascertain that a man claiming to be a Federal Agent had told her that he wanted to see her after the trial about a "white slave" charge. Mrs. Remus claimed that this was a threat from her estranged husband, who had been persecuting her since she arrived in Indianapolis.

Over the next couple of days the prosecution put various witnesses on the stand to testify to the financial arrangements surrounding the purchase of the distillery. Leonard Garver, a Cincinnati broker, testified that he approached two of the defendants, William Lucking and George Landon, on behalf of George Remus in order to raise the $50,000 he claims he paid as his portion of the purchase price. He asserted that the defendants were aware of what this money was for. Then Government agents testified to the discovery of the theft of the whiskey.

Next, Agent "Dynamite Dave" Nolan of the intelligence unit of the Department of Internal Revenue, testified to conversations he had with Arnold Hellmich some time after the discovery of the theft and prior to the Grand Jury hearing. During one conversation Hellmich was alleged to have confessed to Jack Kratz, who had died before he could be brought to trial, that he was "the most worried man in Missouri." Kratz had apparently told him not to worry because "Nat Goldstein, Mike Kinney and Mike Whalen will take care of that." This testimony was corroborated by George Winkler, an Indiana Prohibition agent, who was also present when these alleged conversations took place. Then Edward Miller, the night watchman, took the stand and testified that no whiskey was removed from the warehouse when he was on duty and that there was a policeman there everyday.

Charles Barlow now related how he discovered the water in the barrels. Then a witness testified concerning Senator Michael Kinney's name being used as a reference in the lease of the office in the Arcade Building where the Rex Realty Company was located. It seemed that each time the prosecution put a witness on the stand another defendant was implicated.

Elaborate security measures were taken whenever Remus was in the court room. Informants reported that "Egan's Rats" had contracted to kill him. Surrounded by secret service men, federal officers and his own private bodyguards, he sat in a corner of the courtroom from where he could watch every movement in the room. The federal agents apparently took the threats seriously enough to furnish Remus with a gun for his own protection. Whenever the Court adjourned, Remus remained seated until the courtroom had been cleared, at which time he left by a side door, surrounded by his guards. He was also guarded around the clock at his hotel where he was not even registered on the books.

On December 16th, surrounded by three of his federal protectors, George Remus made his long awaited appearance on the witness stand. He sat down and crossed his legs, seeming calm and confident as he looked over towards the defendants, who, he believed, had double crossed him.

Before Remus could even begin to give his testimony, Mrs. Remus' attorney, Joseph Breitenstein, was on his feet objecting to Remus being called as a witness on the grounds that a husband could not testify against his wife, and although the Imogene and George Remus were estranged, they were still man and wife. Before Judge Baltzell could rule on the objection, District Attorney Ward rose and addressed the Court: "We feel," he said, " that there is too much question about this point to permit such an objection to go into the records." He then proposed a motion to *nolle prosse* the charges against Mrs. Remus. Judge Baltzell sustained the motion. Mrs. Remus, smiling triumphantly, sat back in her chair visibly relaxed.

Remus was on the witness stand for two and a half hours, one hour of which was given over to the cross examination. He described in detail the plot to "milk" the Jack Daniels distillery and the subsequent removal of the whiskey, outlining his part in it and naming many of the defendants as members of the conspiracy. In spite of Mrs. Remus' claim that he would probably faint in court, or do something equally sensational, to gain sympathy, he gave his testimony in a measured, unhurried and very calm manner.

It was evident that he was merely giving the main outlines of the plot without going into too much detail, a decision believed to have been made by the prosecution in order to keep the testimony clear and easily understood, as well as to limit the scope of the cross examination. The defense attorneys would not be able to cross examine Remus on any facts that had not been brought out during the direct examination. This strategy obviously worked. A vigorous attempt by the defense to discredit Remus' testimony met with little success.

Nevertheless, Attorney Ely, who led the defense's attack, managed to ruffle Remus a bit when he questioned him about his being disbared in Illinois. Asked about his reasons for going into the liquor business, Remus declared that he went into it, not for the money but for the "thrill and excitement of the game." Ely then tried in vain to have him admit that he had agreed to testify in order to obtain immunity from prosecution. "In your opinion," Ely asked, "is it not true that Harry M. Daugherty still exerts a powerful influence in the Department of Justice and that you fear you will be prosecuted unless you give the testimony the government desires in this case?" However, a prosecution objection to this question was sustained.

When the defense ended their cross examination, Remus stood down and, accompanied once again by the three federal agents, walked out of the courtroom, passing close to the enclosure where a number of the defendants sat, lowering their eyes as he passed.

The indictment against Remus for his involvement in the Jack Daniels conspiracy was, in fact, dropped in April, 1926, because of his assistance in this case and his testimony before the Senate Investigation into the Justice Department under Harry Daugherty.

The prosecution closed their case with Remus' testimony. They had called 30 witnesses and had implicated every one of the defendants. They were confident that they had made a strong case. Counsel for the defense proposed a motion for the acquittal of their clients, claiming that there was insufficient evidence. Judge Baltzell did not hesitate in overruling this motion.

The defense opened by putting a former Circuit Court Judge, Thomas Hennings, on the stand as a character witness for Senator Kinney. It soon became evident that the defense's plan was to be "every man for himself," and that most of the testimony would consist of character references.

Two former mayors of St. Louis, a chief of police, and various bankers, brokers and other prominent St. Louisans took the stand as character witnesses. Five defendants testified on their own behalf. Nat Goldstein claimed that Remus had approached him in 1923 and had asked him to arrange for a perfectly legal bond on a warehouse deal he was contracting. He said he received $225 as a commission from the bond company and that was the full extent of his dealings with Remus.

Ada and John Gehrum, who had been charged with receiving Jack Daniels whiskey from Remus for resale at the Death Valley farm, denied receiving any liquor and claimed that they had only been implicated because they had once sued Remus for money owed them, and this was his chance to get even. August Walters, a Cincinnati banker, then denied that he had transported and received liquor from Remus, saying that he had been approached by Remus to enter the venture, but he had declined. William Kinney told how he had been appointed gauger at the Jack Daniels Warehouse, but he denied having any knowledge of the activities within the warehouse and even claimed that he did not know where the garage was.

On the 17th of December, the hearing of testimony finally ended, and the closing statements began. John Marshall opened for the government declaring "We are called upon here to wash out the dirty linen of the greatest bootlegging concern in the United States." Then he reviewed the testimony and asserted that the existence of a conspiracy had been proved beyond a doubt, and he labeled it "one of the biggest scandals that has ever gotten into the Federal Court. All that remained for the jury now," he concluded,"was to convict the alleged conspirators." Albert Ward then vigorously appealed for conviction of every one of the defendants, also stressing that this was "the greatest liquor conspiracy in the United States."

The defense, led by Ely, launched a spirited attack on the credibility of George Remus. Referring to him as a notorious bootlegger, Ely charged that Remus had put "more illegal whiskey on the market than anyone else in the country." He also charged that Remus' entire testimony was intended to harm his estranged wife, and he did not care whom else he wronged in the process.

On December 18th, Judge Baltzell instructed the jury. He reminded them that the defendants were being tried on one count: conspiracy to violate the National Prohibition Act; and he stated that the government had proved beyond any doubt that a conspiracy did exist. The jury's task was to determine how many of the defendants were involved and to charge them accordingly. The jury deliberated for just over two and a half hours before returning their verdict to a hushed courtroom. Of the twenty five defendants, they found only August Walter and Ada and John Gehrum not guilty. The rest were found guilty as charged and bound over to receive their sentences on the 30th of December. All of the defendants were in the Courtroom when the verdict was announced, and they all received the news with outward calm.

At the sentencing, Judge Baltzell declared that the Jack Daniel case was: "The biggest conspiracy I have ever heard of." Then he set a precedent by denying freedom on bond to the defendants who had filed an appeal in the Circuit Court of Appeals. He also overruled all motions for new trials except in the case of Michael Kinney, the State Senator, whom he felt had not been sufficiently implicated. One defendant, Don Robinson, who had testified as a government witness was discharged. Of the remaining twenty conspirators, twelve received fines and sentences of varying lengths in the Leavenworth Penitentiary, and eight received terms of less than a year, to be served in the Marion County Jail. The most severe sentences went to those who the Judge felt were the brains behind the conspiracy. He acknowledged that some of those charged were probably unaware of the enormity of the conspiracy they were involved in, but the law had to be respected. The convicted conspirators were further humiliated by being marched through the busy streets of Indianapolis, to join the 225 inmates of the Marion County jail.

One of the jail guards was so surprised at the well dressed, prosperous appearance of the new convicts that he remarked: "This doesn't look like a bunch of gangsters to me." And one of the newly arrived conspirators lamented: "All we did was to buy some whisky and sell it and no one got hurt."

CHAPTER NINE

MARITAL STRIFE

George Remus returned to Cincinnati before the verdicts had been returned in the Jack Daniels trial. Having made so many powerful enemies, he immediately appealed to the Cincinnati Police for protection, and although he was denied a special detail, patrolmen were instructed to watch his house in the course of their rounds.

George and Imogene Remus continued their verbal battle. Imogene claimed that her husband had tried for a reconciliation with her on their arrival in Indianapolis, and when she made it clear that she was not interested, he threatened her. Remus vehemently denied ever attempting reconciliation and declared that his wife had become repulsive to him. He told of her filing for a divorce and how he had counter filed, but he explained that it had been impossible to serve her with injunctions because she had not set foot in the state of Ohio since then. He challenged her to do so in order that the matter could be "thrashed out in the divorce court." He further denied making any threats against her, explaining that he had been in the constant custody of government agents since he had been released from Atlanta.

For the first few months of 1926, Remus was occupied in matters concerning his estranged wife and his upcoming divorce case, which was already gaining widespread attention in the press. For Remus that his wife had left him and taken his money was bad enough, but the thought that she did so with "an officer of the government, sworn to uphold the law," really inflamed him. And to make things worse, he discovered that Dodge had been an active agent in collecting the information that led to the raid on the Death Valley farm in 1921. He now began to believe that his wife had been the informant in that case, and that her affair with Dodge predated that event.

Remus suffered his first blow in his divorce case in March, when Imogene Remus' attorney, Edward Dixon, filed a motion with the Domestic Relations Court in Cincinnati to dismiss Remus' cross petition filed against Mrs Remus and Dodge. He presented depositions indicating that there was no improper conduct between Dodge and Mrs Remus. The motion was sustained, and Remus' cross petition was dismissed.

Remus, however, was still convinced that Franklin Dodge had conspired with his wife to keep him in jail while together they controlled almost $275,000 in cash and a number of his distilleries and whiskey certificates that Remus had left with his wife, who had power of attorney over his affairs. He claimed that when he was released from the Atlanta Penitentiary in September, with only $36 in his pocket, he discovered that a number of his distilleries had been sold at well below market value and that Franklin Dodge had been named on many of the property transfers. He also believed that Dodge, seeking to keep him in jail, had encouraged the Justice Department to appeal Judge Hickenlooper's decision to dismiss Remus' one year sentence on the nuisance conviction.

In March Remus told reporters that his wife had stolen $80,000 from him. He was referring to the sale of the Fleischmann Distillery in Cincinnati, which Imogene Remus had apparently sold for $80,000, well below its value, and had then offered him $100 as his share. He also accused her of using his money to give Dodge expensive gifts such as motor vehicles and jewelry. He even contended that she changed the engraving on their silverware from "R" to "D". Mrs. Remus naturally denied having taken any of Remus' money. Moreover, her lawyers insisted that she was almost bankrupt, having to borrow funds to pay for their services.

On March 24th, 1926, Congressman Fiorella La Guardia of New York entered the controversy. In a fiery speech in the House of Representatives he referred to Dodge as the "ace" of investigators, and he corroborated Remus' charge that Dodge had conspired with Mrs Remus to keep him jail while they disposed of his property. "I would not be concerned in Remus' confinement at this time," he stated, "were it not that I am personally convinced that this persecution is along a carefully laid plan to keep him in jail as long as they can in order to dispose of the property obtained from him through the conspiracy of a Department of Justice agent."

La Guardia claimed that Dodge had met Mrs. Remus early in 1924, at the Atlanta Penitentiary when he was assigned to the case of Warden Sartain and had come to question her husband. In spite of the dismissal of charges against Dodge and Mrs. Remus for improper conduct, La Guardia asserted that the two had become "very friendly." "Their conduct in the very Warden's office," he said, "is too obscene to relate at this time." He charged that Dodge was "travelling around the country violating both the Mann and Volstead Acts with Mrs Remus, and in was in possession of whiskey certificates which belonged to Remus." La Guardia produced one example of the sale of a certificate by a man named John Gray, which he claimed was an alias for Dodge.

The Congressman then attacked the Justice Department for allowing this sort of activity by one of their agents and for allowing the man to resign without any investigation into his alleged illegal or unprofessional activities. Dodge had resigned on August 10th, 1925, and La Guardia claimed that he had done so at the request of the Department. Dodge vigorously denied this accusation,2 asserting that he resigned to accept a position with the investigation department of the National Credit Men's Association.

Finally La Guardia called attention to the disappearance from a government warehouse of cases of whiskey confiscated from the Squibb Distillery in 1921. When the distillery was closed following the raid on Death Valley, 1,500 cases of whiskey were confiscated by the prohibition agents and ordered destroyed. Attempting to get the whiskey back, Remus had Blanche Watson, his secretary, claim it as her own. She entered an appeal with the Circuit Court of Appeals for the return of the whiskey; therefore the whiskey had not been destroyed. The appeal was due to go to Court sometime in 1926, and in the meantime the whiskey remained in a government warehouse. However, 350 cases of the liquor had disappeared, and it was believed that the remaining cases might have been "milked," replacing the liquor with water and alcohol. Congressman La Guardia claimed that the Department of Justice knew about this theft, but had not investigated, hoping that eventually they would be allowed to destroy the remaining liquor and therefore not have to account for the missing cases.

Stung by La Guardia's accusations, the Justice Department finally conducted a full investigation, and several people were arrested and sentenced, but the Congressman was still not satisfied, claiming in July that he believed the important people responsible had been allowed to walk free. He intimated that Franklin Dodge was somehow involved in this theft.

Resenting these charges, an irate Franklin Dodge wrote to La Guardia emphatically denying any wrong doing; moreover, he accused La Guardia of being an ally of Remus. "The charges are absolutely false," he said, "I deny them without qualification; they have no foundation in fact and the attack upon me is wholly unwarranted and manifestly unfair." He denied the accusations regarding his alleged misconduct with Mrs Remus, claiming that he had only met her in January, 1925, and that she was in the company of her husband on that occasion and at all subsequent meetings. He refuted allegations that he had conspired with Mrs. Remus to defraud her husband, claiming that Remus had no money because most of his property was currently in litigation. The rest of his property, Dodge claimed, was hidden away in safety deposit boxes around the country. He concluded by charging that "George Remus is an atheist. He has no regard for the laws of God or man."

Congressman La Guardia resumed his attack on Dodge by furnishing proof of whiskey certificate transactions in which the route was from Dodge and Mrs Remus through her lawyer, Josdeph Brietenstein, to the buyer, Matt Hinkel. La Guardia criticized the Justice Department for ignoring these allegations and even blocking access to Dodge's files. The Bureau of Investigation did actually investigate these allegations with the Director of the Bureau, J. Edgar Hoover, himself assigning an agent to the case. Agent Wilcox, who headed the investigation, spoke directly to Joseph Breitenstein regarding the evidence introduced by Congressman La Guardia, and was told that a transaction was set up between the parties named. Mrs Remus was cited as the seller and Matt Hinkel as the buyer with Breitenstein and Dodge receiving a commission on the sale.

When this information was forwarded to Assistant Attorney General Mabel Willebrandt, she ruled that it did not indicate any criminal act on the part of Dodge because it was not illegal to sell whiskey certificates as long as they were sold for legitimate use. It did appear though that Dodge was secretly acting for Mrs. Remus, and in doing so was possibly conspiring against her husband.

The department files on Dodge contained no evidence that he had been involved in any conspiracy to keep Remus in jail. They did disclose, however, that Dodge's activities had been investigated previously, but there was never enough evidence of misconduct to warrant a dismissal, although instances of his drinking while on duty and having illicit relations with women were cited. After studying a report on the files made by a bureau agent, J. Edgar Hoover wrote to the Attorney General, stating that "the files of the Bureau have been searched and no references have been found therein to any charges, allegations, intimations or interferences to the effect that Dodge was in any way implicated in dealings in liquor certificates while an agent of the Bureau of Investigation." The Attorney General's office was satisified, but an enraged La Guardia was never granted access to the file on Dodge.

On April 2nd, 1926, Remus sued Imogene Remus, Franklin Dodge and Matt Hinkel for approximately one million dollars worth of property which he claimed to be his. This included 95,000 gallons of whiskey currently being stored at the Pogue Distillery, which he still owned. Mrs Remus had sold the whiskey and the withdrawal certificates to Matt Hinkel, and Remus claimed that she did not have the authority to do this. Hinkel had tried to remove the whiskey to the Old Pepper Distillery at Lexington, Kentucky, but he had been prevented from doing so by an injunction filed by Remus.

Seven days later, on April 9th, Remus' luck ran out. The Cincinnati Court of Appeals ruled that he would have to serve his one year sentence in a county jail. Knowing that he would be unable to look after his affairs for another year, he decided to make one final, although illegal, attempt at getting some of his property back.

On May 3rd, he drove to the Pogue Distillery in Maysville where he bribed the guards to let him start loading the whiskey onto his trucks. Unfortunately for him, Hinkel had anticipated this move and had posted his own loyal guards at the distillery. They called the police, who arrived along with Federal Marshalls and a restraining order before a single truck could depart from the premises. Two weeks later a disconsolate Remus was on his way to the Miami County Jail in Troy, near Dayton, where he was finally to serve his sentence on the nuisance charge.

On April 26th, 1927, George Remus was finally released from the Scioto County Jail in Portsmouth, Ohio, to which he had been transferred for six months of his sentence because he complained constantly about his treatment at Troy. He claimed that he was not given enough exercise and that the environment was bad for his health .He claimed that he was incarcerated in "a small cell where I could not see anything--but a portion of the sky. I could not even see the top of the trees." At Portsmouth he was soon made a trusty at the Portsmouth jail and enjoyed special privileges such as walks outside of the jail. He was a model inmate, and once he even helped the prison guards capture two escaping prisoners. Just prior to leaving the jail he hosted a banquet for 56 fellow prisoners. Attired in a white coat, white apron and Palm Beach pants he personally served his guests an elaborate meal featuring chicken and ice cream. This was the third banquet he served and paid for since he arrived at the jail. He also hosted a banquet for the telephone girls. At the farewell dinner he announced that he had given up a life of crime. "I set out to make a quick clean up, but not all the dollars that rolled in could pay for that first night in Atlanta." After his release he paid a short visit to New York City and then returned to his home in Cincinnati.

When he arrived at his house, he found all the doors were locked. He had to climb through a window. He found the house empty except for a bed, a table and a chair. It was later alleged that Remus himself had removed most of the furniture and sent it to his daughter in Chicago, but he always maintained that his wife had stripped the houxse bare with the help of Franklin Dodge. In spite of his claims that his wife had taken all his money, Remus could still afford to reside in a suite in the Sinton Hotel.

He started to work on his impending divorce case. Intending to prove that his wife had been having an affair with Franklin Dodge, he had the couple tailed, hoping to catch them together in some hotel room. In spite of spending thousands of dollars in this pursuit, he never succeeded. He also sought to regain some of the money he said his wife had stolen from him. He even threatened her, claiming that he would follow her all the way to China if necessary if she did not return his property. Undoubtedly Mrs. Remus took this threat seriously; she took to carrying a revolver in her purse. Remus, on learning of this, claimed she intended to kill him if she had the opportunity.

Even before Remus was returned to jail in May, 1926, deportation proceedings had been instigated against him. In March, 1926, Mrs. Remus and Franklin Dodge, who started the action, visited Mr. Coykendall, the immigration officer in Atlanta.

Imogene Remus made an affadavit declaring that "My husband. George Remus, stated at different times and places that he was not a citizen of the United States; that his father never became a naturalized citizen of the United States, but that when the case came to final issue, he, George Remus, would tesify that his father did become a nauralized citizen of the United States before he, George Remus, reached the age of 21 years, thereby conferring United States citizenship on him, the said George Remus; he also stated tha he would testify that his father's naturalization papers 'were lost in the shuffle' and that he could not produce them."

She also indicated that since her marriage to him made her a subject of Germany, she was filing an application for naturalization. However, fearing Remus' reaction to her action, she decided not to sign the affadavit until after the divorce.

Under Coykendall's direction an investigation was made into the charges that Remus' father was not a naturalized citizen, as Remus claimed. In July, 1926, it was announced that the investigations had failed to find any record of Frank Remus being naturalized, and therefore George Remus would have to face a deportation hearing. Remus declared the claim to be idiotic.

Remus' hearing was to be presided over by Judge Thomas in Cincinnati on January 10th, 1927, but it was postponed on recommendation of the Justice Department because of Dodge's direct involvement in the matter. The Department wished to avoid unfavorable publicity, realizing that Remus would ascribe the move to deport him to a vendetta on the part of his wife and Dodge, her alleged lover. The Labor Department concurred; so the hearing was postponed until June, 1927, and then further postponed until September. By this time the Labor Department was having doubts about the strength of their case. They knew that Remus would fight the case and might win. So the case was eventually held over till July, 1928, when Remus was given till October to produce proof of his citizenship; and on October 3rd, 1928, the department announced that they were not dropping the charges against Remus, but were going to allow the case to lay dormant. This meant that the charges could be reinstituted against him at any time, but they never were.

Surrounded by personal bodyguards, George and Imogene Remus appeared in court a number of times in 1927, filing petitions and cross petitions, and accusing one another of having made threats to kill on sight. Remus even charged that his wife carried a gun in her handbag waiting for the opportunity to shoot him. Both sides in the impending divorce case traveled around the country taking depositions for use in the trial, and the pressure evidently began to affect Remus. In Chicago, it is alleged, he attacked one of Mrs. Remus' attorneys, Joseph Breitenstein, and tried to throw him out of a window in a high rise building.

In September, Remus' attorneys, John Druffel and Benton Oppenheim, unexpectedly withdrew from the case, and Remus decided to represent himself. Meanwhile his wife's lawyer, former Common Pleas Judge, Edward Dixon, was pressuring the Court to set a date for the trial. Remus, attempting to stall the proceedings, filed an affidavit of prejudice and bias against Judge Hoffman, who was to preside over the trial. A few weeks later he unexpectedly dismissed his affidavit and declared himself ready to go trial. Judge Hoffman then set the hearing for October 6th, 1927, and announced that the Remus case would be the only one on the docket for two days. He wanted the trial to ensure a final settlement. Then he notified Charles Dean at the Internal Revenue office of the date so that the government would hear any evidence about the alleged large sums of money each side accussed the other of possessing.

BOOK ONE - PART TWO

CHAPTER TEN

CHARLES TAFT: IN THE FOOTSTEPS OF HIS FATHER

Charles P. Taft, 2nd, has become an extremely able lawyer, following well--in personal and professional distinction--the footsteps of his father, Ex-President William Howard Taft, Chief Justice of the Supreme Court of the United States."

"The White House Gang" by Earle Looker

p. 64

In 1678, Robert Taft, the first of his family to come to America, was recorded as living in Baintree, Massachusets. He and his wife had twelve children. Their fourth son, Joseph had a son, Alphonso, who served as Secretary of War in the Grant administration. Alphonso had a son, William Howard Taft, who married Nellie Herron. They had two children, Robert aged eight and Helen aged six, before their last son, Charles was born in the family home in Cincinnati, Ohio, on September 20, 1897. William Howard Taft, was serving his sixth term as federal judge of the Sixth Circuit, which included Kentucky, Ohio, Michigan, and Tennessee, and was already on his way to a prestigious political career. The Taft family, dedicated to public service, was becoming one of the leading families of the country.

Charlie was a very attractive and active child. "He had big, dark eyes, soft, brown curls, very deep dimples, and a charming smile that was always in evidence." An extrovert, he was unhappy when he lacked playmates, and he always wanted to go along when the grown-ups went anywheres. He was well coordinated and seemed to have an endless supply of energy. His mother characterized him: "He is so full of life that he is not still a moment and tears off all his buttons everyday." "He behaves pretty well, but he is so restless as if he had quicksilver in his veins. It tires you to keep up with him.""He disliked wearing shoes. He insists on running barefoot even when he was suffering of little boils on his feet."

Energetic and charming, Charlie occasionally misbehaved, but his father found it difficult, if not impossible, to discipline him. He wrote to his wife:" As to Charles, he is so attractive even in his naughtiness that he will have to grow into a less attractive age before he can have the necessary discipline."

The Tafts spent their summers in Murray Bay, located on the banks of Saint Lawrence River some 100 miles northeast of Quebec. There the children could enjoy hiking, swimming, fishing and playing games. One day young Charlie was the object of a community wide search. His mother could not find him, and when it was seven thirty and he was still missing, she was very worried. Then, as she related it in a letter to her husbvand, "Bob who came in late also started out, and though I thought it foolish, said he would go down on the rocks to look. Sure enough there he found Charlie fishing with Mr. Johnicoueur, the druggist, and some friends, among them Mrs. Mischler, who had taken them supper and lanterns."

Charlie Taft started his life-long travels at a very early age. He was only two years old when he accompanied his family to the Philipines. In April, 1898, the United States went to war to free Cuba from Spanish domination. Hardly any thought was given, at the time, to the Spanish colony of the Philippine islands, in the distant Pacific Ocean, until Admiral Dewey sailed his Pacific squadron into Manila harbor and demolished the Spanish fleet anchored there, without suffering a single casualty. At the Treaty of Paris in 1899, the United States paid Spain two million dollars and was granted sovereignty over the Philippine Archipelago. What to do with the Philippines was hotly debated in the United States. There was considerable anti-imperialism sentiment, supported by Federal Judge William Howard Taft, who did not want his country to become a colonial power. However, when President McKinley declared that all efforts would be made to establish a government under law and liberty leading to eventual independence of the Philipines, Taft agreed to head a commission to implement a peaceful transition to self rule.

Taft, now an international figure, boarded the Manila bound U.S. Army transport *Hancock* on April 17th, 1900 accompanied by his wife and three children, despite warnings that the journey might be hazardous for the children. Charlie had recently recovered from pneumonia, but he still played actively with the other young children aboard. Indeed his amazed father declared:""We call him the 'tornado', he creates such a sensation when he lands in the midst of the children of the ship. He is very badly in need of discipline, and yet I cannot very well administer it in a crowd."

The first stop on the journey was Honolulu where, for four days the island's famous hospitality was lavished on the Tafts, and they were unable to escape without the inevitable Hawaiian leis around their necks. In Tokyo Charlie's parents were received at the royal palace by the Emperor and the Empress, and when the commission moved on to the Philippines, Mrs. Taft chose to remain with the children for a while on the hospitable island. They lived in a bungalow on Yokohama where Charlie was looked after by the Japanese amah, Matsu. She was hard pressed to keep up with the young toddler whose mother wrote in a letter home that she "toddled after Charlie like a dog and he rules her with a rod of iron." Charlie seemed to spend all his time playing and was rapidly becoming the family favorite. He did not even notice the frequent earthquakes which his brother, Robert, meticulously counted, noting thirteen in one day.

The Taft children thoroughly enjoyed life in the Philippines. They had a play room set aside for them, and the court yard was reserved for their use. Charlie often joined the gardener's two sons, Jose and Capito, in playing children's games. As they climbed trees, watched the antics of the monkeys, and flew kites, they communicated in a language that was a mixture of English, Spanish, and Tagalog. The Taft children shared a number of pets including a deer, a monkey, and a young orangutan. Most of all, though, Charlie enjoyed riding his white shaggy pony, "Weary Willie." Young Charlie was a favorite with the soldiers who guarded the children at play, and he tended to be the center of attention at family gatherings. His father wrote that he was "just as notional and just as determined as ever and his mother is just as much a slave to him as she ever was, but she accuses Maria (the family maid) and me of spoiling him whenever we get a chance so that she regards honors as even." A boy with great dreams in his head, Charlie later recalled standing in front of a mirror on one occasion, and declaring: "'I am the Governor of the Philippines Islands." In 1901 Charlie, aged four, went with his family and the official commission party on a tour of the islands, covering eighteen provinces. While the commissioners were busy establishing local governments and explaining the new provincial codes the children enjoyed seeing the dances and festivities provided by the various tribes. They were most impressed by the reception at Bataan where they were met by a fleet of flower-decked boats fifty feet long.

On July 4th, 1901, Charlie looked on with the rest of his proud family, as his father was installed as the very first Governor of the Philippines. It was an impressive ceremony. Thousands of Filipinos in colorful native garb from all over the Archipelago crowded into the Cathedral Plaza to watch as the contingent of American soldiers and sailors stood at attention in full dress uniforms, and as the band blared out "The Star Spangled Banner," William Howard Taft took the oath of office. The next day the Taft family moved into the spacious and ornate Malacanan Palace, the former abode of General MacArthur, who was returning to the U.S.

Six months later, Christmas Eve 1901, only nineteen months after they first arrived in the Philippines, the Tafts were heading homeward. Their father, who had collapsed a couple of months previously, had been recalled to Washington by Theodore Roosevelt, who had succeded to the Presidency after the assassination of Mc Kinley in September of that year. Governor Taft's orders were to return to the United States to recuperate and to testify at a Senate hearing on the Philippines. On arrival in the United States, the Taft children returned to the family home in Cincinnati while their father went to Washington. At first they found it difficult to adjust to the midwest winter and the lack of freedom, but they were soon at home, skating on the pond and making new friends.

In May 1902 Governor Taft was sent on an assignment to Rome for an unofficial consultation with the Pope concerning the friars' lands in the Philippines. His family could not travel with him immediately because Robert was recovering from a mild case of scarlet fever, contracted after a tonsillectomy; but as soon as he was well enough, they set out to join their father in Rome. Charlie, who seemed to get sick before every trip, made the journey while suffering from whooping cough, but he was fully recovered by the time they arrived and was present when the entire family was invited for an interview with the Pope.

While Governor Taft was busy negotiating with the Vatican officials, the rest of the family were touring Rome, guided by Robert, who had carefully studied a number of guide books. They visited the catacombs, the Borghese Gardens, the Forum, and, of course, the Coliseum in moonlight. After a final audience with the Pope, the Tafts departed from Rome. Governor Taft returned directly to the Philippines, but Mrs. Taft and the children toured Europe. Their itinerary included Florence, Venice, Salzburg, Prague, Dresden, Weimar, Nuremberg and Baden Baden, where they stayed for two weeks before returning to the Philippines via Suez.

At Venice the children were delighted that their hotel was located right on the bank of one of the canals. They visited the Palace of the Doges, wandered around St. Mark's, and especially enjoyed swimming in the Lido. At Dresden they were pleased to meet up with the Andersons, friends from Cincinnati. But the children had their best time at Baden Baden where there were horse races, fireworks, and the famous baths. The Taft children liked to go quickly from a warm pool to a cool one and so on. They also enjoyed going to a farm with a Swiss style chalet. Here they were allowed to milk the cows and then drink the fresh milk.

On returning to the Philippines, Charlie was greeted warmly by his former playmates, Jose and Capito, but the Tafts did not remain long in the Islands. President Roosevelt had approached Governor Taft in February 1903 with the offer to join the Cabinet as Secretary of War and by the end of that year he had accepted the position. Before leaving the Philippines, the Tafts gave a final party, a Venetian masked ball and carnival. There were no gondolas, but flower bedecked canoes, rafts, bancos, barges and launches pulled up to the river landing, filled with costumed guests. They were greeted by Governor and Mrs. Taft attired as the Doge and his consort. Young Charlie was dressed as a Venetian youth.

On their return trip the Tafts visited Japan again, and once again they were royally received. While Taft headed to Washington to assume his new post, Mrs. Taft, Charlie and his sister spent the winter in Santa Barbara, California. While there Charlie enjoyed playing baseball with the local chilrdren, and he spoke in Tagalog to the Filipino boys. The family, except Robert, who was at the Taft school in Connecticut, were reunited at the Louisiana Purchase Exposition (1904) at St. Louis, where Taft was promoting the Filipino's exhibition. After enjoying the various exhibits, the family continued on to their commodious, new two storey home in Washington D.C. located at 1631 K Street. The Taft's did not stay settled for long, though, before they were off on yet another trip. In the summer of 1905 William Howard Taft, in his capacity as Secretary of War, was sent to Japan for unofficial, though government sanctioned, visit to Japan. Accompanied by 7 Senators and 23 Congressmen, he held secret negotiations with the victorious Japanese prior to the Peace Conference scheduled to be held in the United States at a later date. He was also given the opportunity on this visit, to show the Asian leaders what he had managed to accomplish in the Philippines.

Mrs. Taft decided to forgo the trip to the Orient, deciding instead to spend the summer in England with her children. They sailed on the *Zeeland* on July 1st, 1905. Charlie by this time was quite at home aboard ship . His mother recalled that "He rushed around the ship with the utmost carelessness, delivering orders in a strange jargon to his little Filipino nurse, who was always rushing after him just far enough behind to be utterly useless in case anything should happen to him." She wondered how he managed to grow up into a decorous young man without caution on his part or restraint on his parent's part.

In England they settled in a house near Oxford. Bob Taft spent the summer touring Scandinavia with some friends, while Charlie and his sister, Helen, enjoyed punting on the river, watching county cricket, and exploring the countryside on the few occasions that the weather permitted. Their journey home at the end of summer was highlighted by a bit of excitement when they were able to see the English monarch as their train arrived at same station in London as King Edward VII's. After a brief stop in Paris to do some shopping, they returned to United States, eager to catch up with friends and family in Cincinnati, before returning to their home in Washington.

THE WHITE HOUSE GANG

Charlie was soon at home in the nation's capital. Accompanied by their French governess, Mlle. Jeanne Marret, Charlie and his sister visited the many statues, parks, monuments, and historic buildings, and they were invited to the White House as guests of the Roosevelt children. Charlie and Quentin Roosevelt soon became fast friends and were delighted to learn that they would attend the same school. The Force Public School, a red brick structure on Massachusetts Avenue, had about fifty pupils, drawn from the immediate neighborhood.

On his first day Charlie was accompanied by his father. But when Charlie came home for lunch he cried and declared that he didn't ever want to return. In time, however, he became an enthusiastic pupil and one of the best readers in his class. He made friends easily, and when Quentin decided to organize a gang, Charlie, who was nicknamed "Taffy," was asked to join. He was a popular member of the gang and was characterized by fellow gang member Earl Looker as "remarkable for his calmness, slowness to anger, good humor, and steadfast determination when roused." The White House Gang, as they became known, numbered seven, and their objectives were "to confound all rules of deportment in high places, mingle in the lives of Presidents and policemen, win victories, taste honor, and suffer punishment, while engaging in escapades that easily reached the pages of the national press."

One escapade resulted in the gang being banished from the White House for a week. Bored with their usual games, the gang decided that the portrait of Andrew Jackson hanging in the upper hall of the White House should be altered to make "Old Hickory" resemble an Arabian dancer. They fired a volley of spitballs at the portrait, before positioning three spitballs on his forehead, one on each ear lobe, and a gob over each of the coat buttons. The gang then spent a peaceful night as guests in the White House, but the next morning they had to face the music, and it wasn't pleasant. President Roosevelt asked who threw the first spitball, and he was upset when three of the gang claimed the dubious honor. Roosevelt said sternly: "It's all very sporting to take the blame from one another, but I--want--the--truth!" After lecturing them on the respect due to property, he meted out the punishment:

banishment for an entire week. Quentin, noted that it would soon be Charlie's house anyway.

On another occasion the gang found it necessary to avoid telling the truth. During a mock battle between the Spanish and American armies Charlie stumbled over a chair and was slightly wounded by Quentin, who was wielding the sabre his father used charging up San Juan Hill.Charlie, displaying great presence of mind, immediately declared that he had injured himself by falling over the chair. Quickly the boys smeared some of his blood on the chair's brass feet and hurried to summon some aid.

The gang felt just as much at home in the nearby State, War and Navy Departments Building, where they amused themselves by sending the elevators to floors where no one was waiting for them. Once they gave so many contradictory orders to an elevator that it short circuited and was stuck between two floors. Another favorite prank was to tie a wallet to a piece of string and leave it lying out in the pathway while they hid behind a nearby hedge. Any unsuspecting person reaching for the wallet would quickly find it pulled away before they could grasp it. The game, however, was abandoned when one quick clerk actually grabbed the wallet with some of their money in it before they could pull it back.

When they were not indulging in sort of mischief, the gang was usually busy playing games. Baseball was their favorite, but with only seven in the gang, they needed more players to field a team. To recruit the best players in the school they let it be known that the games would be played on a diamond laid out on the White House grounds. Their team, on which Charlie played second base, won most of their games. Their biggest fan was President Roosevelt, who would occasionally steal away from his official business to watch a game. His son Quentin, the team's captain, was also in charge of providing lemonade for the thirsty competitors.

Although Charlie was happy at the Force school, the Taft's found it necessary to move him when he began to be harassed by people seeking federal jobs which only his father could provide. Some of these overzealous office seekers would even stuff letters and petitions in his pockets as he walked to and from school. The family finally decided to send him to the preparatory school established by his uncle Horace. But one more wonderful adventure awaited the young boy before then.

AROUND THE WORLD

On August 18, 1907, Charlie left Washington D.C. with his parents, on a cross country trip to Seattle where they embarked on the S.S. *Manchuria* on September 12th for a trip around the world. William Howard Taft was to represent the United States government at the opening ceremony of the First Philippine Assembly, thereby keeping a promise he had made while Governor of the Islands. By this time Charlie was a seasoned traveler, and he quickly adapted to life aboard ship. Watched often by his father, he engaged in athletic contests, pillow fights and boxing matches with the other boys on board. Three days into the journey, on September 15th, Charlie's father celebrated his 50th birthday. The cake served at the birthday party had inscribed on it; "Compliments to Hon. William H. Taft, Our Next President." Rumors were rife that Taft was thinking of running for the Presidency.

The first leg of the journey, the 5,000 mile trip to Japan, took fourteen days, and after a fairly rough passage, they docked at Yokohama, where they received an enthusiastic greeting. The U.S. *Chatatanooga* saluted by firing its ten-pounders while launches and sampans flying American flags gave shrill whistles and the people on the crowded docks shouted "Bonzi." On shore there were signs of welcome everywhere. For miles the fronts of the houses and shops were covered with red, white, and blue bunting along with yellow suns. There was even a balloon flying with William Taft's face pictured on it.

From Yokohama the Taft group traveled on a special train to Tokyo, where they met with another friendly reception. On previous visits the Taft's had been received by the Emperor and Empress, but on this occasion they were highly honored by being asked to stay as the Emperor's personal guests. They were given suites in the Shiba Palace, with its acres of exquisite gardens, picturesque bridges over canals, and an extensive sea water lagoon, where Charlie and his mother were treated to an afternoon of fishing. This fishing, however, was unlike any they had done at their summer home in Quebec.

> Servants in imperial livery hovered about to minister to the anglers, to each of whom was handed a bamboo pole, with a silken line attached. At the end of the line dangled a silver hook. To one attendant was allotted the custody of the basket of honorable worms which served as bait, and the duty of threading them upon the hooks.It was prime fishing.

> No sooner did the hook touch the water than there would come a strike. Hauling in the prize, another servant would release the honorable fish from the barb, and committing the hook to the bait purveyor, place the fish in a tub of water. The fish were a species of trout ranging from eight to fifteen, or sixteen inches in length. They were fairly gamy, and fought hard enough against landing partially to compensate for the somewhat enervating attentions of the man with the bait and his fellow. At the end of an hour the tub was full of fish, most of which were tributes to Charley's piscatorial skill, was borne in triumph to the cook, and served for tiffin.

While his father was busy making speeches and conferring with important officials, Charlie was given the royal treatment. He was granted an audience with the Empress, who gave him a small gold cabinet in honor of the occasion, and he was taken on a tour of the city by group of local newspaper editors. In fact, wherever he went he was followed by reporters and photographers. He was, at that moment, possibly one of the best known boys in the world.

Leaving Tokyo, the Taft party traveled by special coach to Kyoto, the ancient capital, where they visited still more palaces and temples before continuing on to Kobe. Here they caught a boat for Nagasaki, travelling through the Inland Sea which was crowded with the junks and sampans of the Japanese fisherman. In Nagasaki, he was taken by Mrs. John J. Pershing to see a special demonstration of Japanese dancing. From Nagasaki, the party traveled to Shanghai in China. Here, in the foreign quarter where traders came from all over the world to ply their wares, enthusiastic crowds were kept at bay by the tall, bearded, turbaned Sikhs who had been imported to the area many years previously to take up police duties. The next stop for the group was the island of Hong Kong where they once again boarded a ship, this time the army transport *McClellan*, for the trip across the China Sea to Manilla.

The Taft's were greeted in Manila by an overly enthusiastic crowd, who had been given a whole week's holiday in honor of the occasion. After Secretary Taft's address at the opening of the Philippine Assembly, he was honored at a splendid inaugural ball, held at Malacanan Palace. Charlie enjoyed the festivities, and found time to renew his friendship with Jose and Capito. He also accompanied his father on some of his inspection trips, and the two were photographed together at the Igorrote School in Bagnio, the summer capital.

Rear Admiral Hemphill's flagship, the *Rainbow*, carried the Taft entourage from Manila to Valdivostok, Russia's only naval base in the Pacific. Young Charlie found the daily routine of the war ship very interesting and took the opportunity to learn all he could about navigation, gunnery and signaling. He even joined the marines in their morning exercises on deck. The party arrived in Vladivostok to find the situation very tense. Martial law had been declared a few weeks earlier after a mutiny had been put down and a number of sailors had been executed. Armed patrols roamed the streets and provided Charlie with the rare sight of Cossacks, rifles slung across their backs, galloping about on their shaggy Manchurian ponies. The Tafts made the 5,3007 mile trip to Moscow, via the Trans-Siberian railroad, in a special armored train provided by the Czar. They were guarded at every stop by officers of the Russian Imperial Armed Forces, and although nothing untoward happened, they were delayed shortly by a bomb scare at the station in Ufa. The eleven day journey took them through many interesting and historic places, including Irkutsk, better known as "Exile City," where thousands of people lived, exiled and deprived of all rights.

Thanksgiving Day was celebrated as the wood-fueled train wound its way slowly through the scenic Ural mountains. Instead of the traditional turkey, partridge was served, and the Russian baker produced an enormous cake with the year 1662 inscribed on it. Some discussion ensued concerning the true date the first Thanksgiving was celebrated, but Charlie solved the problem by simply eating the part of the cake that had the date inscribed on it.

In Moscow the Tafts received yet another royal and enthusiastic welcome. They were honored by a special tour of the Kremlin and a special performance of the Imperial ballet. They also drove about the city in droshkies viewing the Cathedral St. Basil, the Moscow Bell and other tourist attractions, even venturing into the infamous "thieves market," which was set up to allow people to buy back sentimental or precious objects that had been stolen from them. During this stay in Moscow, Charlie was pleased to have as a companion the young daughter of the Mayor.

The next destination, St. Petersburg, held special interest for the Tafts since Charlie's grandfather had resided there while serving as the United States representative to Russia, and Secretary Taft enjoyed conversing with a number of officials who had known his father. While the Secretary of War visited the Czar at Tzarskoe-Selo and observed the military parade in celebration of the crack Semenovski Regiment's feast day, Charlie accompanied his mother on a tour of St Petersburg which included visits to the Winter Palace and the the Hermitage.

From Russia, the Taft's travelled to Germany, where Charlie and his father were honored guests at a display of German military might, staged on the Dobgenitz Battlefield on the outskirts of Berlin. There they watched an impressive series of maneuvers by crack German artillery, cavalry, and infantry troops, before being escorted to the Prussian Rifle Range for a demonstration of a new German infantry bullet, which was described in detail by the proud inventor.

Mrs. Taft opted to skip Berlin, choosing rather to carry on to Paris to do some shopping. She then met up with the rest of the party in Cuxhaven, where they boarded their ship for the trans-Atlantic journey to New York. The crossing was rough, but by now the Tafts were seasoned sailors, and they arrived in good health and spirits to a noisy welcome from the cheering crowds on the docks. Even the ships in the harbor joined in the festivities by sounding their whistles and spraying water. The Tafts had been gone for four months during which they had visited eight countries. Charlie had just completed his second trip around the world, and was not yet in his teens.

PREP SCHOOL DAYS

When the Taft's returned from their successful world tour Secretary Taft returned to work amongst increased rumors that he was intending to run for the Presidency, while young Charlie was sent off to study at his uncle Horace's prep school in Connecticut. In 1890, Horace Taft who had given up a successful law practice to tutor classics at Yale, eagerly seized the opportunity presented to him by Mrs. Robert Black of Pelham Manor, New York. She founded a boys school as a memorial to her father and offered Horace Taft the position of headmaster. "Mr. Taft's School," as it came to be called, had only 17 boys, and was little more than an oversized tutoring class. Horace himself taught all the classes except for Greek and modern languages.

Three years later, in 1893, the school moved to Watertown, Connecticut. With $10,000 in borrowed funds Horace took a five year lease on an ancient two-storied New England inn called "Warren House" and converted it into a school building. The conditions at first were far from luxurious, with kerosene lamps being used until 1898. This new school boasted six masters including Horace, whom the boys called "King". There were thirty boarders and a few day scholars from the nearby towns. The converted inn served as the school's center for many years, in spite of the addition of several new buildings over the years. The circular banister in the main hall of the old inn continued as the traditional source of much enjoyment over the years, with the boys sliding down it whenever the chance presented itself. When Charlie enrolled in 1911 an extensive annex had been added, but the splendid new main building, which resembled the colleges at Oxford, was still under construction.

The objective of the school, which was based on the English public school system, was "to give boys a thorough preparation for the best colleges, and to make them strong, healthy, and manly men." Horace Taft's own philosophy of education was succinctly expressed when he wrote:"In scholarship I am a perfect Democrat in wishing that every boy should have a chance to show what is in him, but a perfect Aristocrat in feeling that a boy who shows he has the right stuff should have every opportunity for development and that all of our strength should not be expended on the "duffer." The emphasis was on academic studies rather than on practical, utilitarian subjects. The study of Greek, Latin, mathematics and English literature, often learned by rote, was stressed, and debating was strongly encouraged. There was little exposure to the arts although the staging of a school play became an annual tradition. Horace's favorite class was the senior course in Civic Government. In it he sought to inspire every boy to "feel such interest and sense of duty in regard to the subject as will lead him in college and elsewhere to prepare himself thoroughly to do his part in the State patriotically and intelligently." He often reminded the boys that the school's motto was "Not to be served, but to serve." Although Horace was a Unitarian the school was non-denominational and the boys who wished to attend the Episcopal church in Watertown were provided transportation. Athletic competition was encouraged and games were regularly scheduled with nearby schools, and a friendly, but serious, rivalry in academic achievement existed between Taft School and a similar institution on the West Coast. Sherman Thatcher, a close friend of Horace, had a few years earlier founded a boys prep school in Ojai, California, which sent many bright students to Yale where they competed with the Taft contingent.

Charlie Taft attended his uncle's school for five years. He was on the football, baseball, track, and basketball teams, and he managed the tennis squad. He also engaged in many other extra curricular activities. He was assignment editor of the school paper, and belonged to the mandolin club, the banjo club, the debating club, and the drama association. He even played a leading role in the school play when he was just 11 years old. Since the Taft School was not co-educational, the female roles were played by the boys, and in the production of *The Private Secretary* Charlie played the heroine, Eva Webster. After local performances in the Watertown Hall the play was presented in Carnegie Hall, New York. One newspaper asserted that the financial success of the production was assured because the President's son had been induced to act in the play.

Charlie's interest in sports, and other extra curricular activities concerned from his father who advised him to spend less time in social and athletic pursuits and more time studying. Charlie, however, was a natural "all rounder" and was able to excel in his studies too. He won the Scholar Prize four times in five years and in the year that he finished second he made up for it by winning both the Latin prose and sight translation prizes. In his final year The *New York Times* noted that he took "all the class honors, standing 96 against 90 by the other leading students, only four of whom reached the latter mark." The average for the school was 71. His father had reason to be proud of his son when he made the commencement address at Charlie's graduation.

THE PRESIDENT'S SON

Charlie Taft grew up in the world of politics. He was thoroughly at home in the nation's capital and knew many of the leading politicians . When the Republican Party held its nomination convention in June 1908 at Chicago, Charlie was by his father's side at their Washington home. He acted as a messenger boy, dashing about with bulletins and telegrams, including the one that stated that Taft was nominated for the presidency on the very first ballot.

Before starting his campaign William Taft, accompanied by his wife, vacationed at Hot Springs, Virginia. Charlie came down from Connecticut in time to join them for the Fourth of July celebration. An alert New York *Times* reporter filed the following story:"If Charlie Taft, the ten year old son of the Republican nominee for President, escapes tetanus or complete annihilation tomorrow it will surprise many of his friends among the 'grown-ups' here. His traveling bag was so completely filled with explosives that the lock stuck. Finally the bag burst open. A hasty appraisal of the content disclosed:

Two bundles of giant powder crackers
One package dynamite crackers.
Three packages giant torpedoes.
Two boxes torpedoes packed in sawdust.
Two boxes "nigger chasers.
One box tooth powder,
One tooth brush.
One clothes brush.

"Celebrate?" repeated Charlie as he struggled to close the satchel!" "You bet I'm goin, to celebrate Sure the tooth powder,s mine, but the clothes brush is mamma's"

While at the Hot Springs young Charlie got the chance to play baseball with some adults. .The newspaper correspondent played the politicians, and being short handed they asked Charlie to fill in at second base. When he caught a line drive hit by his father, the press corps declared him to be the hero of the game.

On election day Charlie was at Taft School. When it was announced that Charlie's father was elected President of the United States, the boys cheered loudly, and a celebration began that lasted most of the night. They built a large bonfire and danced around it singing and shouting until they were too tired to continue.

Uncle Horace even relaxed the rules of the school so that Charlie could miss his classes and join his family in Washington for the inaguration ceremonies. The parade was held despite the blustery, cold weather that was the aftermath of a snow storm. However, Charlie and his good friend Quentin, shared a chair in the official reviewing stand in front of the White House and remained till the parade ended and the last of the sixty bands marched by. The official oath taking ceremony was held in the Senate Chambers. Charlie's mother in her memoirs recalls:

> Our children were already in the gallery, waiting eagerly.It was an event in their young lives never to be forgotten, and I believe that Robert and Helen were in properly receptive moods. My son Charlie, however, seems not to have been so confident. Charlie is a great lover of adventure stories and it is a favorite tradition in the family now that he carried with him to the Senate Chamber a copy of *Treasure Island* with which to while away the time in case the Inaugural address should prove too long. Charlie was only eleven years old and I consider it a great tribute to his father's eloquence that *Treasure Island* was not opened that day.

That night Charlie joined the family gathered on the South Portico of the White House to watch in wonder the spectacular fireworks display that illuminated the snow blanketed city. He also felt quite grown up when he was allowed to attend the Inaugural Ball in the splendidly decorated Pension Building. The next day Charlie returned alone to Watertown, and with his uncle's help, he dodged the gang of newspaper reporters seeking interviews.

While his father was President, Charlie spent most of his time away at school, but he joined his family at the White house for vacations and special occasions. Although living at the White house must have been an exciting experience for the young boy, on his first extended visit home, he seemed a little bored with the kind of life Washington D.C. had to offer. After being home for only a couple of days he was already begging his father to allow him to spend the summer at a friend's house where they could "go sailing, and play tennis and golf and all those things." When his father refused, explaining that his mother was ill and needed him, Charlie left the room looking disappointed and muttering: "Dog gone the White House anyway; it's no place for kids."

In spite of his complaint, Charlie had many enjoyable experiences in the famous abode. He soon slipped into the house routine and felt completely at home, becoming a favorite with the White House staff. He ran the elevator for his parents and sometimes handled the switchboard during the operator's lunch break. His friends were free to come and go without being checked by the guards and they joined Charlie for games of football and baseball on the White House grounds. Indoors they played guessing games like charades and they used the carriage house and roomy attic for wild games of hide and seek and tag. Even Charlie's father notice how completely at home in the White House his youngest son was and how confident and independent the experience seemed to be making him.

On one occasion Charlie's high jinks were reported in the New York *Times*:

> If there is any place in or about the White House unexplored by Charlie Taft it is probably the top of the flagpole, and this may yet be discovered by the strenuous young son of the President, who is lending the new Administration all the strenuousness that marked the last.
>
> He chose the roof of the White House to-day for a playground in which "tag" figured. Accompanied by some fifteen of his classmates in the public school, he took possession of the broad lawn immediately behind the White House and organized a scrub game of baseball. When the youngsters tired of that they disappeared in the State, War and Navy Building, just across Executive Avenue. Those who had been observing the game were astonished to see the boys appear on the roof of the White House, Charlie Taft's tousled head coming through the scuttle first.
>
> For a half hour they slid down the steep slopes of the roof and dodged and hid behind chimneys. The danger of falling to the ground was lessened by the presence of a marble balustrade that runs around the eaves of the house, but it is not improbable that Charlie will come in for a lecture, if nothing more drastic, when his father hears of it. Both the President and Mrs. Taft were absent from the White House during the afternoon.

The President was amused by the antics of his children, but once he was a little embarrassed. On this occasion, the children and some of their friends were playing charades in the hallway outside the Emancipation Proclamation Room and they were doing their best to act out the word "dynasty." "I was committing hari-kiri," Helen later wrote, "and Bob, who loved Shakespeare, was a writhing Hamlet drinking poison and crying, 'I die, Horatio!'" In the middle of this melee in walked several solemn faced Senators escorting a group of distinguished foreign visitors to the historic room in which Abraham Lincoln had signed the Emancipation Proclamation." After this incident they always had one of them stand guard.

Living at the White House as the son of the President afforded young Charlie many privileges. His father was the first chief executive to make motor vehicles standard equipment in the White House transportation fleet, and at the age of eleven, Charlie took his first driving lesson. A White House chauffeur gave him instructions and found him an apt and enthusiastic learner. After only a few lessons Charlie, accompanied by his instructor, drove the Baker Electric to Fort Meyer and back. His ambition, though, was to drive his father's favorite car, the Stanley Steamer.

One day a District of Columbia police officer driving a bicycle stopped the Presidential car for a traffic violation and was amazed to discover Charlie had taken over and was driving the vehicle! During the summers spent at Beverly, Charlie had many more opportunities for motoring. He later recalled: "I'd just grab hold of the one single steering bar and I'd drive all around Massachusetts."

Mrs. Taft was uneasy with the idea of her son driving around in a motor vehicle, and she felt that the easy availability of this mode of transport might spoil the children. President Taft, however, was more magnanimous. "Let them have a good time while they can," he told his wife. "In four years we may all have to become pedestrians again and I want them to look back upon this portion of their life with the keenest relish. They are not children to be spoiled by a little luxury now."

On June 10th 1909, Charlie watched a flight by the Wright Brothers who took off and landed on the oval south of the White House. Later that day his father presented gold medals of the Aero Club to the two brothers. That flight must have made quite an impression on the young boy, who accompanied his father the following month, to Fort Meyers, Virginia, to see a test flight by Orville Wright.

Great Britain, Germany, and France had already shown an interest in obtaining planes for military recognizance, and so the U.S. Army Signal Corps offered a proposal to the Wrights. They were to receive $25,000 for the delivery of an airplane that had flown with a passenger at a speed of over forty miles per hour over a five mile course for over an hour and landed with the plane uninjured. A bonus was offered for speed in excess of forty miles per hour, with a deduction for a speed lower. On a previous flight a control problem led to a crash in which the passenger, Lt. Thomas Selfridge, became the first air crash casualty and Orville was injured. This time there was rejoicing as the flight was successful, and the U.S. Army was soon to have its first airplane.

In 1910, Charlie and his mother joined a record crowd of 12,226 to watch as his father started a tradition by throwing out the first ball of the baseball season. Then the Tafts joined the local fans cheering as the Washington Nationals defeated the Philadelphia Athletics 3 to 0 as Walter Johnson limited the visitors to one hit while striking out nine.

Although Charlie was an active, and a times a mischievous boy, there was a serious side to him. He showed a deep interest in religion during his years at the Taft school, where he attended Church and was active in the boys' club of the Y.M.C.A. Charlie chose to attend the EpiscopaL Church favored by his mother instead of the Unitarian church attended by his father and uncle. He was confirmed as an Episcopalian during one of his sojourns in Washington D.C.

Until William Howard Taft became President, the family had spent their summer holidays at their retreat in Murray Bay, a beloved second home to them. But, during his term of office, President Taft thought it unwise to leave the country unless on official business, and so a temporary summer capital was set up in Beverly, Massachusetts. Here the Tafts leased the Stetson Cottage, a spacious fifteen room, two storey, wooden mansion situated on six acres of lawns, shrubbery, and trees, located near the end of Woodberry Point and overlooking Beverley Harbor, Salem Bay, and Massachusetts Bay. With a deep water boat landing and two outstanding golf courses nearby the location was perfect for the Tafts. Charlie spent most of his time outdoors, playing ball, hiking with the outing club he had joined, and learning small boat navigation. He now had his own dory, and despite one capsizing he became quite adept at handling small crafts. Family friend Archie Butt noted that "Charlie is never quiet for an hour. When he is not on the water, he wants to go to see Dick Hammond or play golf at Essex or tennis at Monserratt."

In the summer of 1908, the family took a ten day cruise on the government yacht, the *Mayflower*. While his father was busy at every stopover, making speeches and finding every available opportunity to play golf, Charlie was delighted at the chance to fish, and, as one newspaper reporter noted, he was always the first to board ship with a bucket of clams, waiting for the ship to anchor so he could do some fishing.

Shortly before leaving office, in December 1912, President Taft made his fifth trip to the Panama Canal Zone. His mission was to determine if it was time to establish civil government in the zone and to inspect the engineering work on the nearly completed canal. Charlie and his mother joined the entourage.

The Taft party traveled by train down through the citrus groves and the Everglades of Florida to Miami where they boarded a special observation car for the trip on the over-sea extension to Key West. There they sailed on the new dreadnought, *Arkansas*, and were accompanied by the battleship *Delaware*.

They sailed on December 21, and spent three days, including Christmas, in the Canal Zone. While there, they were guests of Col. George W. Goethals, builder of the canal, who accompanied them on a inspection tour of the nearly completed locks. The party was back in Washington in time for the New Year festivities, the last that President Taft would host in the White House. On the first day of 1913, a record setting 6,054 guests attended the final reception hosted by their outgoing President. That evening Charlie, now fifteen and grateful to be wearing long trousers at last, was the host at a dance given especially for his age group. The following month the Tafts moved out of the White House to make room for Woodrow Wilson.

COMING OF AGE: YALE & THE WAR

In 1829, Alphonso Taft, Charlie's grandfather, started a family tradition when he entered Yale at the age of 19. He was the class orator, was elected to Phi Beta Kappa, and helped establish the Skull and Bones honor society. Following in his footsteps, many other Tafts, including Charlie's father, his older brother, and three uncles, selected Yale as their Alma Mater. Also on leaving the White house, his father joined the faculty, as the Kent Professor of Constitutional Law. Charlie had visited the campus on several occasions himself, and was a spectator at the 1908 commencement exercises.

When Charlie took the entrance exam for Yale in 1916, he won the prize in Latin translating, which had been previously won by both his father and his brother, both of whom had gone on to graduate at the head of their classes. Charlie's academic record was also outstanding. He led his class in his freshman year and was second in his sophomore and junior years. However, his greatest achievement was winning, by unanimous vote the Gordon Brown Prize which was presented to the student who summed up best what the school stood for in manhood, scholarship, and the capacity for leadership. He was also elected to Phi Beta Kappa and the Skull and Bones honor society.

Although Charlie's father once again advised him to cut down on extra curricular activities and concentrate on his studies, Charlie found time to join the debating team and to compete in three major sports. at 6 feet 1 1/2 inches tall and weighing in at 190 pounds, he was a natural choice on the sports field. He played varsity football and baseball, but he was most successful in basketball. He was a guard on the Yale team that defeated Dartmouth 36 to 15 on March 12, 1915, to win the Ivy League championship, and was elected captain the next season.

When on April 6th, 1917 Congress declared war on Germany, Charlie was 19 years old and in his junior year. Some of his fellow students went off immediately to Officer Training Schools, while others joined the Navy's First Yale Unit to train as naval aviators. Charlie, however, was below the legal age for officers training, but he was eager to fight for his country, and so, with twenty five fellow classmates, he enlisted as a private in the U.S. Army. Because he was still slightly under the age for enlistment even in the ranks, his father had to accompany him to give the necessary parental consent. Charlie was sent to Fort Meyers, Virginia, and along with ten of his classmates was assigned to the Second Division, 12th Field Artillery, Battery A.

Earlier that year Charlie had met Eleanor Chase at a dance and had fallen in love with her almost immediately. She came from a prominent and wealthy New England family. Her father, Irving H. Chase, had made a fortune in copper and brass and was president of the Ingersoll Waterbury Watch Company. The couple became engaged shortly before Charlie enlisted. While he was at Fort Meyers Charlie received the following advice from his concerned father:

> I would regret it if you got into a battery that had tough soldiers in it, because it would be disagreeable for you. However, with your ten Yale men I should think you might surround yourselves with associates who will avoid the effect of demoralizing comrades. I have every confidence in you, my dear Charley, that none of these fellows can lead you off much as they would like to, and this without regard to your engagement to Eleanor, but I know that gives you an additional stimulus to look with disdain on all the invitations that will be made to you in the wrong direction. It is a great comfort to me that you are a member of the church, that you don't smoke, and that you don't drink, and that you have those high ideals that enable you to elevate the people about you rather than yield to their levelling or lowering tendency.

Charlie and Eleanor, realizing that they would soon be separated for the duration of the war. decided to get married before his outfit was shipped overseas. The wedding ceremony took place on October 6th, 1917, at Rose Hill Cottage, the palatial estate of the Chase family, which was decorated for the occasion with autumnal flowers and with the stars and stripes. The young married couple rented a house at St. Asaph's near Fort Meyer while Charlie's company prepared to be shipped out. Late December they sailed from Hoboken to England and then to France. Charlie was now a Sergeant-Major. He had earned his promotion on merit, without any political pressure being applied by his father. In fact, his father had written to Newton Baker, the Secretary of War: "I am not ambitious for his military promotion, but only for his usefulness." Just before he sailed Charlie received a touching letter from his father:

> And now Charlie dear, my heart goes out to you. You are a constant source of pride and joy to me. Not, my dear boy, in your mental power and application, not in your fine face and form, not in your physical strength and capacity but in your fine character, in your purity of soul, in your high ideals, in your spurning of the low and unmoral...It is hard, my darling boy, to let you go. You are the apple of our eye. But we would not have it different. If sacrifice is to be made who are we that we should escape it...You are a knight *sans peur* and *sans repoche*. God bless and keep you.

The 12th Field Artillery was stationed between Chaumont and Tours northeast of Gondercourt. Charlie was in charge of 27 men. They were completing their training in a relatively safe area when the situation suddenly changed. At 4;50 A.M. on March 21, 1918 the Germans launched Operation Michael with a massive bombadment. They had secretly massed their forces for a final attempt to knock the Allies out of the war before the Americans could bring the full force of their armies to bear. The Germans hoped to rout the British Fifth Army, led by General Gough, and drive a wedge between them and the French forces which would fall back to protect Paris. The British Fifth Army suffered heavy casualties and retreated towards the coast. The situation for the Allies was desperate. All available units were called upon to halt the Germans' advance. Charlie's unit went into action on March 26, 1918, in a place "where shell holes overlapped." On March 28th Charlie wrote to his wife:

> It is quite a feeling to be under fire. Of course I haven't really been under any kind of bombardment, but I've heard them whistle right enough.The ones that have come near to me were all strays, I guess, but lots have wizzed over or off to one side. All of them you can hear coming for several seconds before they hit and its a scary feeling. You have time to duck in if you are near cover always, if you are on the alert, and I will tell you, I am very much on the alert when I get outside the dugout. Yesterday I was walking up the ravine from the French office to the Telephone central, about 50 yards, when I heard her. It whistled louder and louder, and I ducked behind a tin shack, when blouie! she went off on the top of the ridge only about 50 meters away in front.

Then he realized what effect this would have on his wife and he added: "Doggone it, now I've gone and got her all scairt up! when really, me and my French Major's abris are as safe as a church."

The German offensive was finally contained, and Charlie's outfit, which had been under enemy fire for a month, returned to their training camp..

William Howard Taft, realizing that Charlie's outfit probably would be called upon to help stop the German desperate offensive, expressed his family's concern:

> Our prayers go with you. Whatever happens, we know that you will do your duty and face death with a pure heart and a clear conscience and a spirit that either in you or in others will win the war for the right. Your mother said this morning: "I wish Charlie was not over there," but I don't think she really means that. It is a solemn and sacrficial moment, and I am glad you are there, much as it presses on my heart to think of the possibilities. We are all proud of you.

When his month at the front was over, Charlie expressed his opinion that he was qualified to become an officer. However, he was stymied by Army regulations that required that he be 21 years old. He wrote about his situation; "I suppose one ought to be satisfied with what he is doing, and make the most of it. But a sergeat-major is either a clerk or an extra leg. I'm not a clerk, and I find that the organism does very well with two legs." Finally Charlie was ordered to report to the Officers Training School for Artillery at Samur.

On May 1, 1918, Charlie wrote an eleven page letter to his mother describing his trip. His only complaint was that he was not able to visit Paris on the way there. He did, however, call on General Harbord at the office of the Chief of Staff. The general wrote to Charlie's father recalling: "That tall attractive young soldier has come a long way from the small boy that I saw in the Philippines. He is a fine looking young soldier and I congratulate you on his having had the patriotism to enlist while his age prevented him from getting a commission."

At Samur, formerly a cavalry training school, Charlie enjoyed riding horses in his spare time. He successfully completed the three months course, and was commissioned a 2nd Lieutenant on August 1, more than a month before his twenty-first brithday. He was promted to First Lieutenant a month later. Shortly before his 21st birthday, Charlie received the news that he was the father of a baby girl. His very proud father wrote to Charlie's uncle: "Your namesake Charlie is a graduate of Yale, a commissioned officer in the United Sttes Army and a father all before he is 21. Which is going some--a little girl was born to Elanor this morning,"

Charlie had graduated *in absentia* with his class in June. While at Yale he had taken enough classes to earn 56 units, needing only 4 more to graduate. His father had little trouble pursuading the administration to award him six units for his army service. So, he would be elgible to enter law school when he returned home.

However, Charlie had mixed feelings about missing his senior year. He had looked forward to playing a final year on the basketball team. His father's reaction was predictable:

> I was somewhat disappointed at your attitude in respect to your degree. Few of those who went into the army from your class will get a degree. It is a great and clean thing for you to have your degree and to have a year in the army too. Your ambition as to basket ball shows you don't quite realize that your college days are over. You are married and when you come home, you will dig your nose into law. You'll be a veteran. Basket ball will be as far from you and your concerns as Teddy Bears. So brace, up, my dear Boy, and realize you are a man, if you are not twenty-one. You'll now have to give your athletic energies to golf, that old man's game. You'll become a householder. You'll probably be too stiff for basket ball after your training at the front.

At Samur Charlie's duties, after heing commissioned, included guiding 20 enlisted men through a three months course in artillery techniques. Then we was assigned to be Aide-de-Camp to Brigader General W.I. Weservel;t, Assistant Chief of Artillery. He explained his situation to his wife: "A staff job in G.H.Q. might be a permanently bullet proof office job." He worked in the information section of the Chief of Artillery's office, marking on the large wall maps the gains and losses, location of units, supplies etc. On occasion he was called upon to translate French messages into English. Then he was sent on a three weeks inspection tour of all the U.S. artillery units.

As the end of the war seemed to be near, Charlie had to decide what to do when he left the army. He announced his decision in a letter to his mother: "In spite of the hopes that various members of the family have expressed that I should enter professions varying from the ministry to school teaching, I can't help but feel that it takes an education in law to give a man the ability to understand the principles of government and politics; and if there is one thing that the country is going to need when this whole business is over with, it is common sense based on such knowledge. So I'm afraid you will have to abandon me as determined to be a lawyer, descended from lawyers."

His last assignment was to observe for three weeks the progress and readiness for combat of the Field Artillery Brigade of colored troops from Camp Meade under General Sherburne. A few weeks later the Armisitce was signed. In January 1919, Charlie received an honorable discahrge from the army and he returned home to his wife and daughter.

In the fall of 1920 he entered the Yale University School of Law. He was interested in sports although he was not eligible to compete. So he coached the freshman football team's line, and the following year he coached the varsity line. However, his coaching duties did nmot interfere with his studies. He edited the *Law Review* and in the spring of 1921, he graduated first in his class, just four months before his father was appointed Chief Justice of the Supreme Court.

CHAPTER SIXTEEN

A YOUNG LAWYER IN CINCINNATI

After graduating from Yale, Charlie returned to Cincinnati with his family. He was admitted to the Ohio bar and joined his brother's law firm, which expanded a few years later into the prestigious firm of Taft, Taft, Stettinius, and Hollister. Charlie, a reform minded idealist, was appalled by the sad state of his native city. His idealism had been nurtured during his years at the Taft School, where the boys were consciously prepared for active participation in civic affairs. They often attended the Watertown town meetings, and were encouraged to prepare for participation in the political process. Young Charlie had been especially impressed by a guest speaker's account of a reformer's victory over a corrupt political machine in a Chicago ward election. He was thrilled by the triumph of good over evil, and was influenced by the novels of Winston Churchill and Holman Day, whose heroes battled valiantly against corruption. As a young boy he found role models in such characters as Austen Vane in Churchill's *Mr Crewe's Career*, who stood unflinchingly for clean politics and Harlan Thornton in Horace Day's *The Ramrodders*, whose idealism challenged the political machine of his grandfather.

Charlie practical idealism motivated his plunge into volunteer community work. He taught Sunday School in the Episcopal Church and was on the board of directors of The Community Chest, The Y.M.C.A., Children's Hospital, Widows and Old Men's Home, and the Colored Industrial School. He even found time to serve as a Captain in the Field Artillery Reserve Corps. And to top it all, he joined the fledgling Cincinnatus Society.

Established in 1920 by a group of young lawyers and business men, the Cincinnatus Society was a social and debating club where the members could get together to discuss many topics, including the politics of their city. Out of this debating society grew the Charter Party, which, lead by Murray Seasongood, set out to defeat the corrupt Republican machine and reform the city government.

Cincinnati, in the early 1920's, had the unenviable reputation of being the worst governed city in the nation. For decades the city had been run by a Republican machine forged by George Cox, whose successor, Rudy Hynicka governed by remote control from New York where his business interests included burlesque houses. The machine found it easy to remain in power since it controlled 6,800 city jobs and could reward its friends with lucrative city contracts. It also had an experienced vote creating organization. Thus, despite the high taxes and deplorable condition of the streets and poor city services few people dared to complain for fear of still higher tax assessments and difficulties in obtaining business licenses.

The Charterites, dedicated amateurs, set out to defeat this entrenched machine.They rang doorbells, mailed leaflets, kissed babies, and made countless speeches. Charlie made his first political speech on behalf of the Charter Party, in Chester Park in September 1925. He appealed to all civic minded citizens, irregardless of party alignment, by declaring: "There is no Republican way or no Democrat way to pave a street. There is only an honest and efficient way as compared with a dishonest and ineffectual way." He preached the power of idealism in practical politics, and in another speech, given during the 1926 campaign, he attacked the lenient attitude towards gambling. "The Sheriff and Prosecutor plead ignorance of gambling, handbooks, and roadhouses, and act only when shoved by groups of indignant citizens," he declared:

> When Coney Island opens again we may expect the Sheriff to say again that he does not know there is gambling there. The retail merchants of Cincinnati and the friends of the young men and women who destroy their futures by embezzling money to pay their handbook losses demand that the law in Hamilton County be enforced.

On a lighter note, he expressed his life-long interest in baseball by declaring that "If the citizens' ticket wins on August 10th, the Reds will win the pennant." Although the Cincinnati Reds lost the pennant race to the Saint Louis Cardinals by two games, Charlie's party won the election and the Charter was finally adopted, giving the city a new form of government. The city council was reduced from 32 members to 9, six of whom were Charterites. A city manager was installed and city positions were to be filled by civil service examinations instead of political patronage. Also proportional representation in the city council was instituted. Charlie claimed that it was "the fairest way of doing it. It is the only way of assuring the appropriate number of minorities, such as blacks and women, on the council."

In 1926 the Charterites extended their campaign to include Hamilton county, and Charlie was elected County Prosecutor. When in November he took office he seemed on the way to a very successful career in the political arena. He was handsome, a good speaker, well liked, active in many community organizations, and he had a magical last name. Furthermore, he had been brought up in the world of politics. As he was growing up he had impressed people with his charming personality and his self assurance. He seemed to be at ease whether in a palace or a playground, and got along well with the press.

Earle Looker, a member of the White House Gang and its chronicler, writing in 1926 noted that Charlie "has become an extremely able lawyer, following well, in personal and professional distinction, the footsteps of his father, Ex-President William Howard Taft, Chief Justice of the Supreme Court of the United States. Thinking back to the Force School days, and knowing Charlie's steadiness of purpose, one sees that it is quite possible, even then, he may have decided upon his career. Certainly he displayed more concentration than any of his companions."

Charlie had also impressed Major Archibald Butt, military aide to both Roosevelt and Taft, who had been with the family since their early days in the Philippines. He had abundant opportunities to observe the Taft children as he was accepted as a trusted friend and an unofficial family member. The Major asserted the Charlie was "wiser than most of the family in many ways," and he found Charlie's self assurance remarkable, reporting: "He played golf yesterday and posed with the ease of an old politician for the photographers, when they wanted to snap him in action. He is really better broken in to this side of the Presidential business than his father."

Charlie's sister, Helen, was convinced that her younger brother had all the potential necessary for a successful political career. She noted how poised he was in granting interviews to the press on their trip around the world, and many years later, while writing about her brother Bob, she remarked that, in 1909 when her father became President, "If we had been told by a soothsayer that we had a born campaigner in the family, we would have said, It's Charlie, although Charlie was only 11 years old at the time." She commented on how different her two brothers were at this time with Charlie always ready to identify himself as the President's son, and quick to make friends, while Robert "always shrank from attracting attention to himself."

Even President Taft was aware that his youngest son displayed the self-confidence and poise of a natural born leader. He noted in a letter to his wife:"it is very full of humor to think of Charlie sitting at the head of the table in the White House and formally presiding over it as though he were President of the United States. But nothing fazes him."

At his inauguration as Prosecuting Attorney of Hamilton County, Charlie was praised for his public service by Judge Stanley Struble, who joined the ranks in predicting a successful political career for the young reformist. He predicted "a career of great promise, rivaling if you will so to do the great career in public service of your distinguished father," and ended his laudatory speech with a reference to the Adams dynasty, declaring that the "Taft family ought to be able to accomplish the record of the Adams family."

Certainly, a bright future with unlimited possibilities seemed to await the Chief Justice's youngest son. He received national attention when he was invited to be the featured speaker at the dinner celebrating the seventy-fifth anniversary of the founding of the Washington YMCA. It was a gala affair, and Charlie's proud parents were there to listen to him deliver the key-note address to a distinguished audience, which included President and Mrs. Coolidge, Attorney General Sergeant, Secretary of Labor Davis, Secretary of the Interior Work and representative members of the diplomatic corps.

On taking office as County Prosecutor, Charlie found a large number of pending cases left by his predecessor, which he and his staff succeeded in clearing up within six months. He also sponsored an ordinance aimed at preventing crimes and proposed curbing the sale of firearms. The two main provisions in this proposal were, that "no persons convicted of a felony, no alien, no drug addict, no minor, and no insane person shall buy, own or possess a pistol or machine gun," and that "any one desiring to own a pistol must obtain a permit for its purchase, but no person of good character can be refused a permit."

The first important criminal case Charlie's office handled involved a murder committed by three defendants. The trial took three months to wrap up completely, the minimum time possible for a first degree trial in Ohio at that time, and the verdict went in favor of the prosecution. All three men were found guilty and sentenced to life imprisonment.

The next case proved to be more difficult. A bootlegger by the name of "Fat" Wrassman shot and killed a rival bootlegger in a Cincinnati beer joint, and the police court wished to try him on a charge of second degree murder (homicide in a fight, without premeditation). Taft, however, insisted on a charge of first degree murder. Wrassman's defense was handled by a promising young lawyer, Charles Elston, who proved to be a worthy opponent. The prosecution's case fell apart when its key witness and his family simply vanished. Taft suffered his first significant defeat when Wrassman was acquitted.

On October 6, 1927, Charlie Taft wrote a long letter to his parents telling them about celebrating his tenth wedding anniversary, spending a month at Murrary bay, seeing the Tunney-Dempsey fight, and winning a golf tournament. When he arrived at his office, he was informed that George Remus had killed his wife and was in custody. The stage was set for one of the greatest court battles of the century.

Book Two

Combat

"I love Dodge, and when Remus finds it out he will be wild, but it won't do him any good, because he'll either be in jail, out of the country or penniless."

Imogene Remus (Deposition of Mrs. Oliver Long, New York *Times* (October 28, 1927)

"I was never in the presence of Mrs. Remus at Atlanta, Ga. or at Athens, Ga. or at any other place at any time except when she was in the presence of her husband or members of her family or friends or her attorney. I was never alone with her at any time or place in my life."

Franklin Dodge in letter to Congressman Fiorello La Guardia (April 8, 1927)

"Yet she must die, else she'll
betray more men."

"An honorable murderer if you will,
for naught I did in haste, but all in love."

Othello by William Shakespeare (V,ii)

OCTOBER 6TH

October 6th, 1927:

Pittsburg, Pa.

Babe Ruth, who hit a record setting 60 home runs this season, led the New York Yankees to a 5 to 4 victory over the favored Pittsburg Pirates in the first game of the World Series. Ruth had three of his teams six hits and scored twice.

New York City

The gala World Premiere of the first talking picture, Warner Brother's *The Jazz Singer*, starring Al Jolson, took place today, just one day after the tragic death of Sam L. Warner.

Mexico City

General Alfredo Quinato, leader of a failed rebellion, was executed today by a firing squad which he bravely faced and gave the command to fire.

Washington D.C.

Nat Goldstein, serving time in Leavenworth Prison for conviction in the Jack Daniels liquor conspiracy, was paroled.

Appleton, Wisconsin

Five people were killed and eight were seriously injured when a section of the nearby Kimberly-Clark paper mill collapsed unexpectedly.

Cincinnati, Ohio

Charles and Eleanor Taft celebrated their tenth wedding anniversary. They recently returned, with their family, from a month-long vacation at Murray Bay, Quebec.

Cincinnati, Ohio

George Remus, former "King of the Bootleggers," killed his wife, Imogene, this morning on her way to their divorce hearing. His car managed to force the taxi she and her daughter were occupying to pull over and stop. Remus jumped out of his car and ran towards the taxi. Ruth Remus tried to climb out, but her mother pulled her back before opening the door to face her enraged husband. Remus grabbed his wife Imogene by the wrists and pulled her out of the car shouting "Now you decomposed mass of clay I've got you." He then drew a pearl handled gun from his coat pocket and put it to her stomach. She pleaded with him, screaming "Oh Daddy, you know I love you. Daddy don't do it! Don't do it!" Remus twisted her around so that she could look into his eyes, but she wouldn't look.

Holding her to him, he pulled the trigger once. She screamed and fell to the ground while Remus stood over her. Ruth jumped from the taxi and tried to stop her stepfather from firing again. With blood pouring down the front of her dress, Imogene Remus struggled to her feet and with her daughter's help, climbed back into the taxi where the driver was still behind the wheel.

Remus immediately followed her, and the wounded woman made one final effort to get away. Opening the door on the other side of the cab, she jumped out and staggered down the road, her hands above her head, pleading "For God's sake won't somebody help me?"

A number of cars stopped, but the drivers were not eager to get involved. One driver even prevented the wounded woman from climbing into his car. However, the man in the car behind him took her in and drove her and her daughter Ruth to the Bethesda Hospital.

Remus walked calmly away from the scene. His chauffeur had panicked and driven off with his car, but a short way down the road a man, unaware of what had just happened, offered Remus a lift. Remus asked to be taken to the Railway station.

An hour later he walked into the downtown police station and calmly stated: "I want to give myself up. I've shot my wife."

Not long afterwards Imogene Remus died. The bullet her husband had shot into her critically wounded three vital organs and lodged itself just under the skin in her back. She died on the operating table at 10.45 a.m without having regained consciousness. Her distraught daughter's first act was to phone Franklin Dodge at his home in Lansing, Michigan.

Remus was pacing up and down in a cell at the police station when he was told the news.

"Your wife just died." Lieutenant McNeal informed him.

"Very well, gentlemen. I thank you." he replied calmly.

Asked if he had anything else to say, he shook his head, but a moment later he added: "It's the penalty one pays for being contrary to the debt one owes society." He then asked Lieutenant McNeal if he could not arrange for the preliminary hearing to be held soon because he wanted to get it over with and have the case taken to trial as soon as possible.

Remus then accompanied Detective Sergeant Dooley and a couple of assistant detectives to Eden Park to reconstruct the shooting. He claimed that he had driven himself to the scene and that he had thrown the gun away sometime before being picked up on Gilbert street. Neither the gun nor the car were found; his claim that he drove himself to the scene was contradicted that afternoon by George Klug when he surrendered on the advice of George Conners. After listening to Klug's story, the police announced that no charges would be made against him. While Remus was with the detectives at the scene of the crime, his wife's body was being examined by the County Coroner, Fred Swing, who declared that each of the three vital organs which had been wounded had been destroyed to the extent that each one would have been a fatal wound. While her body was at the morgue, hundreds of curious people gathered at the building hoping, in vain, to get a look at the corpse.

That evening a distraught Ruth Remus returned alone to her mother's room at the Alms Hotel. The following day was her twentieth birthday. Her stepfather, meanwhile, was declaring his intentions of disowning her through proceedings before the very Judge who had authorized him to adopt her. Romola Remus left Chicago that evening and travelled to Cincinnati to offer her father her full support. As soon as the cell doors were opened, she flung herself into his arms and kissed him. "I love my father more than anything in the world," she told reporters, "and I'll stand by him to the end. He needs the love and tender care of a woman and I am going to give it to him." Later that evening Remus admitted that the only regret he had was that she would be effected by the situation. In Chicago, Remus' ex-wife told reporters that in her opinion Remus acted in self defense. She insisted that he "wouldn't hurt a fly." .

Soon after his daughter's arrival, Remus held a press conference. Dressed in a smart gray suit with a silk shirt and black tie, Remus shook hands with each reporter and then clicked his heels together. "I see the press is here in all its grandeur" he remarked before taking his seat. He did not seem in the least bit ruffled or nervous. He politely answered every question asked of him, no matter how personal, only showing signs of bitterness when questioned directly about his wife. "I had a moral right to act as I did and I can convince a jury of it," he said, insisting that he had a perfectly clear conscience and that he owed it to society to do what he did.

Remus whirled on one young reporter who asked him why he had not planned his getaway since there was no doubt that he had planned the shooting. "Your youth excuses you for the question you have asked," he replied, "When you have become more matured and have attained a riper age you, too, under similar circumstances would reason differently. Why should I go about the country as a fugitive from justice - a man with a price on his head? If you have a clear conscience, you have nothing to fear and consequently why should I run away? A man who feels that he had performed a duty to society and that he has committed no moral wrong would not run away from the consequences of his act, but would do just as I have done, give himself up."

Asked if he had sought a reconciliation with his wife, Remus replied: "How could I? No sane man could. They think I'm insane. Well I'm not half as crazy as some think I am. I am entirely responsible for the act I committed. I feel that I was justified in doing what I did. I owed it to society, My fate will be in the hands of twelve men, and I will abide by their decision."

Remus then told the reporters that he had chased his wife and Franklin Dodge around the country in an attempt to catch them together and kill them both. He declared:"I am a man of principle, despite what people think of me. I have never smoked, drank, or swore in my life. I cannot stand for the sort of thing this man and Mrs. Remus have been carrying on for a long time." He also charged them once again of conspiring to rob him of his property and have him deported.

Dodge vehemently denied Remus' accusations and referred to him as "a coward and a shameless liar." He claimed to have several iron clad alibis for almost every occasion when he was supposed to be engaging in illicit liaisons with Mrs. Remus. Dodge also accused Remus of offering $8,000 to have him killed. He claimed that because he was a "square shooter" he was tipped off by the man Remus sought to hire. "I dare not reveal the name of my informant because it would mean death to him but I will say he was a Southern gambler and bootlegger who had been close to Remus in the liquor trade." { This description fit Willie Haar, who had been in prison with Remus at Atalanta.} Dodge ended his tirade by characterizing Remus as one who "would never personally offer violence to anyone except to a woman or a child, but who would hire assassins, if necessary, to remove enemies from his path."

The following day Remus arrived at the Court House dressed smartly and in a seemingly good mood, laughing and shaking hands with friends and reporters. Police officers said that he had had a disturbed night, although he claimed to be feeling as good as could be expected. He was extremely calm when his name was called in the Courtroom, and he approached the Judge. After pleading not guilty, he asserted that he was ready for trial and waived his right to a preliminary examination. He then requested that his case be put before the Grand Jury as soon as possible so that in indictment could be returned and the case could go before the Common Pleas Court without delay.

The next sitting of the Grand Jury was scheduled for the 10th of October, the following Monday. Remus was returned to the jail, where he had a private cell on the top floor. James Kilgallen, a crime reporter with Hearst's International News Service, later told of visiting Remus in this "cell."

> I went to the jail on the chance that I might be able to see Remus. It was no trouble at all....He had private quarters on the top floor. Unlike the other prisoners he was not confined to a cell. He greeted me warmly, and showed me his books and his wardrobe of about 20 suits of clothes. He had liquor available although he never drank. Whenever he wanted to he could go up on the roof and exercise to keep himself fit.

On one of Kilgallen's visits Remus actually outlined his strategy for influencing the jury in his favor. He seemed extremely confident about the outcome of the trial.

Remus spent most of the first weekend conferring with George Conners, who had immediately rallied to his side. On Sunday he attended a religious service in the jail. Then he was interviewed again by news hungry reporters. He announced that, should he be indicted, he would enter a plea of justifiable homicide, and he outlined his defense pointing out that the testimony he would produce would have ramifications for both prohibition officials and national bootleggers. He spoke of large whiskey rings that, he asserted, had used his wife to get at him and his whiskey concerns. "I will bring witnesses to the trial," he stated, "who will reveal the secrets of the entire American illicit whiskey trade."

He also announced that he would conduct his own defense in spite of claims that he would hire the best criminal lawyers money could buy. He dramatically declared: "Remus will defend himself. After all it is I who will be tried for murder. Death is staring me in the face, and I say to you frankly that I will defend myself. Remus will play a lone hand." He again asserted that he had no money and therefore could not hire any big name attorneys. However, he did have offers of legal support. He showed the reporters telegrams from Hugh J. Daly, a former Assistant United States District Attorney, and W.W. O'Brien, a partner in the law firm of Clarence Darrow, offering to defend him gratis. Remus did concede, though, that he would need an attorney to assist him and said that he was considering Charles Elston, a young criminal lawyer and former prosecuting attorney, who was currently defending a Cincinnati bootlegger, "Fat" Wrassman, on a murder charge. Remus decided that if Elston procured an acquittal in that case, he would ask him to act as co-counsel. Shortly thereafter Wrassman was acquitted, and Charles Elston became Remus' co-counsel.

On Monday, October the tenth, the new Grand Jury was impaneled, and the first case they considered was that of George Remus. The County Coroner testified that Mrs. Remus died from a bullet wound inflicted by George Remus. Twenty four witnesses were called, including Ruth Remus. Most of them had witnessed the shooting. Remus, who was not present at the inquest, was indicted and charged with first degree murder. While the Grand Jury was deliberating Mrs. Remus' body was secretly being placed in a private vault at the Rosehill Cemetary in Chicago with only the family present.

On October 14th, 1927, the Grand Jury charged that George Remus had "unlawfully, purposely and of deliberate and premeditated malice, did kill and murder" his wife. The following day Remus pleaded not guilty, and the trial was set for November 14th with Judge Chester R, Shook presiding.

Intent on proving justifiable homicide, Remus motioned the Court to allow him to take depositions from seventy five people outside of Cincinnati to prove that Franklin Dodge and Mrs. Remus conspired against him. He asserted that these depositions would show that Dodge had waited for him in Hamilton on October 6th, with the intention of killing him and that three gunmen had been sent to the Hotel Sinton that morning to wait for him. He also claimed that Dodge had been in Mrs. Remus' room that morning and the depositions would prove it.

He claimed that the depositions would also show that $20,000 had been paid to five St. Louis gunmen with instructions to kill him. Finally he recounted how only the presence of John Marshall saved him from being killed while in Indianapolis. Permission to take depositions was granted, although few were actually entered as evidence in the trial.

PRE-TRIAL PREPARATION

During the month leading up to the trial Remus and Conners were busy gaathering evidence of Imogene Remus' unfaithfulness. They also launched an all out search for Remus' lost fortune. They placed full page advertisements in twenty three newspapers in the United States and Canada requesting information about the $1,8000,000 Remus accused his wife of stealing from him.

On October 27th nine officials watched as a hole was drilked into a saftey deposit box in the vault of the Rogers Park National Bank in Chicago. It was empty.

The search now turned to Michigan. Conners located a safe deposit box in the American States Saving Bank in Lansing which had been rented in September 1926, by a Mrs. Holmes. The bank manager showed Elston and Conners the photo that had been submitted with the application for the box, and they identified the person as Imogene Remus.

Elston obtained a court order to have the box openned. The State of Michigan, anticipating a large inheritance tax if the lost fortune were found, sent officials to monitor the proceedings. Franklin Dodge disclaimed any connection with the safe deposit box. He declared: "If she had a safety box here or visited Lansing, I know nothing about it." However, the assistant custodian of the bank vault identified a man matching Dodge's description as visiting the vault with the woman known as Mrs. Holmes. The box was drilled open, and once again nothing was found.

In Chicago Remus' lawyers, Charles Elston and Henry Pritzker, started digging into Imogene Remus' past. They learned that she received only $832 in alimony settlements in her previous divorce. They claimed that this was evidence of her limited resources before she married Remus, implying she married him for his money. To back this up they had the testimony of A.W. Brookway, who asserted that Imogene had indicated that she would get Remus' money even if she had to marry him.

Further damaging information was provided by Mrs. Alice Webber who quoted Imogene as saying she would "get that guy" and that she would send him back to jail again or have him departed , and , if that failed, she would kill him and plead self defense. Mrs. Weber also stated that Mrs. Remus had declared her love for Franklin Dodge and telephoned him in

Lansing to warn him about Remus being out of jail. She said that during the conversation Mrs. Remus referred to Dodge as "dear" and "honey" and declared "You know I love you, dear." In addition, Charles Clapper, a former Chicago hotel employee, declared that he once found Imogene Remus and Franklin Dodge together in a hotel room. And Warden John W. Shook said that he heard rumors that the couple were "travelling around together."

Even before Imogene Remus' death in October, 1927, George Remus' name had become virtually synonymous with sensationalism. His marital problems with its plethora of accusations received unprecedented coverage. His histrionics in the Chicago Courts were widely known, as was his flamboyant and unruly behavior during his trial for conspiracy to violate the Volstead Act. With Remus defending himself in the upcoming trial the newspaper editors knew that they would have plenty of sensational copy to keep their readers amused and interested. This was going to be a high profile trial, and both Remus and Taft were aware of it. Only Remus, though, was intent on using the press to espouse his cause.

Taft was advised by his father to speak to the press as little as possible and seek to have the case tried in Court, not in the newspapers. The Chief Justice wrote to his son about a month before the trial began:

> Remus' idea of a defense seems to be a sensational appeal through the newspapers and ultimately to the women on a jury in favor of the rights of a man to kill his wife for disposing of his property while he is in jail and changing to the home of another man. Of course I don't know what your Ohio ideas are, but certainly such a defense would not have appealed to the juries in my day. He talks so much that he may prove himself to be suffering from mental abberation, but I should think he was suffering only from the poisoned atmosphere of this bootlegging, divorce making, sensational press publicity, and that he is normal in the view of those who enjoy nothing else. You are going to have difficulty in preventing him from lying with the facility of the loosest kind of a tongue about what he believed and had reason to believe as to the schemes of his wife and her alleged paramour, because you are going to find some limitation upon your right to disprove what he charges against her, because such proof would be regarded as not competent except possibly as impeaching his veracity, or on the issue whether what he did was premeditated or only an outburst of momentary wrath. I can conceive that some puzzling questions on the subject of evidence will arise not only in the trial but in your preliminary consideration as to what you shall introduce. I see you are going to have your two strong assistants to aid you, and while it is going to be in a troublesome case and involve you in the hardest kind of work and study and may lead to a disappointment in not securing all you hope, it is a real

opportunity for usefulness and for added experience. Remus is bound to advertise you in his course of advertising himself.

Judge Chester Shook, who was to preside over the proceedings, was aware that many newspaper reporters would converge on Cincinnati to cover the trial, and he was determined to control their activities without curtailing their rights. He banned the use of all typewriters, telegraph equipment, flashlight photography and tripod cameras from his courtroom, but he provided the adjacent courtroom, which Judge Thomas Morrow had vacated for the duration of the trail, for their use. Here they were allowed to set up whatever instruments or paraphernalia they wished. Judge Shook informed them: "This case must be tried without confusion and in the usual dignified, calm manner. The atmosphere pervading the Courtroom must be consistent with the best traditions of American Judicial Procedure." [5].

Pressured constantly by reporters, County Prosecutor Taft at last disregarded his father's sage advice and spoke to the press. He made it clear that he considered Remus a common criminal who had committed a cold blooded murder for whixch he would be electrocuted. He was also confident that he could prove that Remus murdered his wife to keep her from testifying that he had killed Sheriff William Van Camp about four years earlier. Remus replied that this accusation was totally ridiculous, but Bert Morgan, former Prohibition Commissioner for Indiana, admitted there were rumors to that effect, although there was no concrete evidence.

On August 20, 1923, a farmer called the sheriff in Brookville,Indiana, reporting that two suspicious men were parked in a car in the woodshed area of his farm. The sheriff, acompanied by nearby farmers, rushed to the scene and engaged the intruders in a gun battle. After firing a couple of shots, the sheriff was fatally wounded, and his assailants escaped. It was generally believed that the men responsible for his death were bootleggers, and it was noted that the sheriff had been very active in the war against bootleggers in his county.

---

[5]Chief Justice Taft, who followed the case closely, was very critical of Judge Shook. "I have no use for that judge. He seems not only to be lacking in what a judge must have, namely the power of decision, but also in any knowledge of the law. It would not hurt him to study constitutional law so that he might understand as a State judge the difference between State jurisdiction and Federal jurisdiction. It is really too bad that a man so totally lacking in what is necessary to make a useful judge should be put upon you in a case that involves such really difficult issues as the Remus case. (Chief Justice Taft to Charles Taft, Dec. 18, 1927.)

Despite a $2,500 reward offer and an area-wide search in which even trains were stopped, the suspects were not apprehended. Four men were eventually questioned but released. Several months later a convict in the Ohio Penitentiary serving a 20 year sentence for bank robbery confessed to killing Sheriff Van Camp. There was talk about his being pardoned and extradited to Indiana, but no action was taken. When this information was brought to Prosecutor Taft's attention, he admitted knowing about the confession, but indicated that, notwithstanding, he had conclusive evidence that would prove that Remus killed the sheriff.

It is not known what basis, if any, there was for this serious accusation. It could have been based on an incident related by Remus' right hand man, George Conners, in a remarkable ten installment series on Remus' career written by Paul Anderson of the St. Louis *Post Dispatch,* {January 9, 1926}. Conners told how two rum runners from Chicago were near Brookfield, Indiana, with a load of whiskey in their car when they spotted a car parked by the roadside with eight armed men around it. Naturally, they took them to be hi-jackers, and so they crashed their car through a fence into a farm yard and crouching behind it exchanged gunfire with the hi-jackers.

One of the rum runners broke into the farmhouse and phoned Death Valley for help. Conners, Remus, and two city detectives who were there drinking, got into Conners' Marmon and sped to the scene, but they took a wrong turn and got lost. Meanwhile the two rum runners drove back to Cincinnati after a running gun battle in which, although their car was hit by bullets, they escaped unharmed.

Taft might have read this account, or Remus might have bragged to his wife that he was involved in the gun battle and that he shot the sheriff. It is not even known if this was actually the incident in which Van Camp was killed. Conners' account places the events as near Brookfield, but he could have been confusing it with Brookview as there is actually no town named Brookfield in Indiana. It is also very unlikely that Conners would have told the complete truth about the incident if he and Remus were actually involved in the killing. Imogene Remus probably knew the whole story, but she took it with her to the grave. Strangely enough, the incident was never mentioned in the trial.

As the trial drew nearer, the antagonism between Remus and Prosecutor Charles Taft, increased. On November 3rd, Taft incurred Remus' wrath when he requested that the Hamilton County Sheriff, William Anderson, produce the County jail book in which all visitors to Remus' cell had to sign themselves in and out. Remus objected, arguing that some of these visitors came to see him with information which he could use in his defense, and he was afraid that should they discover that the County Prosecutor was going to have immediate access to their names, they would stop supplying him with this information. He asserted that this violated his fundamental rights and hindered his preparation of a valid defense. Remus petitioned the Court to issue an order forbidding the prosecutor from further interference of this nature. His petition was granted.

The following day, Remus received a box of candies in the mail. The package had been opened by the Chief Clerk, and then delivered to Remus' cell. He opened the box, offered one to his guard, Sam McQueen, and then took one himself. No sooner had he put it in his mouth than he spat it out. He had recognized a foreign taste, which he identified as very much like strychnine. He thought that this was an attempt to poison him, and he shouted to McQueen to warn him, but the guard had already swallowed his candy.

Remus' suspicions seemed to be well founded when McQueen began to feel ill. Remus retrieved the piece of candy that Mc Queen had thrown into the spittoon and handed it, with the rest of the box, to George Sherber, the Hamilton County Jailor, who put them in the jail vault until they could be analyzed. The substance was identified as quinine, not strychnine. Obviously the sender did not intend to kill Remus, as quinine would merely cause pain and discomfort. However, Remus immediately took advantage of the situation by petitioning the Court to submit the facts of the incident to the alienists who had been assigned by the Court to study him so that they could determine whether such incidents were apt to produce mental disturbances which might effect his ability to control his emotions or actions.

Most of the week before the trial officially began was devoted to entering in the Court record the depositions which had been collected. Remus looked positively bored as he sat listening to the monotonous tone of the stenographer as she read out each deposition. When he was not in Court, he could be found in his cell-office in the court building, working with Elston on his defense.

At first Elston also favored the justifiable homicide defense. He told the press: "We expect to prove conclusively that Mrs. Remus and Franklin Dodge, Jr. carried on a love affair and that they conspired to deprive Remus of his property while he was in jail. It is a clear case of the unwritten law." However, after learning that the justifiable homicide defense was not recognized in Ohio, Elston suggested that Remus change his defense to insanity. Remus virtually exploded. Nevertheless, he eventually capitulated when Elston convinced him that justification was not a legal defense in Ohio.

His only hope was to plead temporary insanity, the defense he had used when representing William Cheney Ellis thirteen years previously.

Although Elston had managed to convince Remus that an insanity plea was his only option, Remus was obstinate and sought to postpone the final decision until the very last moment. However, a new Ohio law stated that if an insanity plea was to be used in a murder case, it had to be announced prior to the date set for the trial so that an insanity hearing could be set. At this hearing a jury of twelve would decide on the defendant's sanity, requiring only nine votes to secure a verdict. Should the jury find the defendant sane he would not be allowed to plead insanity during the murder trial.

Thinking that Remus might enter an insanity plea, the prosecution had ordered him to be examined by Hamilton County Court Alienist, Dr. W.C. Kendig. The results of this examination were never made public. Remus, unaware that he would eventually have to plead temporary insanity, declared: "Anyone who thinks I am insane needs a mental examination himself"

On October 17th, Elston went before Judge Shook to appeal against the new Ohio law, citing it as unconstitutional. First, he argued, it was unconstitutional because it adhered to the majority vote of nine jurors instead of a unanimous decision of twelve. He also claimed it was discriminatory because if the defendant was found to be sane, the prosecution could make use of that evidence, but the defense could not; and finally he claimed that by requiring the defendant to submit his defense prior to the trial, he was essentially being required to testify against himself.

Judge Shook listened to Elston's arguments patiently and then overruled the motion stating that if the defense planned to set up a plea of insanity they had until the following day to do so. However, Elston indicated he would challenge the constitutionality of the ruling, and at a conference it was decided that to save time the pre-trial sanity hearing would be skipped and the trial would begin as scheduled.[6]

---

[6]Chief Justice Taft wrote to Charlie:"I shall watch with a great deal of interest your insanity law. I hope that it may prove to be practical, and after the question of sanity has been settled avoid in the regular trial the disturing and confusing issues which a long trial with experts on the doubtful subject of insanity always clouds the real issue of guilt If your State has succeeded in getting a remedy of that kind that will work, it will doubtless be quickly followed by other States, as it ought to be." (Oct. 23, 1927)

JURY SELECTION

At 11 a.m. on November 14, 1927, the State of Ohio versus George Remus trial began in Courtroom number two at the Hamilton County Jail in Cincinnati, Ohio. As the doors opened a crowd of people who had been lining up since early that morning began to stream into the Courtroom, pushing and shoving in an desperate attempt to secure one of the 110 seats available. Some lawyers not involved in the case also came to see the remarkable spectacle of a lawyer defending himself in a murder case. And several off duty judges attended sessions as guests of the Court. Within a few minutes, the spectators' area was full, and two deputy sheriffs stood guard at the closed doors.

George Remus had entered the Courtroom earlier, immaculately groomed and carrying two law books under one arm and a steel document box under the other. He was soon joined by his co-counsel, Charles Elston. Three Court appointed alienists, Dr. David Wolfstein, Dr. Charles Kiely, and Dr. E.A. Baber, were seated on a raised platform directly behind the judge. They would be present throughout the trial to observe Remus and finally determine whether he was insane at the time of the killing, and whether he was still insane. They had the authority to stop the trial at any time if, in their opinion, Remus was showing signs of being mentally deranged. If they did so, the trial would end, and Remus would be sent to the State Hospital for the Criminally Insane at Lima, Ohio. Remus waived his right to have alienists of his own present, agreeing to accept the findings of the State's experts.

The selection of the jury was the first order of business. The difficulties facing the prosecution had been commented on recently by Chief Justice William Howard Taft, who declared: "The method of selection ought not to be such that counsel for the defendants by the exclusion of worthy citizens may bring about the selection of jurors of weak intelligence, little experience, and subject to emotions easily aroused."

Remus' first challenge was to obtain a satisfactory jury. Remus hoped to obtain as many women jurors as possible."Women jurors," he said, "will first ask whether I was justified when they consider their verdict and they will see the justification I feel." Even after he changed his plea to one of insanity, Remus never once admitted, even to his own co-counsel, that he had not been justified in killing his wife, and he never expressed any regrets for his actions.

Remus and Elston were aware that the subject of Remus' bootlegging would become a pivotal issue in the choosing of jurors. Remus was proud that he only sold pure whiskey and that he never cheated any of his customers. He believed that this would favorably impress the potential jurors, the majority of whom, he was convinced, were not opposed to the consumption of alcohol.

Ohio law granted the defense sixteen preemptory challenges and the State four. Obviously this was advantageous to the defense. Eventually twelve jurors would be selected to serve. A thirteenth juror would be chosen as a possible substitute. This juror would sit with the jury and listen to all testimony but would not take part in the deliberation unless one of the initial twelve jurors was unable to continue.

Remus was determined to make good use of every advantage to influence the jury. As he told a reporter for the Cincinnati *Enquirer* shortly before the trial commenced; "Remus the lawyer is fighting for Remus the defendant, and he will make the fight of his life for his life." Remus almost always referred to himself in the third person. He especially used this procedure in the courtroom. He explained to James Kilgallen: "In the courtroom I'm a dual personality. In defending myself, I forget there is a physical George Remus. I feel detached from him. I am the lawyer pleading his case." He claimed that at times when he was practicing law in Chicago he would use this dual personality technique to imagine what it was like to be the defendant as well as the lawyer. In this case he did not have to pretend.

Each prospective juror was questioned as to his feelings regarding capital punishment, the insanity plea, his willingness to make factual decisions based on the evidence and to accept guidance from the Judge as to points of law. He was also asked if he was acquainted with anyone who was even remotely connected with the case. Although Remus was pleading temporary insanity, the prosecution, fearing that the inadmissible "unwritten law" defense would be a factor, asked each prospective juror whether or not a plea that a man had taken the law into his own hands would influence him. One venireman was excused when he exclaimed: "I've been in the same kind of trouble. I had a wife who ran away with my money too."

During the proceedings Taft motioned that the jury be sequestered for the entire period of the trial, beginning with the tentative jurors. This was unprecedented in the Hamilton County Court where tentative jurors were allowed to return home until they were confirmed as jurors. However, the Remus trial had already garnered unprecedented news coverage. Moreover, Charlie Taft feared attempts would be made to tamper with the jury. He had been warned by his father that "Remus, unscrupulous as the devil, will doubtless have money enough to attempt to corrupt your jury." Judge Shook granted the motion, and arrangements were made to supply the prospective jurors with needed personal items.

By the end of the day six tentative jurors, four men and two women, were selected. They were still subject to preemptory challenge. The first day of the trial had taken place on Remus' 50th birthday. There was no celebration, just a card from his daughter saying "I hope your next birthday will be spent in happier circumstances."

The first day of the trial passed relatively quietly, but soon the spectators and reporters witnessed an eagerly awaited display of Remus' legendary temper and histrionics. Remus and the Assistant County Prosecutor, Carl E. Basler, nearly came to blows during an argument that occurred during the questioning of John Trautman, the 23rd venireman. When Basler asked whether Trautman knew "this man Conners, called Remus' lieutenant?" Remus immediately leapt up and loudly objected to the use of the word lieutenant. "He's not my lieutenant, he's my secretary," he insisted. Judge Shook sided with Remus. Now it was Basler's turn to object. "With all due respects to Your Honor, we will not refer to this man Conners as Remus' secretary." Remus once again jumped up and pulling off his glasses, gesticulated in Basler's direction. "I object to Mr. Conners being referred to as 'that man Conners'," he shouted. "Mr. Conners' character is as good as Mr. Basler's!" Basler eventually rephrased the question and asked, "Do you know this Conners who served time in Atlanta the same time as Remus did?" Once again Remus was on his feet, as was Charles Elston. Red in the face and waving his left arm in a manner that was to become characteristic, Remus strongly objected to the question, claiming its only objective was to prejudice the jury. Remus smiled as Judge Shook sustained his objection.

The defense now took over, and Remus arose to begin his interrogation. Immediately the prosecution objected, maintaining that Remus, by virtue of his plea of insanity, should not be allowed to interrogate his own prospective jurors. Basler insisted:"It is ridiculous to think that an insane man should question and examine jurors.".

"The claim of the defense is that the defendant was insane at the time the crime was committed," Elston replied, but Basler asserted that this was ridiculous. Judge Shook immediately declared a recess, and after consulting with one of the alienists, he ruled that Remus could continue as long as he made the distinction between his role as a lawyer and his role as the defendant. Prosecutor Taft objected vociferously, but in vain. and Remus continued his interrogation of the prospective juror, John Trautman.

Remus unleashed a volley of question at Trautman, who at times was only able to nod or shake his head in reply. He was asked whether he would be prejudiced by Remus' bootlegging activities or the fact that he had spent time in Atlanta Penitentiary and had been disbarred in Illinois. He was even asked whether his own marital relations might have a prejudicial effect on his decisions.

Remus then questioned Trautman concerning expert witnesses. Pointing to the three alienists, he asked: "If these alienists conclude that the defendant was sane at the time of the murder, would you be guided entirely by their expert opinions to the exclusion of any or all testimony adduced?" This brought a strong objection from Taft, who felt that Remus was asking the juror how he intended to evaluate the testimony. Judge Shook ordered the veniremen and tentative jurors to be removed from the Courtroom while the point was argued. Taft's objection was finally overruled, and Remus was permitted to ask the question. Trautman answered that he would take into consideration all of the evidence provided throughout the trial and would not rely solely on the opinion of the alienists. Trautman became the seventh tentative juror, after seven others had been excused because they were opposed to the death penalty.

After Trautman had been accepted, Elston resumed the questioning on behalf of the defense. Apparently Remus, as shrewd as ever, had specifically chosen to question the venireman at this stage to force a decision on his eligibility to question jurors. He probably realized that should the jury find him insane, then any subsequent sanity hearing would have to recognize that the Court by allowing him to interrogate his own jurors considered him to be sane at that time.

Remus had reason to rejoice on the second day of the trial. Not only did he gain the right to interrogate his own jurors, but also a large number of his possessions were discovered in a garage after an anonymous telephone tip. Four truck loads of goods were recovered. Remus was especially pleased to recover his law library of over 2,500 volumes, which he could use in preparing his defense.

As the jury selection continued, Remus sought to capitalize on the unpopularity in Cincinnati of the 18th Amendment. While Basler was examining a potential juror about her attitude towards bootlegging, he asserted "that every law-abiding person is supposed to be prejudiced against crime and criminals." Remus immediately sprung to his feet and loudly declared that "moral turpitude is not affected by the liquor laws; a violator is not placed in the category of a criminal." Remus did not want to be portrayed as a criminal but as a man who supplied the thirsty public with the liquor they wanted and which their elitist government, represented here by Charles Phelps Taft II, refused to let them have.

The next dispute was over the procedure to be employed in determing a person's sanity. Prosecutor Taft explained to one of the venireman that "the Court will charge you that there are three legal tests of insanity which the jury must apply in their consideration of this case," and then asked him if he would follow the Court's ruling. Remus immediately objected, and the tentative jurors were sent out of the room while he argued with Judge Shook over the decision to limit the procedure for determining sanity to three questions. According to Ohio law the jury had to be asked these questions:
"Was the accused a free agent in forming the purpose to kill?
Was he at the time capable of judging whether the act was right or wrong?
Did he know at the time that it was an offense against the laws of God and man?"

Remus argued that these three tests were far from sufficient to determine whether a man was insane or not, and the decision of the jury should not be limited to these tests alone. Claiming that there were more than two hundred tests for insanity, he offered to show sixty such tests which he used in defending William Ellis in Chicago. However, in spite of Remus' offer and his heated appeal, Judge Shook overruled his objection.

Remus not only lost his appeal on the insanity tests, but he also lost an earlier motion to have the Secretary of Labor, J.J. Davis, subpoenaed and instructed to produce all documentation relating to attempts to deport Remus. He claimed that the evidence will show that the deportation case was instituted by the deceased Mrs. Remus and Franklin L. Dodge Jr., and the records are of paramount importance in presenting the defense of this defendant. Taft opposed the motion, claiming that the Court had no jurisdiction over Secretary Davis. Remus replied with a long, eloquent speech, but Judge Shook obviously shared Taft's views and sustained the prosecution's objection; he reprimanded Remus and warned him not to waste any more of the Court's time. Remus, intent, as usual, on having the final word, then demanded that the Court instruct Taft to reveal the whereabouts of Franklin Dodge so that the defense could serve him with a subpoena. Judge Shook also refused to do this, but newspaper reporters later informed Remus that Dodge was staying at a downtown hotel where he had already been questioned by Taft, who intended to use him as a rebuttal witness.

On leaving the courtroom Remus was asked by a reporter whether he had found any precendents for acquital on the grounds of transitory insanity. He replied: "There never was a case like mine. No husband was ever so betrayed. To come back from prison to find that the love your wife bore you is gone--that your money is gone."

On November 16th, George and Mrs. Conners, along with Remus' brother-in-law, Gabriel Ryerson and the caretaker of his Price Hill Mansion, William Meuller, and Conners' brothers Harry and John were subpoenaed to appear before the Grand Jury. Taft would not reveal the reasons for this action, stating only that the Grand Jury was in the middle of an investigation. Elston claimed, however, that this was the result of wild rumors and insinuations that Conners and the others had conspired with Remus in planning the murder. He stated that he had instructed Conners and his wife of their right to refuse to testify. The charge of conspiracy was not to be taken lightly because under Ohio law any persons found guilty of conspiring in a murder case were liable to the same punishment as the actual killer.

The previous day Mrs. Conners outwitted and embarrassed the Prosecutor's office. Taft sent an officer to bring her in for questioning. Mrs. Conners excused herself to phone her attorney, Elston. She was gone only a few minutes when a car drove up to the house and Mrs. Conners ran out and got into the car which sped away while the surprised officer watched helplessly.

During the questioning of the final juror on November 18th, Remus and Taft and Basler were involved in another heated exchange that almost came to blows. When Remus asked the prospective juror if he would be prejudiced by the fact that Remus had been disbarred in Illinois because of his bootlegging activities, Basler objected, and Judge Shook ordered the jury out of the room before Basler was allowed to explain his objection. Basler then asserted that the prosecution had information proving that the Chicago Bar Association had been attempting to disbar Remus for ten years and had merely taken advantage of the bootlegging situation when it arose.

Remus immediately objected, and Judge Shook reminded him that he did not need to voice his objections because the jury was not present. But Remus insisted on being heard. "The press is here. Every word uttered by the Prosecutor's office and by this defendant goes throughout the country and this civilized land." Judge Shook, visibly annoyed, declared, "So far as I know, the case is not being tried in the press. It is being tried before the Court and jury. I am trying this case as though there were not a newspaper man in the room." Turning to Taft, he then asked the Prosecutor to state the objection. Taft replied that he thought they had already told him that and repeated the claim that Remus had not been disbarred solely on reasons pertaining to his bootlegging activities.

When he had finished, Remus, red in the face and gesticulating wildly, launched a verbal barrage: "A nice statement to be made by the son of the Chief Justice of the Court please!" he exclaimed. "He knows that the defendant is charged with murder and he makes these statements for no other purpose than to cause prejudice as a result of these newspaper men that are here." Charging that Taft knew this type of accusation was not permissible in any court in the country, not even in the Supreme Court, Remus then once again called attention to the Prosecuting Attorney's relationship to the Chief Justice of the Supreme Court. "It has been the pleasure of this defendant," he said, "to appear before that High Chief Justice, but the specimen as given by the offshoot of that great, renowned character is pitiful." He concluded his startling oration by asserting that "five hundred Judges and members of the Chicago bar have volunteered to come down here as character witnesses and, just because the son of the Chief Justice in this wonderful United States makes that kind of assertion." Then advancing towards the prosecution table where Taft sat dumbfounded, he shook his fist under his opponent"s nose and with tears streaming down his cheeks, he threatened: "Man, if I had you in the corridor, I would wreck you physically!"

Immediately Basler was on his feet threatening Remus. "Get back on your side or I'll punch you!" He then asked Judge Shook how much more of these accusations the Court would allow, but Remus simply turned on him. "When you were on the Eastern trip you drank two pints of whiskey."" {He was referring to the trip both the prosecution and defense made to collect depositions prior to the trial.} Basler implored Judge Shook to put an end to this vilification. Remus, now enraged, directing his remarks to the press section, continued to harangue Basler about the amount of alcohol he consumed on the trip. Basler protested that Remus was speaking for the benefit of the press and "not for the benefit of the Court at all."

Judge Shook eventually ended the fracas by ruling that Remus could ask the question that had started the whole uproar, but he also ruled that the prosecution could ask similar questions. Remus seemed about to object again when one of the deputy sheriffs stepped forward to restrain him. Remus, however, had changed his mind. By this time he was perspiring freely and, taking out a handkerchief to mop his brow, he turned to the press section behind him. "Did I make an impression?", he asked. Meanwhile, Dr. Wolfstein and Dr. Baber had rushed over to the Judge's bench, where they held a long, whispered confidential conversation. During the entire debacle, Charles Elston was silent, dazed and amazed at what was occurring.

The jury returned to the room, but Remus never continued the line of questioning that had caused the furor. Then Taft asked Judge Shook if there was nothing he could do to prevent further outbreaks of this kind., The Judge replied that if necessary he would rescind his permission for Remus to act as his own counsel. Legally, however, Judge Shook did not have the authority to do this. If Remus, in his capacity as a lawyer, were to disobey the orders of the Court, he could only be charged with contempt. If found guilty of contempt, he would be given a jail sentence, but at this time he was not only already in jail, he was also on trial for his life. If he was found guilty of murder, a sentence for contempt would mean nothing. Remus' outbursts could be stopped only by the use of force. Deputies would have to be assigned to watch him and prevent him from leaving his chair when it looked like he was going to cause problems.

When Remus was asked about Judge Shook's threat, he replied that it was immaterial considering the fact that his very life was at stake. "They may bind Remus," he continued in his glib, dramatic fashion, "they may truss him; they may entangle him in chains, but they will never halt his mind, and they will never silence these lips." This was the challenge that faced Judge Shook in a trial that had scarcely begun.

By the end of this unforgettable day, twelve jurors and the reserve sat in the jury box. Remus' fate now would be decided by: Joseph Lambert, machinist; Mrs. Ruth Cross, housewife; Joseph Schwab, farmer; Henry Hulting, cigar maker; Mrs. Anna Ricking, housewife; F.H. Oberschmidt, baker; Robert E. Hosford, contracting painter; Matthew J. Normile, produce dealer; Harry G. Byrd, food salesman; G. Henry Sandhager, retired liquor dealer; James E. Clark, machinist; and John Trautman, farmer. Their official duties began almost immediately; they were taken to the scene of the killing in Eden Park and then to the Price Hill mansion.

Court was adjourned until the following Monday so that Judge Shook could see the Ohio State-Illinois football game at Columbus. The weekend was far from quiet though. On Saturday Taft received reports that armed men were roaming the streets demonstrating their support of Remus, and one had reportedly waved his revolver and threatened that there was "a bullet in there for anybody who thinks Remus is going to be tapped for this racket."

Franklin Dodge was also in the news that weekend. He was seen nervously leaving a meeting with Willie Haar, who was in Cincinnati as a friend and witness for Remus. Dodge refused to talk to reporters about the visit, and Remus accused him of attempting to intimidate his witness. Haar denied that Dodge had tried to intimidate him, claiming that he had simply paid him a friendly visit. The two had met when Haar was incarcerated in the Federal Penitentiary in Atlanta and Dodge was the Prohibition Agent who worked up the case against him. Haar told reporters that they just talked, adding that Dodge had told him that he did not think Remus would be sent to the electric chair, but that he would wind up in an insane asylum.

Charles Taft spent most of the weekend working on strengthening the prosecution"s case. Disregarding his father's advice once again, he agreed to being interviewed by the press. He told reporters that Remus killed his wife because she knew too much about his business, and was going to reveal all in the course of the divorce trial. He further asserted that Mrs. Remus had evidence that would implicate Remus and a number of his associates in crimes that would result in them being returned to the penitentiary, and that Remus and his associates wanted to get hold of this evidence. When all their attempts, including a plot to kidnap her, failed they decided it was necessary to kill Imogene Remus. Taft claimed that they decided that Remus would carry out the killing because he was the one with the most obvious motives, and his arrest would divert attention from the real reason for the killing.

Remus, meanwhile, spent most of his weekend preparing his opening statement, although he claimed that he did not have to do much work on it. "I have lived with my opening statement and my memories for weeks," he said, "My address will be entirely extemporaneous. I will require no notes."

MONDAY, NOVEMBER 21ST

Early on Monday morning a crowd of people eager to listen to Remus deliver his opening statement gathered outside the Courtroom. As they waited impatiently for the doors to open, some fell prey to con artists and pickpockets. Some gullible people were swindled by con men selling fraudulent tickets to the trial, paying $1.25 each. As usual, the Courtroom was filled minutes after the doors were opened, and Judge Shook allowed some spectators to stand up against the walls. The corridors were still crowded with people hoping that someone inside would leave and relinquish his seat. Security was tight. Five extra deputies were on duty. Two deputies stood behind both the defense and prosecution tables, and one circulated around the room. A number of people were searched, and Remus himself had his papers and his document box carefully examined by Sheriff Anderson.

Judge Shook began by setting the rules for the opening statements. "Each side will be limited to two hours. "Each side will make a plain statement of its case. There will be no emotion and no argument. There will be simple statement of the facts that the evidence will bring out." At this point Remus stood up and, pointing to his throat, croaked hoarsely "Your Honor, I have a very bad...," but Judge Shook had been advised of Remus' condition, and he simply told him to be seated. The many people who came to hear Remus' opening statement were obviously disappointed.

Walter K. Sibbald, a youthful, tall, bespectacled assistant prosecutor, at once announced that the charge was murder in the first degree calling for death in the electric chair. He declared that the State would prove that the murder was planned on the night of October 5th. "The State's evidence will show that George Conners, George Klug and Blanche Watson of Covington were with Remus in his room at the Sinton that night. We will show that they plotted to kill Mrs. Remus." Sibbald pictured Remus as a cold blooded, determined killer, who when he had no opportunity to kill that night, returned the next morning and waited for his prey to appear.

He then asserted that the State would not only prove that Remus killed his wife, but that he did it with pre-meditated intent. He described how as Remus "approached his wife, who had left the taxicab, his actions were so deliberate that as he walked to the taxicab he slowly drew his revolver from his pocket and that as he fired he said something abusive to the woman he was killing. After the shooting Remus put the revolver in his pocket and calmly walked away from the scene." Sibbald insisted this proved that Remus was not insane when he killed his wife.

Sibbald then claimed that the State would prove that Remus had not prepared a defense for his divorce hearing because he had planned to kill his wife before that hearing took place, and that he had followed her on that fatal morning and killed her as part of a pre-determined plan. Remus listened intently, making copious notes and sucking on a lemon to soothe his throat.

Charles Elston delivered the opening statement for the defense. "We will introduce evidence to show that for two years prior to the killing George Remus was insane and that on the morning of the killing the insanity was brought out by a series of circumstances and facts which had turned this otherwise normal man into an insane man." At this moment he poimted to Remus, seated at the defense desk, surrounded by notes and law books. (The prosecution had already tried in vain to have the period of analysis of Remus' mental health limited to within three months of the shooting, but Remus and Elston insisted that they needed to go back at least two years to trace the development of Remus' insanity.) Elston admitted that Remus killed his wife, but he denied that the killing "was with deliberate and premeditated malice which the law says must exist for murder." He emphasized that the defense was one of insanity, stating that "at the time of the slaying George Remus was not a free agent, he was not a sane man, he was not a normal man, he was not able to entertain deliberate preparation and malice such as the law contemplates in a first degree murder." Elston declared that Remus' insanity was caused by his knowledge of the intimate relationship between Franklin Dodge and Imogene Remus; and he asserted that the defense would prove that this relationship existed; and, moreover, they would produce witnesses to prove that the couple conspired to keep Remus in jail and that they even hired assassins to kill him.

Then Elston traced Remus' life from the time he entered the United States as a young child. He related how Remus worked hard, long hours to qualify as a pharmacist and then to become a lawyer. He did not hesitate to tell of Remus' great success in the bootlegging business before being sent to Atlanta, about which time, he claimed, the affair between Mrs. Remus and Franklin Dodge began. He described how affectionate relations were between Mr. and Mrs. Remus before he went into jail and how they changed once Dodge appeared on the scene. He alluded to the conspiracy Mrs. Remus and Franklin Dodge had formed to strip Remus of his worldly possessions while he was incarcerated in Atlanta. Elston also informed the jury that Remus had not known that his wife was carrying on behind his back until he was served with divorce papers, and even then he hoped that a reconciliation was possible. "He learned the truth after he got out of prison in 1925," Elston declared, "and we claim that since then he has been insane."A thousand times at night and a thousand times by day he has had the bitterness of it all before him. It was more than a mortal man could stand."

Elston then described how Remus came out of jail to find his home stripped bare and how he discovered evidence of Dodge having stayed at his house, and even having slept in his bed "while he was occupying a prison cot behind bars." "We expect to show his mind snapped because these things bore down so heavily on him. Because after all he is just human." Elston admitted that Remus had been at the Sinton Hotel the night before the killing, but denied that there was a conspiracy, and he challenged the prosecution to prove otherwise. Elston finished his statement in fifty minutes, using only half the time allotted to him.

With the introductory statements over, the prosecution called their first witness, Mrs. Ethel Bachmann, a part-time clerical assistant for Mrs Remus who was staying with her at the Alms Hotel. She testified that the night before the fatal event Mrs. Remus had gone out at about 7 o'clock and had not returned until midnight when she went to bed.

Next Charles Stevens, the driver of the taxicab Mrs. Remus hired on the 6th of October, told how the other vehicle cut him off and how Remus walked towards the taxicab with his right hand in his coat pocket. He said he lost sight of him and Mrs. Remus when they passed to the rear of his cab, but he could hear Remus swearing and Mrs. Remus pleading "For God's sake, don't do it. For God's sake, come over and help me." He heard Remus answer: "I'll get you." At that moment, before he could come to her assistance, he heard the revolver go off; however, he claimed that he did not see the actual shooting. He then told how Mrs. Remus returned to his cab, crawling onto the back seat, but being forced out again by Remus. At that point, he said, he drove off in search of a policeman, but when he returned to the scene, Remus was gone, and Mrs. Remus had already been taken to the hospital.

On cross-examination Stevens admitted that he did not offer Mrs. Remus any assistance and had actually remained remarkably calm throughout the incident. The jury listened intensely to Stevens' account while Remus sat listening, seemingly unmoved.

Then Mrs. Audrey Stewart, a window trimmer, testified that she saw Mrs. Remus "crouching, not just kneeling, on the sidewalk with a look of pain on her face."

William Smith now took the stand and provided a moment of laughter to the grim proceedings when he admitted that he "stood perfectly still until the man was clear down the road and out of sight."

At this moment Ruth Remus entered, dressed in black mourning garb. When she saw her stepfather, she started to cry, and Remus, on the verge of tears, reached for his handkerchief.

Before returning to his cell, Remus smugly showed reporters a check for $100 that he had received from Charles M. Rau, manager of the Steamfitters Protective Association, with a letter thanking him for his work on behalf of organized labor in Chicago and offering more money if he needed it.

TUESDAY, NOVEMBER 22ND

Witnesses to the shooting continued to testify. Although most of them did not actually see Remus shoot his wife, they did see her running down the road, blood streaming down her dress, calling for help. One saw Mrs. Remus crouching on the ground while her husband stood over her with a gun in his hand. John Matthews, an attorney who saw the incident from his car, testified that he saw Remus with "something in his hand. They struggled. Something happened and the woman was struck down." He admitted that he was near enough to hear the report of the revolver, but he could not say that he actually witnessed the shooting.

Evander Austin, the man who took Mrs. Remus to the hospital, testified that he picked her up after the driver of the car in front of him had refused to help her, and that he had driven her and her hysterical daughter directly to the Bethesda Hospital, stopping only to pick up Lieutenant William Knight. Three physicians then took the stand to describe the wounds from which Mrs. Remus had died.

Remus sat chewing gum through most of the eye-witness testimony, not even looking at the witnesses, whom he and Elston chose not to cross-examine. He did show some agitation, though, when Dr. Howard Fischback, the surgeon who operated on Mrs. Remus, described his futile attempts to save her life.

After the noon recess, Remus, having recovered from his cold, got involved in a protracted verbal duel with Judge Shook when Remus motioned the Court to hand over all the papers and documents pertaining to his possessions which were now held by the prosecution. Judge Shook denied the motion, but even with the aid of two bailiffs he could not silence Remus. Finally exasperated, Judge Shook agreed to provide the defense the opportunity to examine the papers in question.

The prosecution next introduced witnesses to prove the existence of a conspiracy. Mrs. Luella Glover, a room inspector with the Sinton Hotel, identified Blanche Watson and claimed that she had seen her often around the hotel, where Remus had a suite. An attempt to have her identify Conners as another frequent visitor to Remus' suite failed since Conners was not in the Courtroom and could not be located.

Under cross-examination by Remus, she admitted that the suite Remus rented was used as an office for business purposes and many people visited it daily. Remus' attempt to establish that Blanche Watson was merely his secretary failed when the witness stated that she did not know what Miss Watson's occupation was. Asked whether the door of the suite was open or closed when women were present, Mrs. Glover replied that the door was open practically all the time. This corroborated Remus' assertion that he conducted a legitimate business from the suite. Under re-direct examination, the prosecution asked what kind of business Remus was engaged in, but the witness replied that she did not know.

Robert Clark, a waiter at the hotel, testified nervously that he had served dinner to four people in Remus' suite the night before the shooting and that he had been told to hurry up with the order. Under cross-examination he admitted that Remus was the only diner he could identify. When Remus tried to prove that the other three were not Conners, Klug and Blanche Watson, as the prosection claimed, but rather Jack Shevlin and August and Mrs. Bruck, the witness said he did not know any persons by those names but would be willing to identify them if necessary. Judge Shook ruled that Clark could be recalled at a later date to identify them if they were brought into court. Clark said that he knew George Conners, but could not remember if he was present during the meal. He further testified that he was requested to hurry because one of the diners was worried about missing a train he had to catch.

Edward Dixon, Mrs. Remus' divorce lawyer, took the stand next to bolster the prosecution claim that Remus had not prepared a defense for his divorce hearing, an indication, they claimed, that he had planned to kill his wife before the trial began. Dixon testified that he had concluded that Remus had no case when he learned that the defendant had not filed for any witness subpoenas, standard procedure in any trial.

Elston objected to this line of questioning, stating that the record of the case should be introduced as evidence rather than the opinion of the opposition lawyer. His objection was sustained. Remus, however, managed to get into the record the fact that he had obtained a number of depositions for use in his divorce hearing.

George Klug, Remus' chauffeur, who was being held on $10,000 bond for his possible connection with the alleged conspiracy, was the final prosecution witness for the day. The prosecution considered him their star witness for the conspiracy charge, but Klug proved to be a big disappointment. His testimony seriously contradicted previous statements he had made that were favorable to the prosecution. When asked to state his profession, Klug announced that he was a pipe fitter, but that he had been employed as a chauffeur for both Remus and Conners since April. When asked what was Conners' occupation, he replied that he was Remus' secretary, and when asked what was Remus' occupation, he replied, "Not any I know of." "And Conners was Remus' secretary?" Sibbald asked, calling attention to the absurdity of a man with no occupation hiring a secretary. Klug merely answered "Yes" and did not elaborate.

Klug claimed that he had slept most of the day preceding the shooting because he had been working the night before parking cars at an alleged gambling club on the outskirts of town. Continuing his testimony, Klug said that he woke up at about 5.p.m. and went to a local cafe where he received a telephone call from Conners instructing him to meet Remus at the Sinton Hotel to pick up the keys to the car, which was normally kept at Conners' house in Cumminsville. He said that he met Remus in his room, at which stage Sibbald interrupted him.

"Don't you recall that two weeks ago in the Prosecutor's office you told us you met Remus in the lobby and left the lobby with him and got into the machine?" he asked.

"No I don't." Klug replied.

"Don't you recall you said you got into the machine and drove away?"

"I do not."

"Didn't you make that statement to me?" Sibbald asked, beginning to show signs of annoyance.

"I don't think I did." Klug replied calmly.

"Don't you recall telling me you also saw Conners and got the keys to the machine from him?" Sibbald insisted.

"I'm not positive about seeing Conners. I can't remember saying that." Klug replied.

At this point Elston objected to the way Sibbald was interrogating his own witness as though he were under cross-examination. Sibbald replied that he was surprised by the testimony Klug was giving and concluded that he had become a hostile witness. Judge Shook overruled the objection and allowed Sibbald to continue under notice to the jury that the witness was hostile to the prosecution. Sibbald continued to question Klug, but he continued to receive conflicting statements. Klug insisted that he met Remus in his room at approximately 7 o'clock and that he stayed there for five to ten minutes, during which time Remus was the only other person present. This directly contradicted the prosecution's claim that the murder of Mrs. Remus was planned in that room at that time and that Remus, Klug, Conners and Blanche Watson had all been present. It also contradicted an earlier statement by the waiter, Robert Clark, who testified that he had served dinner to Remus and three other people in the room at 7 o'clock.

"Do you remember telling Mr. Taft, Mr. Clippinger and myself that there were several people in the room?" Sibbald continued.

"I didn't. No such thing." Klug replied.

"Don't you recall telling us you talked with Conners at the hotel?"Sibbald asked, referring to the telephone call the witness claimed he received at the cafe. Klug replied that he had spoken to Conners, but he was not sure now whether Conners was speaking from the hotel or his house. He then went on to contradict his statement regarding the whereabouts of the car he was to pick up, and finally stated that he could not remember if he picked it up at the hotel or at Conners' house.

"Who have you been talking to about this case?" Sibbald eventually asked out of frustration.

"No one," Klug insisted.

Frustrated and angered, Sibbald tried to impress Klug with the seriousness of his situation. "Didn't we tell you we considered you squarely in the middle of this case?" Klug seemed unconcerned. After further futile questioning about where Klug picked up the car, Sibbald, obviously upset, asked "Do I understand your mind is blank about everything that happened that evening?" Remus' immediate objection to the question was sustained. "We have got nothing but suppositions and guesses out of this witness," Sibbald attempted to explain, but his remarks were ordered to be stricken from the record.

Continuing with his testimony, Klug said that he had driven Remus to the Alms Hotel and parked outside the entrance where they sat for ten to fifteen minutes. He said that Remus had told him that he wanted to speak with his wife and that they had discussed the upcoming divorce case. He then testified to driving Remus home and receiving instructions to return the following morning at 7 o'clock, after which he went to the Boomer club where he worked until 6.30 the following morning. He claimed that he went straight from the club to Remus' house in Price Hill. Once again Sibbald challenged him on the truth of this testimony. He produced a sheet of paper which Klug identified as the statement he had signed at police headquarters on October 7th, in which he stated that he had kept the car at his house and Remus had called him at about 7 a.m. and asked him to pick him up. Klug acknowledged that the signature on the statement was his and that of the witness was

George Conners', but he claimed that he had not been able to read that bit of the statement when he had signed it.

Remus objected to the admissibility of the statement, asserting that all the circumstances surrounding the giving of the statement at the police station should be presented to the Court. Taft replied that he would be willing to provide the necessary details at any time, and this satisfied Judge Shook who allowed the questioning to continue and the first paragraph of the statement to be read into the record. After claiming that he did not know why he had given the police that information and admitting that he had been drinking some that day, and could not remember what he might have said, he continued with his testimony, insisting that he arrived at Remus' house soon after 7 o'clock after having had no sleep or breakfast.

Klug was on the stand for 45 minutes before Court adjourned. He had not finished his testimony, and the following day promised to be an interesting one. Reporters surrounded Sibbald asking him if Klug would be charged with perjury. Sibbald avoided a direct answer, but he did issue a warning that:""Any witness in this case who testifies falsely, whether he is a State witness or a defense witness, will be prosecuted by the State." When a newspaper reporter suggested that Klug's testimony might jeopardize the prosecution's conspiracy case, Prosecutor Taft fielded the question and replied: "On the contrary. It will make our case. We know what Klug had sworn to and what he had told us, but we did not know what he would testify to today." Sibbald emphasized that Klug contradicted himself so much while he was on the stand that it destroyed his credibility, and he considered this to be dangerous for Klug in the long run since he was one of the conspirators. He also charged that Klug's testimony during the day was the fourth different version he had given.

WEDNESDAY, NOVEMBER 23RD

Klug maintained his hostile attitude during five more hours of gruelling questioning. Sibbald began by reading the transcript of Klug's Grand Jury testimony, but Klug, looking puzzled and shaking his head, claimed that he could not remember having made the statements that were read to him. Klug then described how he arrived at the Remus mansion on the morning of the October 6th and was told by Remus that he wanted to be taken to the Alms Hotel. He insisted that this was all Remus said to him, but Sibbald challenged this statement, asserting that Klug had told them previously that he and Remus had chatted and joked in the kitchen while Remus ate his breakfast. Remus objected and accused the prosecution of intimidation of the witness prior to the trial. The jury was sent out, and Judge Shook prepared to listen to arguments from both sides.

Klug maintained that he was threatened while in the Prosecutor's office. He said that he was given just five minutes to answer a number of questions. He also claimed that Prosecutor Taft had virtually ordered him to say that he had driven Remus to the Pennsylvania Station after the shooting and that Sibbald instructed him to answer in under five minutes. When he refused to answer the questions, he was locked in a cell where, he claimed, he remained for two days before being allowed out on bond. He also said that the prosecutors had referred to a prison sentence that he had once served and told him that it looked like he was going to get another one.

Sibbald immediately denied that Klug was given just five minutes to answer any questions. "We gave Klug a long opportunity to tell us all he knew about the killing. He studied, stammered and finally declined." Sibbald handed a sheaf of papers to Klug who identified them as the notes that Sibbald had been taking during his interrogation. Judge Shook interrupted to ask Klug if he had been physically threatened. When Klug admitted that he had not and that he had told all he knew of his own volition, the Judge ruled that there was no evidence of intimidation.

The jury was recalled and informed of the ruling before the direct examination continued with Klug claiming that he did not see Remus at all once he got out of the car in Eden park, and that all he heard was a shot and a scream, at which time he drove away. This contradicted his statement to the Grand Jury that he saw the incident in the rear mirror of the car. However, when pressured by Sibbald he admitted that he might have looked back, but he wasn't sure. He also claimed that, as far as he knew, there was no revolver in the car that day. After the shooting, he testified, he basically blacked out and could not remember what route he took back into town, but he did know that he did not, at any time, go to Pennsylvania Station. This contradicted the prosecution's theory that he had picked Remus up further down the road and had driven him to the station. Sibbald then managed to get Klug to admit that he had gone to both George Conners' and Blanche Watson's houses after the shooting, in spite of his earlier claim that he went straight to the Price Hill mansion. Remus objected to the line of questioning stating that Klug's movements after the shooting were irrelevant, but Sibbald asserted that this helped to prove the State's conspiracy theory. At this juncture, Judge Shook excused the jury so that he could hear arguments on the conspiracy theory, which the prosecution was trying, so far in vain, to establish through Klug's testimony.

Sibbald explained that Klug's testimony was vital, but that he had constantly lied on the witness stand. He insisted that Klug's being at the wheel of the car which had cut off the taxi was evidence of his aiding Remus, and his visiting both Conners and Watson after the event was evidence that they too were involved. Remus then asserted that, "it will be shown that Klug's hands were not on the wheel when the motor car headed into the curbing and halted the taxicab. It will be proved that Remus at the time controlled the car." This contradicted previous eye-witness statements which put Remus in the back of the car and therefore physically unable to steer the car. Klug himself had testified that he drove the car with Remus in the back and had obeyed his order to cut off the other car, although, later in the afternoon, he once again contradicted himself when he stated that Remus had actually had his hands on the wheel when they cut off the other car.

After listening to arguments on the conspiracy charge for over half an hour, Judge Shook ruled that Klug's testimony, and that of other witnesses was insufficient to prove a conspiracy and that the prosecution "must first show there was a conspiracy not only to murder but to conceal the facts of the murder." If they could not prove that the actions of the accused parties were directly related to the committing or concealing of the crime, then the testimony concerning events occurring after the killing would be inadmissible. This ruling was extremely advantageous to the defense. The onus was now on the prosecution to produce concrete evidence regarding the alleged conspiracy.

After the recess, Klug was cross-examined by Elston with prompting from Remus and frequent objections from the prosecution. The questioning focused on the Klug's state of mind after the shooting and at the time of his reporting to the police station. By establishing that Klug started drinking heavily soon after the incident and was intoxicated when he was questioned in the police station and later in the Prosecutor's office, Elston hoped to counter the charge that Klug's testimony contradicted his previously sworn to statements.

On re-direct examination Sibbald tried to get Klug to tell from where he got the liquor, but he refused to answer the question, and the defense objected to the question even being asked. Judge Shook then called Klug to the bench where they conversed for a short time before the Judge sustained the objection. Remus, unable to resist the opportunity for a little showmanship, leapt up and, with a broad smile on his face, said "Thank You Your Honor." He received a stern look from the Judge and was ordered to sit down. Klug was allowed to step down shortly afterwards.

The prosecution then sought to establish that after the shooting Remus was driven to the Pennsylvania station in a blue car, the color of the car Klug drove for Remus. However, their effort met with little success. Two cab drivers testified that they saw Remus at the station, but they could not identify the car which dropped him off. Lester Ruele, the cab driver who drove him from the station to the police headquarters, testified that Remus drove up in a blue car, but he could not tell what type of car it was. Another witness, John Cassidy, testified that he saw Remus pull up at the station in a dark blue sedan, but he was unable to identify the driver, although he knew George Conners and he thought there was a chance that it might have been him. This was stricken from the record though because it was not a definite identification. Cassidy was also acquainted with Remus, and he testified that he greeted Remus at the station and when he asked him if he was leaving town, Remus replied that he was. Cassidy said he then asked him whether he was not supposed to appear in court that morning. Remus replied, "Not today," before walking across the road and getting into Ruele's cab.

Just before Court was adjourned, the detectives who accompanied Remus to Eden Park that afternoon to search for the revolver testified concerning their unsuccessful search. Remus, always mindful of the media, issued a Thanksgiving Day statement, which he ended by saying; "Thankful! Yes a million times thankful for the peace of mind, soul and being, that no verdict can rob me of, and which now, on this day of thanks is my solace."

THURSDAY, NOVEMBER 24TH

There was no Court session on the 24th because of the Thanksgiving holiday. Remus celebrated with a turkey dinner in the company of the other 150 inmates of the Hamilton County Jail. Called upon to make an after dinner speech, Remus vividly described the harsh treatment he had received in various prisons and told the inmates that, although they were in jail, they still had much to be thankful for. He told them that they had Sheriff Anderson to thank for their above average living conditions. He informed them that this was the only time while he was incarcerated that he did not have to pay for favors or privileges.

Remus spent the rest of the day setting up an office for himself in a small, unused, room in the jail. On newly constructed shelves around the room he placed the law books which had been cleaned up after being discovered in a garage the previous week. "Those books have saved many a life,"' he told reporters, referring to his career as a criminal lawyer in Chicago. He seemed confident that they would save his life too. After holiday dinners with their families, Taft and his assistants spent the day working and were expected to start wrapping up their case the following day. The jurors were treated to a turkey dinner and then taken on a bus trip to Harrison's tomb near Cleves.

Many of the newspaper reporters were guests at a Thanksgiving Day party hosted by John S. Berger, an exposition promoter and self-styled millionaire. Berger, a boyhood friend of Remus', had come to Cincinnati to help his friend. Bragging about his generosity, he proclaimed: "It cost me several hundred dollars. I introduced them to a lot of women. They had a good time."

Hungry for copy, some reporters speculated about the forthcoming testimony of Ruth Remus. Would Remus himself cross-examine the young woman whom he had adopted as a child and who had once been his greatest admirer? Remus himself seemed unsure about whether to cross-examine her himself or not, stating that he would be the ideal choice because of his intimate knowledge of her and her life. "My inclination will be all against it. Not that I would have any compunction for I have no respect for her as a woman. She was an accessory before the fact in this colossal conspiracy between her mother and Franklin Dodge against me and knowingly condoned her mother's relations with the man."

FRIDAY, NOVEMBER 25TH

The prosecution was determined to prove that Remus had not prepared any defense for his divorce hearing because he planned to kill his wife before the hearing took place. The first witness, John J. Schmidt, a Deputy Clerk of the County Court, was asked if Remus had sent out any subpoenas for the hearing. Remus' immediate objection was overruled. However, Remus still insisted on being heard, and the jury was sent out while he argued the point. Waving a briefcase, Remus told the Court that it held a number of depositions that he had intended to use in his defense and which he had with him on the day of the killing. Judge Shook, however, stuck to his original decision and overruled Remus' objection.

The jury was recalled, and the witness was allowed to answer the question. He replied that no subpoenas had been issued. Under cross-examination Remus referred to depositions he claimed he had received and to witnesses who had offered to testify on his behalf. The prosecution objected to this introduction of evidence, and his remarks were struck from the record, but he had achieved his objective; the jury had heard the remarks and would undoubtedly find it difficult to disregard them altogether.

Next, Mrs. Gabriel Ryerson, Remus' sister, testified, tearfully, that she and her husband lived with Remus at his Price Hill home, and she had seen him leave in the morning of the killing. She also admitted that her husband had been informed of the shooting by a telephone call from Blanche Watson before they received the news through official channels. The prosecution intended to use this as evidence that Blanche Watson had been involved in the killing.

After the noon recess, the long awaited testimony of Ruth Remus began. Dressed in black, she made her way to the witness stand carefully avoiding looking at her step father. When Assistant Prosecutor Sibbald asked her if she was the daughter of Imogene Remus, she wept silently and just nodded her head. During the ensuing testimony she spoke in such a quiet, faltering voice that Judge Shook often asked her to speak louder, and ocassionally the court stenographer had to read her answers. Many of the jurors were visible afftected, and Ruth Cross, the youngest jury member, was crying.

Ruth then tearfully related how she accompanied her mother to a conference with Judge Edward Dixon, her mother's attorney, the night before the fatal shooting. She testified that after breakfasting in their rooms at the Alma Hotel the next morning they took a taxi to go to Judge Dixon's office. She stated that when they became aware that Remus was in a car, a blue buick, following them, her mother asked the driver to stop, while she asked him to go faster. Then when the Remus car finally got around the cab, the driver jammed on the brakes and brought the car to a stop. "Mother opened the taxicab door and started to get out, and Mr. Remus approached her and grabbed her by the wrist and pulled her out of the cab. It took me some time to recover myself, but I followed."

After crying for a few minutes, she was able to continue. "I asked him what he was going to do--but he had already shot her. Then he hit her on the head. He held the muzzle of the pistol close to her body.I heard her scream 'Oh Daddy, dear, you know I love you! Daddy, you know I love you!' He swore at her--terrible language. Then she said 'Don't do it, Daddy, don't do it.' I saw the pistol in his right hand. After the shot was fired, I grabbed him by his coat label and said ' You don't know what you are doing.' He answered:' She can't get away with that!'"

The bereaved girl continued her emotion ladened testimony reluctantly relating how her mother made her way through the cab out onto the street and, bleeding profusely, ran down the street "crying for someone to take her to a hospital. That she was shot. I caught up to her and got her into a car." Ruth then sobbed as she described how on the trip to the hospital "Mother was lying on the floor. I was trying to help her--but she was suffering terribly, although conscious and able to talk. She said 'I know I'm dying.' I said ' No you're not.' I couldn't believe it Then she said 'Isn't it terrible of George to do this?'" She then told of her mother being taken into the operating room. When Sibblad asked her: "Did you see your mother after the operation?" she barely managed to answer: "Yes--after she was dead."

Ruth Remus still faced a final heart wrenching ordeal. She was asked to describe the clothes her mother was wearing the day she was shot. Then the blood stained flimsy garments with black bullet holes-the black silk dress, the pink slip, the brassiere- were draped over the railing in front of the witness stand and shown to her for identification as she shrank in horror. Through her entire testimony, her step-father sat just five feet away from the witness stand listening intently but showing no emotion.

Elston conducted the cross examination. First he established that George Remus paid for her tuition while she attended the Cincinnati

Conservatory of Music. He then asked her where she and her mother had lived when Remus was in the Atlanta penitentiary. Miss Remus replied that they did not have a permanent address and that they went about a lot, travelling between Atlanta, Cleveland and Cincinnati. She denied that she and her mother had ever lived in Lansing, Michigan, where Franklin Dodge lived, but she admitted that they had visited there some time ago.

Then Elston questioned her concerning her claim that she had to leave the Cincinnati Conservatory of Music because Remus was disagreeable. Elston asked whether he had been disagreeable to her specifically. "Well," she replied, "He had men stationed at the school to take my car away from me." However, Elston got her to admit that her car had not actually been taken away by Remus but by officers carrying out Court instructions, although she insisted that Remus was the instigator of the Court action. This incensed Remus, who turned to Elston and stated just loudly enough for the jury to hear: "They had three cars. I had none."

Next Elston asked whether she had told investigators after the shooting that Remus was "acting insanely" in Eden Park and that she even described his demeanor as that of a madman. Prosecutor Taft and his assistants immediately objected. Judge Shook dismissed the jury and allowed Miss Remus to step down while the point was debated. Elston and Remus contended that this was the only subject on which they could discredit her testimony , and they insisted that they had every right to ask the disputed question. The prosecution innsisted that Elston was trying to establish the basis of Remus' insanity through this cross-examination, and they furthermore asserted that this was not permissible under the law. After a prolonged argument concerning the legal aspects of the situation, Judge Shook announced that it was such a delicate point of law that he did not feel he could make a ruling without first consulting his law books. He declared that he would postpone his decision until then.

SATURDAY, NOVEMBER 26TH

On this day the alienists filed their eagerly awaited report on Remus' state of mind. All the concerned parties had been given a copy the evening before. The report, signed by the three alienists, was presented as a provisional report, subject to modifications at any time during the remainder of the trial. The conclusion read:

> Basing our conclusions upon conversations with and examination of, the said George Remus, including our observations of him in the Courtroom during the progress of the trial thus far, we are of the opinion that the said George Remus is now sane and was on October 6th 1927, sane.

Judge Shook kept the report from the jury, ruling that the information was for the attorneys and was not to be considered evidence in the trial. Both sides could, however, call the alienists to the witness stand at anytime to give testimony if they so wished. In fact, Judge Shook declared that if neither side called any of them to the stand, then he would. The actual findings of the report were naturally advantageous to the prosecution, but Judge Shook's decision to withhold the findings from the jury favored the defense. Rising from his seat, Remus approached the bench and, in an emotional voice, thanked Judge Shook for his decision.

Elston, however, unhappy with the conclusions of the report, objected to the filing of it at that time. He maintained that it was incomplete and only based on observation of Remus during half the trial. Judge Shook overruled his objection and read into the Court record a transcript of the previous proceedings when Remus and Elston had both agreed that they would adhere to the findings of the Court alienists. Judge Shook also pointed out that the report had to be filed at that time because the findings had direct bearing on the rest of the case. If the alienists had found Remus to be insane at the present time, he would have been unable to continue to represent himself, and with the defense about to open its case, it was a pivotal factor.

In a surprise move the prosecution now called to the witness stand William Hulbershorn, who only the day before had informed the Prosecutor's office that he had driven the defendant downtown on October the 6th.

Although they knew that his testimony would provide the finishing blow to their almost discredited conspiracy theory, they felt that, in all fairness, they had to put him on the stand.

Elston objected to Hulbershorn being called as a prosecution witness, claiming that the defense had planned to call him themselves. When Judge Shook overruled his objection, Elston requested that earlier testimony regarding the identification of the driver of the car that dropped Remus off at the station be stricken from the record and that both Klug and George Conners be offered an apology by the prosecution. His request was denied.

Hulbershorn related how he had seen Remus walking hurriedly through Eden Park on that morning and offered him a lift. He stated that the two men did not speak until they had reached the train station, at which time Remus asked him if he knew who he was. When he replied that he did not, Remus identified himself, Although Hulbershorn was aware of his reputation, he did not believe that this was the famous man. At that point, he testified, Remus turned to him and said "I have just done some shooting in the park." He then left the car and walked across to a taxicab on the other side of the road.

William Hulbershorn concluded his exculpatory testimony shortly before noon, and Prosecutor Taft arose and declared that the State rested. Elston then motioned for the Judge to issue a directed verdict of not guilty, but Judge Shook denied the motion. Elston then motioned that all the State's evidence and remarks regarding the conspiracy theory be stricken from the record because of their failure to prove the existence of any conspiracy. Judge Shook took the motion under advisement.

Then Elston arose and motioned that the alienists be removed from the dais behind the judicial bench where they had been sitting since the beginning of the week. The judge explained that the doctors were sitting there at his request, but he was prepared to have them seated elsewhere if there was some objection. Elston stated that he did not want the jury to think that the three doctors were official in the case. Remus interupted him and asked that Elston's request be disregarded and that the alienists be allowed to sit wherever they wished. Elston was visibly annoyed by Remus' interference, as was Judge Shook. Instead of reprimanding Remus, however, the judge simply instructed Sheriff Anderson to use force if necessary to ensure that only one attorney from each side be allowed to speak at a time. Elston reluctantly withdrew his request, but Judge Shook decided that they should be seated elsewhere in the room, and they took seats behind the high jury box.

The defense now called its first witness. Wasting no time in introducing the subject of Remus' prior mental health, Elston called Leo A. Burke to the stand. Burke, a Cincinnati attorney who had represented Remus on a number of occasions, was questioned by Elston concerning Remus' mental condition during the time he represented him. The prosecution immediately objected to this line of questioning, and this triggered an argument regarding Remus' present mental state.

Judge Shook asked Elston precisely when the defense felt that Remus had recovered his sanity.Elston denied that he had made any statement about Remus' present mental condition, but Judge Shook pointed out that Remus had gone on record with a claim that he was sane at the present time, and that this statement was noted in the record as the opinion of the defense.

In spite of a direct request from Judge Shook, Elston refused to state whether, in his opinion, Remus was sane or insane at the present time, maintaining that the defendant's present mental health was not really the issue here. He stated that the defense was concerned only with his condition prior to and including the day of the killing. Judge Shook warned Elston that he would not stand for any kind of subterfuge. Elston answered sharply that there will be no subterfuge in this case while he had anything to do with it. He finally stated for the record that it was his contention that Remus was insane for a period of approximately two years prior to the killing and that he was insane when the act was committed. He simply refused to elaborate, and Judge Shook, conceding to this, allowed the questioning of the witness to continue.

Then Elston asked Burke if he could conclude from his observations of Remus whether he was sane or not? Burke replied that he could, but he was prevented from stating his opinion by an objection from Taft. The jury was sent out, and the two side argued over the permissibility of a layman's opinion. Taft maintained, and Judge Shook final ruled, that lay witnesses, before being allowed to give their opinions concerning Remus' sanity. would have to relate the factual events that lead them to the opinion which they held concerning Remus' sanity.

The jury was returned to the Courtroom, and Burke was asked to relate the incidents that caused him to form his opinion on Remus' mental condition. He told the Court how Remus would react when Mrs. Remus and Franklin Dodge were mentioned. "Remus would become much worked up, strike his body, raise his hands above his head and to my mind appeared like a maniac." He continued, "He would quiet down, apologize, and then go back and do the same thing over. It occurred twice in one conference. His face would become contorted." He claimed that Remus reacted the same way six times in his presence.

Taft cross-examined Burke himself; this was the first time he had questioned any witness. Taft got Burke to admit that he had decided Remus was mentally imbalanced about three weeks into their association, but that he had not tried to have him observed by a professional, and he had continued to do business with him. Burke admitted that he had no medical knowledge of insanity and could not define exactly what sort of mental imbalance Remus seemed to be suffering from, only that he seemed unbalanced. He also insisted that he had spoken about Remus' condition to a number of people during the time he had been representing him.

Lee Beaty, a former Assistant United States District Attorney, took the stand next to testify that he too had come to believe that Remus was insane when, during the Jack Daniels trial in Indianapolis in 1925, Remus had made a visit to his office. "He talked incoherently and raved in my office for fifteen to twenty minutes." Beaty also claimed that Remus made various accusations at the time that he knew to be untrue. He later told the Court that these accusations centered around a story Remus had been told about a conspiracy the government had formed with the Egan's Rats gang and Franklin Dodge to assassinate him. Beaty also told how Remus raved for no apparent reason when he was transferred from one jail to another. Under cross-examination he admitted that, on the occasion that Remus raved in his office, he had a United States Marshall remove him, but he had not attempted to have him confined on reason of insanity, although under Federal law he had the authority to do this. He also admitted that he had instituted the proceedings to send Remus to Troy jail where he served on year on a nuisance charge, "just as though he were any sane defendant."

The following day Remus worshipped at a service held for the inmates of the jail and delivered a sermon about leading a better and more upstanding life after being released.

MONDAY, NOVEMBER 28TH

Monday's morning session began with a legal argument regarding Remus' pleas of "transitory insanity" and the testimony that would be necessary to prove this. The argument started when the defense called Franklin Edward Shaw to the witness stand. Shaw, a race track employee, was to testify concerning the behavior of Mrs. Remus, but Prosecutor Taft objected on the grounds that this sort of testimony went to show justifiable homicide, which was not the defense plea. He contended that it is simply a subterfuge to get before the jury evidence of justification. He called attention to the fact that prior to the trial Remus had stated that his plea would be one of justification, but that he had changed his plea to fit the laws of Ohio. Elston denied that this course of questioning went to proving justification, but rather that it showed the cause of Remus' insanity. Elston asserted that Remus'insanity began two years ago, but he couldn't say if it still existed.

Judge Shook now ruled:"There must be independent evidence of a diseased mind introduced in this case in view of the development of the case and opening statements of counsel and the interrogation of the prospective jurors." Later in the day, after hours of legal battling over the admissibility of testimony linking Imogene Remus and Franklin Dodge, Judge Shook ruled that enough evidence had been introduced to establish that Remus had a diseased mind and that the defense might show the cause of this condition. This was a very important victory for the defense.

Elston was now able through the testimony of Richard Simmons to introduce some testimony regarding the activities of Mrs. Remus, which lead to Remus having one of his outbursts. Simmons, an attorney for the Ohio and Kentucky Distilling Company, in which Remus had a controlling interest, described vividly one of Remus' hysterical fits, which occurred when he held a conference with Remus, his daughter and Blanche Watson, his secretary. The day before the conference he and Remus had discussed the creation of a trust fund for his daughter and together they had drawn up the agreement. Remus was "perfectly rational" at this meeting, Simmons said, but the next day, when the time came for Romola to sign the document, Remus suddenly jumped up and shouted out: "That beautiful little daughter of innocence shall never sign a paper bearing the name of George Remus, declared by all to be the arch conspirator of all the ages!" He said that Remus "beat his clenched fists on his breast as he talked. It sounded as if he were beating on metal." When asked what had caused this outburst, Simmons said that he had told Remus earlier how his wife had tried to embarrass him and the corporation by instigating an Internal Revenue investigation into the business accounts, which resulted in the filing of liens against the corporation's finances.

While the trial was proceeding, Remus was informed that Franklin Dodge was finally served with a defense subpoena. This was an important personal victory for Remus because it meant that Dodge had to remain in Hamilton County until he was summoned, and, if he failed to appear, he would be held in contempt of court.

Remus was pleased to hear the news about Dodge, but he was unhappy to learn of the indictement of one of his potemtial witnesses, Vernon Chumbley, for perjury. Chumbley, who had been released from Atlanta Penitentiary on a writ in order to appear in Court when necessary and was currently sharing Remus' "suite" in the Hamilton County jail, where he was doubling as a secretary for the defendant, was charged with perjuring himself in a deposition he signed for use in the Remus divorce case stating that he had served as secretary to the Warden at Atlanta. Taft claimed that the deposition contained false information about Mrs. Remus and further charged that Chumbley was never secretary to the Warden.

TUESDAY, NOVEMBER 29TH

William Mueller, Remus' caretaker at the Price Hill mansion, testified that he had seen Franklin Dodge at the house with Mrs. Remus on at least three occasions while Remus was in prison.

"Did you ever see Franklin L Dodge at the Remus home?" Elston asked him.

"Yes sir, I did," he replied, and then told how, on August 1st of the previous year he had seen Dodge at the house sitting in Mrs. Remus' car, but claimed that when Dodge saw him, he covered his face. On another occasion, he looked through the window and saw Dodge inside the house with Mrs. Remus, and Dodge pulled the blind down. He saw the two together at the house for the third time in December 1926. They were about to drive away when Mrs. Remus reportedly saw him and called him aside.

He was prevented from continuing by an objection by Prosecutor Taft. The jury was sent out, and Taft asserted that the testimony being given was irrelevant because it pertained to justification and not the defendant's sanity. He stated that only testimony which had been directly communicated to the defendant and had effected his mind was relevant. He added that he did not mind how the story was told or how many times it was repeated, but only the person who actually told it to Remus should be eligible to testify.

Judge Shook agreed with Taft and informed the defense that proving that a conspiracy existed between Dodge and Mrs. Remus was irrelevant, unless it could be established that knowledge of the conspiracy caused Remus' insanity. He made it clear that "facts, whether proved true or false, if brought to the defendant's knowledge previously to October 6th, are competent testimony, but the facts must have been communicated." He also reminded the defense that it was their burden to prove insanity in the same way that it was the prosecution's burden to prove murder.

Taft, worried that defense witnesses would give testimony and falsely claim that it was communicated to Remus, asked the Judge how the State was to protect itself against this kind of abuse, but Judge Shook merely told him that they had the right to object to any testimony which they felt might violate the ruling. The argument was eventually resolved when Elston agreed to give his professional word that he would only question witnesses about facts which had been communicated.

The jury was recalled, and Mueller took the stand again, but a sustained objection prevented him from relating what Mrs. Remus said to him when she called him aside.

"Did you see her leave?" Elston asked, returning to Mueller's testimony.

"Yes, she left with Dodge," Mueller replied, and he then described how they left the house totally bare except for a bed, a table and the kitchen range. He explained how Remus had to climb through a window to gain entry to the house on his return from prison and how it took a locksmith two days to unlock all the doors inside. He testified that Remus was outraged by the state of the house.

Mueller also testified that on one occasion Mrs. Remus gave him a screwdriver and instructed him to remove a clock from the wall. When he refused, Mrs. Remus told him not to be afraid. "Mr. Remus will never come back here," he quoted her as saying, "We are going to have him deported. Everything is fixed up. He will go back the way he came - without any money."

When Mueller finished his testimony, Taft moved that all of it, except for the description of events that occurred in Remus' presence, be stricken from the record. The jury was sent out for another twenty minutes while Taft argued his point, after which Judge Shook agreed to take the matter under advisement.

Next, former Judge of the Court of Common Pleas, Benton S. Oppenheimer, told about visiting Remus at the Price Hill mansion when it was devoid of any furniture. He related how Remus walked from room to room "wringing his hands, uttering cries of amazement that he had been treated in that manner." Remus' clothes, he said, had been dumped in a pile on the porch, and his bed had been stripped of all bed clothes, and to aggravate matters, there were over sixty pairs of woman's shoes in a cupboard in one of the rooms.

The former Judge, one of Remus' divorce attorneys, said he came to the conclusion before October 6th that his client was insane. He based his opinion on Remus' obsession that Dodge conspired with his wife to strip him of his property. Oppenheimer described how Remus would talk about how he was convinced Mrs. Remus would return to him despite the divorce proceedings, and then he would suddenly change the topic to Dodge and the alleged conspiracy against him. "We would be talking about matters entirely foreign to that," Oppenheimer told the Court, "and Mr. Remus would give way to an outburst. Uncanny laughter would resound through my office." He said that during these outbursts Remus "raved, and raved, and raved. His eyes became glassy. He told me he was being watched by detectives and gunmen--and left my office without making one coherent statement." Oppenheimer was not permitted to provide anymore information about Remus' accusations, except to say that one of them involved an incident in St Louis. Remus' strange behavior,Oppenheimer maintained, led him to withdraw from the case.

Under cross-examination Oppenheimer was asked why, if he considered Remus insane, he had continued to represent him in his divorce case and had even filed a cross petition when he knew that, according to Ohio law, an insane person could not get a divorce. He replied that he had not concluded that Remus was insane overnight, and had, up until the time he withdrew from the case, been of the opinion that Remus was entitled to a divorce. When asked why he had not had Remus examined by a professional in the mental health field once he came to the conclusion that his client was insane, he replied that he felt that course of action would have been unseemly. Questioned about the divorce negotiations, he admitted that an offer had been made through another attorney to Mrs. Remus of $100,000 for an uncontested divorce. Mrs. Remus had agreed to a divorce only on condition that she received 50% of the Remus property, which Remus had not considered a viable proposition.

Alan Curry, a former United States District Attorney from St. Louis, was next on the witness stand. He also claimed that Remus was insane prior to the killing. He told how he and the defendant were going over the evidence in the Jack Daniels case when Remus suddenly exclaimed: "That man Dodge has taken my wife's affections. Franklin L. Dodge has taken my wife after I trusted her and ruined my life forever." Curry described how Remus paced backwards and forwards, wringing his hands and crying. "His muscles were contorted, his face was drawn and his eyes were glassy." He testified that Remus was unable to concentrate on the trial at hand because of his obsession with Franklin Dodge and his belief that the prohibition agent had conspired to put him in jail. Curry also claimed that Remus was convinced that he was being followed by detectives and gangsters intent on killing him. "He left my office without making a coherent statement with reference to the Daniel case," he concluded.

Under cross-examination, Assistant Prosecutor Carl Basler attempted to discredit the witness by charging that he had been asked to resign because of personal misconduct and under threat of impeachment. Curry replied that he had not been asked to resign, and Elston objected angrily to the line of questioning, asserting that it was just intented to prejudice the jury. Basler replied that he had obtained his information from "the highest source," and Judge Shook overruled the objection. The source was Assistant Attorney General Willebrandt, whom Taft had spoken to on the telephone while Curry was undergoing direct examination.

WEDNESDAY, NOVEMBER 30TH

William Mueller was back on the witness stand in the morning to face cross-examination. Taft immediately questioned him concerning the removal of Remus' furniture and possessions. Taft maintained that Remus himself had striped the house and hidden the furniture so that his wife could not get it, and he hoped to prove this through cross-examination of Mueller. "Don't you know the furniture was removed under the order of Remus?" Taft asked.

""No sir," Mueller replied, but he did admit later that he had been on vacation when the furniture was removed and that Remus had been in charge of the house at that time, and he also admitted that he had read in the newspaper that Remus had sent the statuary to his daughter, Romola, in Chicago.

"How many truckloads did Remus remove?" Taft shot at Mueller, in an attempt to catch him off guard, but Mueller, unflustered, replied that he did not know.

Taft had motioned the previous day to have all Mueller's testimony stricken from the record, and now he tried to get Mueller to admit that the incidents he had related the day before may have happened, but that they were not communicated to Remus and were therefore irrelevant; but the witness insisted that he told Remus everything, except that Dodge had hidden his face on one occasion. Taft, however, seeking to discredit his testimony, did get him to admit that he had once been employed by Remus as a watchman at the Jack Daniels Distillery in St. Louis. The prosecution sought to establish that Mueller was involved in bootlegging activities and was not merely the innocent caretaker. Taft also tried to impeach Mueller's testimony that Dodge and Mrs. Remus were at the house alone, by proving that Mrs. Remus' brother,Harry Brown, was at the house with them, but Mueller denied seeing him there. The prosecution was obviously disturbed by Mueller's testimony. The week before he had told Assistant Prosecutor Clippinger that he knew nothing about Remus or his wife that would be of any importance in the trial, and now he was offering testimony valuable to the defense.

John B. Marshall took the stand next, coming all the way from Juneau, Alaska, to testify. Marshall, the former special Assistant Attorney General who prosecuted the Jack Daniels case, was responsible for Remus' protection and appearance at the trial. Elston began the direct examination by asking Marshall about his connections with Remus before and during the Jack Daniels case. The prosecution objected, arguing that the line of questioning did not have any bearing on Marshall's opinion of Remus' sanity. Elston pointed out that he would not be asking every witness what opinion they formed about Remus' sanity. Asserting that Remus' insanity was the only real question at hand, Basler concluded that "if Marshall formed any opinion it must have been sane since he used Remus as a witness in the Jack Daniels case." When the interrogation resumed, Marshall told the Court that he had received a telephone call from John Rogers, a reporter with the St Louis *Post Dispatch*, who informed him of an alleged plot to kill Remus and that he had relayed the information to Remus. He added that the following day Remus pointed out a man in the hotel lobby who he claimed was a Chicago gunman named Mullins. He later saw this man again at the railway station in the company of a known St. Louis gunman, Dan O'Neil.

Basler objected to this testimony on the grounds that Remus' fears for his life were normal considering the nature of the bootlegging business and the fact that he was testifying against criminals. Elston retaliated with a scathing attack on Dodge in which he again charged that Dodge had conspired against Remus and had even tried to have him killed. "If those things would not influence a state of mind in a man what would?" he questioned. Basler now reminded Elston that the defense's burden was to prove insanity, not simply a "state of mind." The two attorneys continued their bitter verbal exchange until they were surrounded by bailiffs and ordered by Judge Shook to sit down. Marshall was dismissed, and the prosecution immediately moved that his testimony be stricken because it had no bearing whatsoever on the sanity of the defendant. Judge Shook postponed his ruling till the following morning. He also allowed the prosecution the right to recall the witness for further cross-examination.

Then August Bruck testified that he and his wife, along with Jack Shevlin, dined with George Remus at the Sinton hotel on the night of October 5th. He denied that Mrs. Remus was the subject of conversation, explaining that he took care not to mention Mrs. Remus in her husband's presence because of the hysterical outbursts that usually resulted. He said that he had witnessed Remus' outbursts on more than one occasion, and he described how once he had seen Remus so upset that be was butting his head against a wall.

Next, John T. Rogers, Pulitzer Prize winning reporter of the St. Louis *Post Dispatch,* kept the courtroom spellbound as he told about frequent meetings with Remus over a period of two years in which Remus went beserk whenever the names of his wife and Franklin Dodge were mentioned. He informed the jury that he was so convinced of Remus' insanity that he had not been surprised when he was informed that Remus had killed his wife. He said that he had expressed his opinion to his editor as early as the summer of the previous year.

John Rogers met Remus in December, 1925, when he was researching a newspaper special on the life of the famous bootlegger. He spent several weeks in his company, sometimes travelling with him to Washington D.C. and Chicago. Once at the Mayflower Hotel in Washington Remus thought that his wife and Dodge were registered there. He exclaimed:"My God, could it be possible that they are at this hotel? My wife and Franklin Dodge. Their names are on the register here." Rogers related how excited and emotionaly disturbed Remus was, and how difficult it was to get Remus into his room and calm him down. They found out the next morning that the the suspected couple had already left, so they could not be certain that Dodge and Mrs. Remus had stayed at the hotel.

Rogers also testified that he also spent time with Remus during the Jack Daniels trial in Indianapolis where Remus, Dodge and Mrs. Remus occupied separate rooms in the Claypool Hotel. He informed Remus that Dodge and Mrs. Remus had reportedly paid $15,000 to have him killed and that Dodge boasted that he had two loaded pistols for Remus. Rogers said that he immediately told John Marshall, who asked him to stay with Remus until a special agent could be assigned to protect him. Rogers agreed to do as he was asked, but when he arrived at the hotel he found Remus in a such a frenzy that it was obvious that he had already been told of the plot. "He was in an agitasted state of mind and behaved like a wild man" Rogers testified that it took him about an hour and a half to subdue Remus. He then described how that evening he, Remus, and Conners had gone downstairs for dinner, but when they passed through the lobby they saw Dodge on the other side of the room. Remus made a dive for his adversary, but Conners and Rogers managed to grab him and hold him until Dodge was safely in the dining room. They took Remus back up to his room, and "from that time on we had our meals sent up," he said. While this was being related to the jury, Remus seemed visibly shaken and ill at ease.

Then Rogers described a meeting Remus had with Mrs. Remus at the Alms Hotel. He related how Mrs. Remus greeted her estranged husband with a display of open affection, putting her arms around him and telling him that she was glad to see him. However, Remus took her hand gently from his coat and put her gently away from him. Rogers then testified that when he was alone with Mrs. Remus, she implored him to persuade Remus to drop his counter suit against her. He told her that he didn't have that much influence on Remus, and when she asked him to help bring about a settlement, Rogers said: that he couldn't do anything as long as she was associated with Franklin Dodge. When he expressed his concern that somebody might get hurt, she merely replied that she did not think Remus would hurt her, although she was afraid that he might do something to Dodge.

Rogers continued his testimony descrbing other occasions when Remus would break into a maniacal rage, or a "brainstorm" as he called them, whenever Dodge or Mrs. Remus were mentioned. Judge Shook questioned the witness as to whether Remus' speech was coherent on these occasions. Rogers replied that it was, but that Remus never finished his sentences. He also said that he had concluded during his dealings with Remus since the killing on October 6th, that the defendant was now sane. In fact, he had noticed a marked difference as early as the Sunday after the shooting when he had visited Remus in his cell and found him calm and tranquil. Rogers was on the stand for three hours before Court was adjourned. A correspondent for the Cleveland *Plain Dealer* concluded: "He was more than a match" for the prosecuting attorneys, and Elston hinted that he was willing to rest the defense case right then and there.

Meanwhile in the Probate Court a legal battle for the administration of Mrs. Remus' estate, which Remus claimed was actually his money. was taking place. Mrs. Grace Campbell, Mrs. Remus' sister, was eventually appointed administrator. Remus claimed that Mrs. Campbell had no right to act as administrator because she was not a resident of Ohio, but her attorney, Edward Dixon, who had represented Mrs. Remus prior to the killing, provided evidence that she had legally been a resident of Cincinnati since 1923, and that although she now ran a hotel in Florida with her brother, Harry Brown, she still spent most of her time in Cincinnati. Remus, who was represented by Charles Elston and J.P. Goldberry, could not refute this claim, and as a result Judge Lueders appointed her as administrator. The estate was estimated at approximately $100,000 in real estate and $25,000 in other assets, although Remus insisted that the actual amount was much larger.

THURSDAY, DECEMBER 1ST

John Rogers resumed tesifying. He described Remus' reaction upon being informed that Dodge and Mrs. Remus were hosting a cocktail party. "Remus at once flew into a rage." He added that it took fifteen minutes for he and Conners, who was present, to subdue Remus, who insisted that they allow him to stand up for his honor. "His struggles were so violent I was knocked to the floor," Rogers added.

The prosecution asked Rogers only a couple of questions. Taft questioned him about another meeting he witnessed between Remus and his wife at the Alms Hotel in June, 1926. Rogers testified that he witnessed the meeting and admitted that Remus did not fly into a rage on this occasion. This contradicted defense testimony that Remus always flew into a rage when confronted by his wife or told of her actions. Taft then asked him why, if he considered Remus insane, did he not seek to have Remus committed to an insane asylum. Rogers replied that he did not think it was his duty. adding that he believed the man had spent too much time in prison anyway.

John Marshall was now recalled for further cross-examination by the prosecution after Judge Shook denied the State's motion the previous day to have his testimony stricken from the record. Basler immediately asked him about his offer to come all the way from Juneau to testify, and then asked whether it was not true that his hotel bill was being paid by Blanche Watson. Marshall answered that he knew the bill was being paid by someone, but he did not know who. He was then asked about a number of pre-trial conferences that he had with Remus and Elston, and he readily admitted that they took place and that they discussed the trial. Marshall was then questioned about the condition under which Remus tesified at the Jack Daniels trial. "I promised to use my influence to get Remus off from a year and a day jail sentence on a nuisance charge," Marshall admitted, and he explained how he wrote a letter to Mrs. Mabel Willebrandt and appeared before the Board of Pardons and Paroles on Remus' behalf. "I urged the Parole sincerely and earnestly," he insisted. Basler then brought up the question of Remus' sanity at the time of the Jack Daniels trial. Marshall declared that he thought Remus was sane and explained that Remus restrained himself because of the relationship between them.

Marshall also testified that he had *nolle prossed* the indictment against Mrs. Remus in the Jack Daniels case, but he denied that he had done so out of friendship for Remus, although he did admit that, at the time, he considered resigning from his government post to work for Remus as a divorce attorney. He said that he had believed at the time that some sort of settlement should be worked out between Mr. and Mrs. Remus, and he felt that he could bring it about.

Under re-direct examination, Elston tried to show that Remus testified in the Jack Daniels case because he knew that legally the case against his wife would have to be dismissed if he did so, but Marshall denied having discussed anything of this sort with Remus. He then asked Marshall whether during the federal investigation into the Jack Daniels conspiracy he had discovered that Remus had been fleeced of $500,000, but the witness was not permitted to answer. Elston did manage, however, to confirm that Mrs. Remus had been indicted through evidence uncovered during investigations into the conspiracy and that her husband had had nothing to do with that indictment.

Mrs. August Bruck was then called to verify her husband's statements the previous day that they had dined with Remus at the Sinton Hotel on October 5th, and that at no time was Mrs. Remus mentioned. Under cross-examination the prosecution still attempted to establish that some sort of murder plot was planned that night, but Mrs. Bruck said that the only conversation she could remember revolved around a trip her husband was about to make.

Orin Weber, a farmer in Paw Paw, Michigan, took the stand shortly before the luncheon recess and hesitantly related how he came to the conclusion that Remus was insane. At first he seemed reluctant to give details about particular incidents and chewed nervously on a corner of his glove while Elston worked hard to draw each bit of testimony from him. He explained how he told Remus about incidents involving his wife and Dodge: how she had bought a car for him, how she had changed the initials on the car doors, and how she had given him whiskey certificates belonging to Remus. "Everytime I told him something he would fly off the handle," Weber said."I told him she had four guns and wanted to get him. Remus walked around the room, shaking his head. He was kind of wild. He was mad."

After lunch, Weber related details of a trip he took with Mrs. Remus to Charlotte, Michigan, on which occasion she carried with her pillowcases packed full of valuables. He said that when he related these details to Remus, the defendant went extremely red in the face and "his eyes bulged out." This sort of reaction, he said, made him believe that Remus was insane. Basler at this point asked whether that was his opinion now. Weber replied, "Yes," which brought a stern look of warning from one of Remus' cronies, and Weber quickly tried to correct his statement by declaring that it was not his opinion now. To help him out, Elston then asked him when he thought that Remus was insane? Weber hastily replied that it was when he shot his wife.

Under cross-examination, Weber conceded that his father rented an office from Remus in Chicago, but he claimed that he was not aware that his father had once worked for Remus, and he did not even know what his father's occupation was. Basler also had him writhing and stammering as he contradicted himself over facts concerning the mortgage on his farm. He was attempting to get Weber to admit that Remus had paid the mortgage, but Weber at first claimed that he had no idea who paid the mortgage, and then said that the mortgage had not been paid, although he had he had the money to pay off a portion of it. Basler then asked him if Remus had given him this money, but he said that he had earned it himself by transporting vegetables. Throughout the cross-examination Elston sat in his chair looking more and more dejected, and he was visibly relieved when Weber finally left the witness stand.

The afternoon session was given over to testimony by Willie Haar, former rum runner, who was a fellow inmate of Remus' at the Atlanta Penitentiary, and was a neighbor of his on "millionaires' row." He reminisced openly, claiming that when they were sent to Athens, Georgia, for six months during the investigation into corruption at Atlanta, they spent a joint total of $24,000 "remodelling" the jail. "We all had private rooms," he testified gleefully, "and a bath for each room. We had big banquets and a party every night. We got up about noon and played handball and baseball for two, three hours. There was a jail worth breaking into." The defense attempted to show through his testimony that a loving relationship existed between George and Imogene Remus before Franklin Dodge appeared on the scene. Haar described how Mrs. Remus visited her husband often in Atlanta and Athens, and he testified that when she was not able to visit, they would talk to each other on the telephone. He added that Remus always referred to her as his "little bundle of sweetness" or simply "sweetie."

Assistant Prosecutor Basler began his cross-examination of Haar with an attempt to highlight his criminal activities and discredit him as a viable witness.

"You are known as the Admiral?" he asked.

"Not until I got up here. I didn't know I was an admiral," Haar replied, but he admitted that he had operated a fleet of twenty rum boats between Nassau and Savannah.

Basler prompted Haar, who was perspiring freely and looking decidedly uncomfortable by this stage, to give the Court details about Mrs. Remus' attitude towards her husband when she visited him in jail, especially in the Athens jail, which was not as strictly run as the Atlanta Penitentiary, and he told how she cooked for him and brought him fruit, and even got down on her hands and knees to sweep the floor of the cell for him. Basler attempted to show that even at this stage when relations between the two were relatively normal, Remus was still subject to the type of violent outbursts and rages that witnesses had testified were brought on solely by mention of Mrs. Remus and Dodge. At first Haar was reluctant to admit to this and merely stated that Remus sometimes got a little excited, but Basler did not let up, and after being shown a deposition which he had signed for use in the divorce case, Haar eventually acknowledged that "Remus would often bluff or want to fight or be disagreeable." He also admitted that relations between Remus and his wife were not always as affectionate as the defense tried to portray, and told how he had seen Mrs. Remus crying and that she told him how Remus had verbally abused her and accused her of misbehaving. He also admitted that he had never seen any kind of improper displays of affection between Mrs. Remus and Franklin Dodge.

Basler also asked Haar whether it was true that Remus would get mad when the inmates called out to each other, "Who ate the cheese?" and then replied, "Remus the rat." Elston objected to the question and while he and Basler were arguing over its relevancy, Remus, who had been quiet up until then, suddenly jumped up and yelled,: "There wasn't a man down there big enough and strong enough to insinuate such a thing!" Basler, irritated by this interruption, turned to Judge Shook and asked if there wasn't "some sort of rule" against these outbursts of Remus'. This simply incensed Remus even more. "You're the man who drank pints of liquor on the Eastern trip, you hypocrite!" he shouted. He was quickly surrounded by Sheriff Anderson and his bailiffs, who forced him to sit down. Then Judge Shook ruled that Haar could tell the Court whether the inmates at Atlanta ever called Remus a rat.

"They did," he replied. Immediately Remus jumped up and objected. Basler faced him looking ready to fight, and Judge Shook had to intervene once again to restore order. When they calmed down, Haar was dismissed. The prosecution seemed pleased with the way the cross-examination had gone. It was important to them to establish that Remus had a violent temper before the time that the defense claimed he went insane. This would show that his outbursts, which were at the heart of the defense's case, were simply temper tantrums and were nothing new.

The last witness for the day was John S. Berger, a suave looking gentleman in an expensive suit who pompously introduced himself as "a promoter of high-class expositions throughout this land." Berger, a childhood friend of Remus', announced that he had not had time to confer with Elston regarding his testimony so he thought that it would be best if he narrated his version of events in his own way and promised that he would "lay bare some very important facts." Berger told the jury that he had not seen Remus for eighteen years when they met up in St. Louis in June, 1925, where Berger was setting up an exposition under the auspices of the St. Louis Chamber of Commerce. He said that they had dinner together and Remus told him all about his domestic problems.

Berger then admitted that he offered Mrs. Remus money in the Hotel Statler, in St. Louis in November of that year, but denied that he attempted to blackmail her. He told Remus:"She wouldn't take the few hundred thousand dollars I offered her to return your property and accept an uncontested divorce." She said no, that she wanted her divorce and would keep everything because she loved Mr. Dodge. Berger claimed that when he told Remus about this conversation, Remus ranted and raved for a full twenty-four hours, and would not eat, sleep or take any medication. "Remus was absolutely insane." The following day I said to Mr. Remus:"Your wife and her heavy lover, Dodge, will kill you at sight. They have hired a lot of gangsters to kill you, and they are trying to get you deported so they can confiscate your property throughout this land. Mr. Remus tore his clothes off. He took of his collar and his coat and vest. Why, he actually tore them right off! Then he took off his shoes and threw them out the window. This fit lasted for hours and hours."

Berger then described Remus' violent reaction when he told him that he had seen his wife and Dodge together in a state of near nudity. Remus was so enraged that Berger had to use physical restraint to keep him from going out and shooting Dodge. That drew smiles from the spectators as Berger was much smaller than Remus and obviously nowhere near as strong. It would have taken a superhuman effort for him to successfully restrain the larger man. Berger then testified that during the Jack Daniels trial in Indianapolis he told Remus that the two were hugging and fondling, and Remus wanted to break down the door to get at them. "I told Remus his wife was not a fit woman for him to live with," Berger continued, glancing arrogantly around the Courtroom. I told him how Dodge and Mrs. Remus were travelling around the country. I told him how they had connecting rooms and suggested that he catch them and prosecute them." He next testified that when he told Remus that the couple had instigated deportation proceedings against him, Remus had reacted violently. "I thought Mr. Remus was going to tear his ears off," Berger said. "In fact he did tear it down quite a way." At 5 o'clock, Judge Shook interrupted his seemingly endless narration by adjourning the Court.

A correspondent for the Cleveland *Plain Dealer* described Berger's performance on the witness stand:"His manner was dramatic and may have impressed the jury as being a trifle over-eager, a little too willing to help make out a case for the school companion he had traveled across the continent to help."

That evening members of the defense team evaluated the day's proceedings as counter-productive. They felt confident that they would be victorious and that Remus would be acquitted, but they agreed that they could not risk anymore damaging cross-examinations. Their best option, they decided, would be to wrap up the case as soon as possible. They also discussed whether to call Remus as a witness, with some claiming that it would be damaging to their case not to have him testify, while others felt that the prosecution would take full advantage of the opportunity to bait him and cause him to lose his temper and that this would make him look bad. No final decision was reached that evening, although Elston later revealed that he had no intention of ever putting Remus on the stand.

FRIDAY, DECEMBER 2ND

John Berger returned to the stand expecting to be there all day. However, Elston, obviously eager to get rid of him, asked him only two questions.

"Is it your opinion, based upon what you have related here, that George Remus was sane or insane?"

"He was insane," Berger replied.

"Is he, in your opinion, sane or insane now?"

"He was insane up to a short time ago. Now he is sane," Berger answered, and with that, to his surprise, he was handed over to the prosecution for cross-examination.

The previous day when reporters had mentioned that he would most probably undergo a stiff cross-examination, Berger had shown them a number of letters of recommendation that had received from various Mayors, Governors and Chambers of Commerce. "If the prosecution gets cute," he warned, "I'll flash these on 'em, and sink 'em." He also admitted stretching the truth. He explained ; "I figured they would discount all I said 50%, so I gave 'em 200% of the truth."

Berger seemed confident as Prosecutor Taft rose from his seat to conduct the examination. Taft questioned Berger regarding the first time he saw Remus in one of his outbursts. He answered that it occurred at approximately 8 o'clock on a September evening in 1925. When Taft pushed him for more information he shook a finger at the prosecutor and said: "Now, Mr. Taft, I'm talking plainly and there's no use in your trying to puzzle me up." Then he stated that the event took place in St. Louis on about September 10th and lasted for approximately fifteen minutes.

"Isn't it true that in your direct examination you testified the first outbreak lasted twenty-four hours?" Taft inquired. Berger replied that he had been referring to the second outbreak he had witnessed. Taft then concentrated his questioning on this twenty-four hour outburst which sounded extremely exaggerated, but he could not get the witness to admit that he stretched the truth even a fraction. Berger insisted that he remained with Remus for the entire twenty-four hours.

"Did you control him?" Taft asked. Berger replied that he did, but when he was asked if he did so physically, he explained that he controlled Remus by simply speaking to him.

Taft next interrogated Berger concerning his visit to Mrs. Remus in the Statler Hotel in St. Louis. Taft asked him if it was not true that he had threatened Mrs. Remus and asked her to pay him $25,000. He vigorously denied this. Taft then asked him if it was not true that he had told Mrs. Remus that her arms and legs would be broken if she did not return the money to George. Berger answered that it was a manufactured lie. Taft then asked if Berger had not told her that the same would be done to Franklin Dodge, which he denied as well. Changing the subject, Taft asked him if he had ever been arrested or convicted of a crime. Berger admitted he had been arrested, but he explained that he was not convicted. Taft cut short his attempt to explain by asking another question.

"Is Remus sane now, in your opinion?" Berger replied emphatically that he was.

"Then shooting his wife made him sane, did it?"

"I would think so," Berger replied after staring at the ceiling thoughtfully for a moment.

"Even though Mr. Dodge is still alive?" the Prosecutor asked.

"In my opinion he ought to be where she is," Berger snapped back. Many spectators loudly voiced their approval and received a stern warning from Judge Shook. Taft then asked Berger if it was not true that he had been asked to leave Remus' room in Indianapolis because of the stories he insisted on relating to him. Berger admitted that this was true, and the admission was greeted with laughter by some spectators. Berger, showing signs of being agitated, was ovbviously upset at being the apparent butt of a joke. He leapt up, pulling his package of recommendations from his pocket, and handed them to the Judge, but Taft objected to them being read and announced that he was finished with the witness anyway.

John T. Rogers, the St Louis *Post Dispatch* reporter, was recalled by the prosecution to answer some questions regarding his opinion that Remus was insane and which seemed to be contradicted in a ten-part special written for the newspaper by his colleague, Paul Y. Anderson, in January 1926. The article maintained that "Remus can bear comparison with the outstanding captains of industry. He has a mind like a steel trap." Elston objected to this line of questioning. but Remus stood up, smiled and declared that he was flattered.

Under redirect examination, Elston returned to the article that the prosecution had referred to and asked Rogers to read another paragraph. It clearly stated that Remus was incensed by the way his wife had left him and was inclined to break out into a rage whenever she was mentioned.

In the afternoon, Paul Anderson testified that Remus was completely sane on every subject except that of his wife. "On that subject," he said,"he was crazy as a bedbug." Anderson then related how during the Jack Daniels trial he was walking with Remus and a number of other people from the Claypool Hotel to the courtroom when they met up with Mrs. Remus. When she saw her husband, Anderson testified, she threw up her hands and screamed, "Oh Daddy don't kill me. Oh don't let him hurt me!" but Remus just ignored her and crossed the street to get away. Anderson then told how, when they arrived at the courthouse, Mrs. Remus asked him if he had heard about Remus' attempt to kill her. When he said that he had not, she told him that Remus had run into her on the street corner and threatened to kill her. "I ran, and he followed me all the way to the courthouse steps shouting and cursing. Isn't that a good story for you?"

Anderson said that he informed her that he did not believe her and explained that he had walked with Remus to the courthouse and didn't see anything like the incident she described. He said that when he told Remus about the incident, he was enraged and shouted "That's what I get for being tied up with a bag of filth like that. She took my property, stripped my house of the furniture and goes around the country with that lover of hers, spending my money on him. Now she tries to blacken my reputation through the press!" Anderson said that he could not remember much more of what Remus said, but he did remember that much of it was incoherent and that he raved on for several minutes. "His neck swelled up like a cobra's," Anderson exclaimed as he described how Remus tore at his collar as if it was choking him.

Next, Anderson testified that when he visited the Remus mansion he found it to be almost completely bare, with very little furniture and no pictures on the walls or rugs on the floor. He said that Remus took him through the house describing the various items that had once embellished the rooms and given the house its reputation for opulence. When they returned to the drawing room, Remus started pacing up and down the room, shaking his fists and pulling at his collar as he spoke about his wife and how he had given her everything a woman could desire only to have her run away with the man who put him in prison. "It's driving me mad. It's more than I can stand." Anderson then explained that Remus' entire countenance was apt to change in seconds with the mention of Dodge and Mrs Remus. "One minute," he said, "Remus would be as solemn and sonorous as an Archbishop, but when his wife and her lover were mentioned, he would jump up like a man with a hornet in his pants, and rave like a maniac." Elston then asked if these action had led Anderson to form an opinion about Remus' sanity. He said that he had. "I formed the opinion," he said, "that on every other subject except that of his wife and Dodge he was not only sane but unusually shrewd and intelligent," but on that one subject, Anderson considered him completely insane. The prosecution objected and stated that Anderson should make a blanket statement as to whether he considered the defendant sane or insane, but Anderson said that he was unable to do that. Judge Shook took the matter up with the alienists and then conferred with the attorneys, before he ruled that the answer could stand as it was.

Basler took up the cross-examination for the prosecution and immediately asked Anderson if generally speaking he considered Remus sane. Anderson replied that this was so. Basler then questioned him about Remus' demeanor on the witness stand during the Jack Daniels trial, and he agreed that Remus was calm and testified in a" clear and connected way." "His memory was very clear on that occasion wasn't it?" Basler asked. Anderson replied that he did not know how good Remus' memory was because he never knew how much Remus knew in the first place.

"It was sufficient to convict his little playmates in that conspiracy wasn't it?" Basler continued, intent on obtaining an answer.

"I wasn't on the jury," Anderson retorted, "so I don't know whether it was Remus' testimony that convicted them or not. But they certainly were convicted." After getting Anderson to admit that Remus was calm and unruffled while facing cross-examination on that occasion, Basler changed the subject and asked Anderson whether he considered Remus to be sane now. Anderson said that he could not make an informed opinion on that because he had not seen the defendant in over two years. With that he was allowed to step down.

Professional bondsman, Clarence Owens, testified after Anderson telling how, when he paid Remus' bond in September 1925, the defendant raved on about his how his wife had run off with the man who put him in jail. He then told how he had been offered $5,000 by a man named MeHaffey to surrender Remus to him on bond. He claimed that Mrs. Remus and Franklin Dodge had supplied MeHaffey with the money intending to keep Remus in jail and then have him deported before he could testify in the Jack Daniels trial. Owens said that Remus "raved and threw his hands in the air" when him this. Owens also related how when he informed Remus that he had seen Dodge wearing one of his hats in Indianapolis, Remus went wild and threw Owens out of the car they were in. Owens asserted that this kind of behavior convinced him that Remus was insane.

George Conners took the stand after Owens. Smartly dressed and neatly groomed, with a natural marcel wave in his black hair, Remus' best friend and business partner looked out at the courtroom with steely, hawk like eyes and spoke with a slow Southern drawl. When asked if he had formed an opinion about Remus' sanity, he replied that he had determined that Remus was insane, and he proceeded to graphically described a series of incidents in which Remus raved and was temporarily out of his mind. Once when Remus was in jail at Troy, Ohio, Conners told him that his wife was going around the country with Dodge and having someone mail her letters to him so that he would think she was in Cincinnati. Conners claimed that Remus grabbed him and shook him and shouted out that he had picked his wife up out of the gutter and "she was only fit to stay there." Conners expressed his belief that at that moment Remus was out of his mind. When asked what was the basis of his conclusion, he replied, "I base it principally on the way he dragged me around the corridor. Why you couldn't see the pupils of his eyes."

Conners then testified that on another occasion he told Remus he was unable to raise the $50,000 bond required to keep him out of jail in St. Louis. On hearinng this, Remus immediately called his lawyer and had a will drawn up leaving all his possessions to his daughter Romola. Remus then broke down and cried: "I'm gone! I'm gone!"

"What did he mean by that?" Elston asked.

"I told him he was going to be killed in jail at St Louis," Conners replied., "I told him there was a plan to put three or four gangaters in jail with him and stage a fake fight. When it was over, Remus would be dead, and no one would know anything about it." He said that Remus claimed that he had also heard of the plot, and then he began raving again and eventually went into convulsions.

Conners told of still other instances when Remus would burst into a rage whenever he saw Mrs. Remus or her name was mentioned. For example, when he went to the Price Hill mansion and learned that she had taken out an injunction barring him from his own house, he had wrung his hands and cried and shouted about the injustices in the world, before trying to beat up the watchman and finally fainting. Conners testified that Remus was in such a hysterical state that he hardly recognized him. Conners then corroborated

Rogers' testimony concerning the incident in the Claypool Hotel in Indianapolis when Remus had seen Dodge in the lobby. He described how "Dodge fairly skated across the floor to make the dining room, but we grabbed Remus and held him away."

Conners also testified that Remus was virtually penniless when he was released from Atlanta. He claimed that his friend even had to borrow money from him to buy things like underwear and other necessities. Conners gave his testimony in a confident, forthright manner and described in detail each incident, He was constantly interrupted by the prosecution's objections that these gripping orations had little bearing on Remus' sanity. However, each time the prosecution objected, Conners would explain that these incidents led him to the belief that Remus was insane, and each time the objection was overruled.

SATURDAY, DECEMBER 3RD

George Remus, suffering from a cold brought on by a sudden cold snap, spent the week-end in bed under the care of a physician. Conners continued his graphic description of Remus as the harried, persecuted husband of Imogene Remus. He related a seemingly endless number of incidents which caused Remus' "mental breakdown" and led to the "transitory maniacal insanity" that possesed him during the fatal shooting. First he corroborated Roger's testimony regarding the payment of $15,000 to the" Egan's Rats" gang by Mrs. Remus for the killing of her husband. Conners said that Rogers told him of the deal, and after he investigated it and was satisfied that it was true, he told Remus, who was in Indianapolis with his sister, being guarded by federal officers. "Remus flew into a rage," he said, "and wanted to rush to St. Louis. I could only control him by telling to think of his sister." Then he told of reporting to Remus that Dodge and Mrs. Remus had been caught naked together in a Cleveland hotel room, and explained that he had to lie and tell Remus that they were not there any longer because Remus wanted to go to Cleveland at once to kill Dodge.

On another occasion, Conners related, Remus created a scene in front of a downtown store. Remus had found some unpaid bills belonging to his wife, and he had gone to the stores and paid them, but he was so enraged that he stopped outside one store and shouted: "If I get hold of her I'll take her by the back of the neck into every store in Cincinnati and make her pay her own bills."

Then Conners described Remus' reaction after being told about yet another plot to kill him; this time John Marcus, a former partner, had been offered $10,000 to do the deed, but he refused because he was a known enemy of Remus' and feared he would be the prime suspect. On hearing this, Remus "stroked his face and broke into a sweat and said 'Conners I've had word she is going to have another gang kill me. I got it straight.' He paced the room and raved.while crying out that'they would have to watch themselves.'" In graphic detail Conners then related how Remus confronted his wife after learning that she had gone to Atlanta to check on deportation proceedings against him. When she told him that she had gone there to have the proceedings quashed, Remus, in disbelief, flew into such a rage that Conners had to forcibly restrain him from chasing her as she fled from the room.

The prosecution vigorously objected when Conners produced a copy of the *Congressional Record* for July, 1926, which contained Congressman La Guardia's scathing attack on Dodge and Mrs. Remus. However, Judge Shook ruled that "anything that was brought to the mind of the defendant which tended to arouse reactions that caused the witness to form an opinion as to his sanity is admissible." Conners now was free to relate how he had shown Remus the text of the Congressman's speech along with photostats of whiskey certificates that Mrs. Remus had stolen from Remus while he was in jail in Troy, Ohio. Conners decalared that Remus went berserk. "He was ill for two days."

Conners continued his scathing attack on Imogene Remus' reputation by claiming she and Franklin Dodge had violated the Mann act. He claimed that he overheard two detectives talking at the Hollenden Hotel in Cleveland about how they had checked on a room rented by a lone woman and found her and a gentleman together. The man had been ordered to leave at once, and the woman had to leave the next morning. Conners said that he sent private detectives to the hotel with photographs of Dodge and Mrs. Remus, and the hotel employees immediately identified them as being the two occupants of the room. This testimony and more like it was admissible because each time Conners swore that he had told the same story to Remus and that each time Remus flew into an uncontrolable rage.

Conners next told of threats against his own life and attempts to have him killed. He described how he was on his way to the Remus mansion in Price Hill to replevin one of Remus' cars while Mrs. Remus still occupied the house, but as he approached the house Brady, A Newport, Kentucky, gunman, tried to kill him. "I prevented myself from being killed by running Brady down with my automobile." That night, he claimed, Mrs. Remus phoned him and warned him that if he continued to visit Remus at the Troy jail and persisted in helping him, she would have him killed. Assistant Prosecutor Walter Sibbald strongly objected, but once again Conners was allowed to continue because he asserted that he had told Remus about the incident, and once again Remus became hysterical.

Then Conners described how Remus was enraged when he returned to the Price Hill mansion on his release from jail, and found a pair of men's shoes not his size, which he automatically assumed belonged to Franklin Dodge. On this occasion Remus spent a week at Conners' house. During the day, Conners tesified, he could get Remus' mind off his trouble, but at night Remus said that he could see his wife and her lover before him.

Finally, Conners described an incident that occurred in 1926, when Conners met with Mrs. Remus to discuss a possible divorce settlement. The discussion was not going well when Mrs. Remus jumped up and shouted "I'll settle things right now." She then opened her purse and pulled out a handgun. Conners said that he managed to stop her before she could use it. The gun was the same pearl-handled pistol that Remus later used to shoot his wife.

Walter Sibbald cross examined Conners, who freely admitted that he was in the bootlegging business when he met Remus in 1919, and that prior to that he had been an agent in the Department of Internal Revenue. Sibbald asked him if he had known Remus and his bootleggers at that time and immediately drew an objection from Elston on his use of language. Sibbald argued his use of the term "bootleggers" with the assertion that both Remus and Conners were confessed bootleggers so he was fully entitled to refer to them as such. Judge Shook ruled that he could use the term, but Remus pointed out that in 1918, when Conners was a federal agent, there was no such thing as prohibition, and therefore neither of them could be called "bootleggers." Judge Shook smiled and admitted they had all overlooked that proposition, and a disgruntled Sibbald continued with his cross-examination.

He then asked Conners if he was acquainted with Miss Blanche Watson, and Conners replied that he was, but he denied that she was also a bootlegger and that she was associated with Remus. "She is in the legitimate whiskey business," he insisted and then explained that he and Miss Watson had a business partnership in the Kentucky Distributing Company, which sold legitimate medicinal whiskey. The cross-examination had only gone on for fifteen minutes before Court was adjourned. Conners would take the stand for a third time on the following Monday, and Taft announced that Conners could expect to be on the stand for the whole day again because the prosecution would "make it very thorough, upon the assumption that Remus will not appear as a witness."

The advantages and disadvantages of Remus tesifying had been debated at length in the Remus headquarters. Elston refused to tell reporters whether anything had been decided, only admitting that, in his opinion, the defense could have rested a number of days ago, but he was not in full charge of this case. Obviously Elston and Remus did not always agree on the best strategy to employ. The following day they they announced that it was virtually certain that Remus would not testify. They told reporters that everything Remus could say on the stand had already been related by witnesses; however, they emphasized that his failure to testify did not mean that he would not get a chance to argue his case, because he intended to deliver the defense's final plea to the jury. Thus Remus would be able to present his case unhampered by the rules of evidence and without having to face a prosecution cross-examination, which would undoubtedly be fierce and could be very damaging.

Franklin Dodge's appearance as a witness was also doubtful. Most of his testimony would not be admissible because it did not matter whether or not allegations about his relationship with Imogene Remus were true or not as long as they were related to Remus.

During a Court recess, Ruth Remus released a statement to the reporters praising her mother and attacking Remus for his constant lies in the Courtroom and the way he used the press to disseminate his propaganda. She stated that her mother was a good woman, a good mother and a good wife and that Remus knew this. "My mother had not a single enemy in the world except this man she loved and slaved for and finally died for." She claimed that her mother had put up with Remus' antics because she loved him, and she thought that if she held on long enough he would give up bootlegging and go into a legitimate business. She attacked the newspaper reporters for writing "as if they had forgotten that a murder had been committed and that the important thing now is to get 'poor Remus' out of jail." In conclusion, she predicted that that Remus would kill again if he was released. "He has long believed that he is outside the law or above it, and that he can get away with anything."

MONDAY, DECEMBER 5TH

Remus, having recovered from his cold, returned to the Court and announced that he would not take the stand on his own behalf. He then asked the Court to find Dudley Nichols of the New York *World* in contempt for an article he wrote based on an interview with Ruth Remus in which she publicly condemned Remus and which Remus claimed was libellous. He also criticized the sarcastic tone in which the reporter attacked Judge Shook's ruling on the permissibility of evidence. "The entire civilized world is interested in this case," Remus shouted. "I say we have gone far in a civilized country when a reporter can write such libellous articles reflecting on the integrity of the Court and the facts of this case. I say there should be an investigation Your Honor."

Charles Taft countered with the contention that Remus had "issued a stream of publicity ever since the murder" and that his objections came with "very bad grace." He claimed that a number of the statements issued by Remus had been read by the jury before they were all sequestered, and "if any contempt was committed, it was committed at that time." "Remus does not dare take the witness stand," he concluded. "He is afraid to be cross-examined." Now Charles Elston entered the fray. He declared: "Mr. Remus is not taking the stand because I so advised him." He then explained that, although Remus wanted to testify, he felt that everything had been testified to and he wanted to save time. "Moreover," he continued, "we admit the facts of the killing." Assistant Prosecutor Sibbald then requested that the Court take note that the defense had admitted to the murder. Elston quickly claimed that he had said "killing" and not "murder," and he warned Sibbald not to "pull that cheap stuff." Not content to let that lie, Basler argued that Elston had definitely said murder. "I heard Remus prompting him," he said, "and he said murder distinctly."

Judge Shook finally ended the argument. He then informed the jury that under Ohio law the defendant may choose not to take the stand, but that references to this decision could be made by the Court and the prosecution before the jury. Judge Shook then considered the motion concerning the Dudley Nichols' article. "The press has indulged with a great deal of liberality in comment on this trial, but this court does not control the press." He continued: "'I have read the articles cited in the motion. They make no reflection on the Court's ruling in this case. The motion is overruled."

The trial had entered its fourth week with Conners back on the stand to face five hours of relentless cross-examination by Walter Sibbald, who almost immediately attacked him on the nature of Remus' business. When Sibbald asked what business Remus was in, Conners replied that Remus was not involved in any real business, but had retained a suite at the Hotel Sinton to co-ordinate the collection of information for use in his divorce suit. "It kept Remus, myself and a dozen lawyers busy for two years and we haven't got it yet," he said. He then repeated his claim that Remus had virtually no money during this time and borrowed extensively from him. He testified that he, in turn, borrowed from people like Blanche Watson to help Remus.

Sibbald, in an attempt to prove a business connection between Remus and Blanche Watson, then showed Conners a collection of sixteen checks, which he asserted were signed by Remus and endorsed by Blanche Watson, and he asked him to identify the signatures. Immediately both Remus and Elston objected to the relevancy of this testimony, but their objections were overruled. After taking his time to study each check, Conners finally stated that he could identify Remus' signature on one of the checks, but not that of Blanche Watson, and on the others he was altogether unsure about the validity of the signatures.

This line of questioning brought a further objection from Remus. "If we are going into all of the Remus operations," he stated, "we will never get through." Remus eventually withdrew the objection, and Conners was asked if Remus owned the Old Lexington Club distillery and two others, one at Rugby, Kentucky, and the other at Lawrenceburg, Indiana. He replied that Remus had owned them, but he was not too sure about whether he still owned them, or when he may have sold them if he had. When asked about the Remus building in Cincinnati, Conners replied that he knew Remus had once owned that too.

"Don't you know that he owns it now?" Sibbald exclaimed, charging that he had put it in the name of Leonard Garver to protect it from seizure by the Internal Revenue Services. Conners replied that he did not know anything about that.

Sibbald also tried to get Conners to admit that, contrary to claims by the defense, Remus knew about the disposal of his property by his wife and that they had corresponded at length about the various transactions. Sibbald asked if it was not true that Blanche Watson held a $35,000 mortgage on the

Remus home, a part of which Mrs. Remus had paid off with proceeds from the sale of the Fleischmann Distillery.

"Didn't George Remus tell you he had asked his wife to sell the distillery and pay off the mortgage?" Sibbald prompted.

"I can't recall," Conners evasively replied. Sibbald then showed him a statement of payment by Mrs. Remus and signed by Blanche Watson, but Conners once again claimed that he could not identify the signature.

Next Sibbald showed Conners other letters that he claimed had been sent to Mrs. Remus by her husband and which contained details about his possessions. Conners studied each one slowly and deliberately, and each time he answered that he was not sure if it was Remus' signature. On some he claimed that the Remus part of the signature looked correct, but that the "George" was different, or that Remus' handwriting was bigger than that on the letter. Not once did he identify the signature or the writing as definitely being that of Remus. "Knowing conditions at Atlanta, I couldn't swear to anything about letters sent from there," he said and then explained that a lot of letters purportedly sent out from men there had never been written or signed by them. He also denied that he had ever heard Remus tell Mrs. Remus to sell the contents of the Price Hill mansion. During Conners' testimony regarding the signatures, Remus, unable to restrain himself, jumped up and exclaimed that the signatures were not his. Judge Shook now instructed Elston to restrain Remus from making statements of evidence, especially as he had declared his intention not to take the stand.

When almost seventy letters and documents had been introduced for Conners to examine and testify as to the signatures, Judge Shook told Conners to read only enough of the documents to identify the handwriting or signature. The prosecution was disappointed when Conners refused to make any positive identifications.

In spite of Sibbald's claims to the contrary, Conners denied knowing that Mrs. Remus refused to sign any divorce settlement because she claimed that Remus was hiding the full extent of his assets. Prosecutor Taft had claimed that Remus killed his wife because she intended to reveal this information during the divorce trial. Conners did admit, though, that Remus held stock in a Chicago taxicab company which was worth about $15,000 and that he was part owner of the Cincinnati Baseball Team, but he denied that he owned any racehorses. He claimed that Remus had no money and therefore could not have afforded racehorses "unless they were given to him for nothing." He also denied any knowledge of Remus' purported interest in the Springdale race track.

Sibbald then attempted to establish that Remus himself had sent his wife to meet Dodge to try and obtain his early release from the penitentiary. Conners denied any knowledge of Remus having any dealings with Dodge, and stated that Remus had actually warned his wife to stay away from him."He did tell me that he wished to get her away from Dodge."

Sibbald then introduced a number of letters written by Remus to Mrs. Remus in which Dodge's name was mentioned. In one letter Remus stated that it was important for him that she look up Dodge. But Conners, unrattled by the constant stream of questions, denied that he had any knowledge of these letters.

The prosecutors' prolonged cross-examination of Conners did little to discredit his testimony. However, they believed that his evasive answers and his failure to identify a number of the documents or the signatures on them would be beneficial to their case because they created doubt as to whether he was telling the truth or not.

Near the end of the day Elston announced that the defense planned to call only a few more witnesses before resting their case. Most of these witnesses would be called to testify to Remus' character, and among them was Clarence Darrow. Interviewed by the Asssociated Press in Chicago, Darrow stated: "Remus is a man who likes to help people. I like men who are that way." Taft's reaction was to promise that if Darrow testified, he would call on Judge Keeshaw Mountain Landis, Baseball Commissioner and former Federal Judge, to rebut the testimony. "I am informed that Landis knows something about Remus' character as well as Darrow," he declared. Remus had argued several cases before Judge Landis in the Chicago Courts that had ended in bitter clashes between the two, with Remus being ejected from the Courtroom.[7]

---

[7]Judge Landis also clashed with Darrow on many occasions. He refused to sign a petition attesting to Darrow's good character when Darrow was charged with suborning a jury ("Darrow A Biography, Kevin Tierney p. 260)

TUESDAY, DECEMBER 6TH

Assistant Prosecutor Walter Sibbald made a concerted effort to show that Remus had problems with the Internal Revenue Service and that he had hidden assets which his wife had threatened to disclose. He also returned to the State's conspiracy theory and attempted to show that Conners and Blanche Watson were involved in hiding these funds and had conspired to kill Mrs. Remus when she threatened to disclose all the details. Conners, however, emphatically denied that he or Blanche Watson held any of Remus' money, and insisted that Remus himself hardly had a dollar to his name, although he did admit that Mrs. Remus had spoken to the Internal Revenue Commissioner in Washington and had given him information regarding Remus' finances.

When Sibbald asked him about the documents which the prosecution had introduced during his cross-examination and which Remus said he had been trying to get hold of for almost two years, Conners replied that Remus had wanted them because he believed that they held evidence sufficient to convict both. Mrs. Remus and Dodge on violation of the Mann Act. He also hoped that if he could get them into Court, he would be able to get his property back. The State's contention was that he wanted these documents because they could be used to show the full extent of his assets.

During the cross-examination Sibbald went over Conners' Grand Jury testimony, but he had difficulty getting relevant answers. Eventually Conners asserted:"Practically all of my grand jury testimony was hearsay. I volunteered it. It was gotten by me from others. I was taken advantage of by the grand jury."

Conners then related how he and John Rogers met in St. Louis with members of the Egan's Rats gang. Rogers, who was acquainted with and respected by many important gangsters, told these men that Conners and Remus were friends of his and that if anything happened to them, he would personally see to it that ten gangsters were hanged. As a result, Conners claimed that a number of gang members actually accompanied them to Indianapolis to make sure that nothing happened to Remus. This contradicted defense testimony that members of the gang were in Indianapolis during the trial with the intention of killing Remus. When questioned about Dan O'Neill, the gunman who had been seen with John Marcus in Indianapolis, and who was suspected of being there to kill Remus, Conners replied that O'Neill was not a member of the Egan's Rats.

Sibbald then asked Conners how many barrels in the Jack Daniels distillery Remus owned. He replied 60%. "With the St. Louis crowd?" Sibbald asked, consciously not using the term "gang" which had drawn an earlier objection from Remus. But Remus, in the mood to argue, objected: " It wasn't a St Louis crowd," he said,"There were more than St. Louis men in it."

Sibbald immediately objected to this comment claiming that it constituted the introduction of evidence. Judge Shook reminded Remus that he had to restrain from giving evidence and suggested that if he wished to give evidence "there is a way to do it," meaning that Remus should take the stand himself. Remus replied that he had tried criminal cases all over the country and knew how to "propound and couch an objection." This brought a further warning from Judge Shook, who ordered him not to criticize the Court. However, Remus continued to argue, and Judge Shook threatened to hold him in contempt of Court if he continued. When Remus still refused to sit down and be quiet, Sheriff Anderson and two bailiffs urged him to do as he was ordered. Romola also tried to calm her father down and tugged on his sleeve in an attempt to make him sit down. Remus eventually sat down, but, still intent on being heard, he turned to Sheriff Anderson and shouted: "My life is at stake here, and I know what my legal rights are!"

While the bailiffs worked hard to calm Remus down, Judge Shook sat nervously paging through a book and trying to ignore the fracas until quiet was restored. He then called the attorneys from both sides to the bench for a private conversation. The jury was recalled and Judge Shook informed them that he was "trying to administer justice fairly and squarely in this case" and did not want to show favor to either the defense or the prosecution. "Upon reflection," he said, "I feel that the language of this Court was unnecessary and you must disregard it." A few minutes later Remus apologized for his actions and declared that he was laboring under a great strain.

Sibbald now challenged Conners' testimony concerning the incident in the Claypool Hotel lobby. Sibbald asked Conners if it wasn't true that Remus had followed him into the dining room and sat quietly eating just two tables away from Dodge, but Conners denied that that happened. He also denied that Remus told Mrs. Remus in Indianapolis that he would "get" her and that he later told her that he "would take from her every shred of her reputation and bury her in a pauper's grave."

During the afternoon session Conners testified about a conference that was held to arrange a financial settlement. He freely admitted that Remus had not ranted or raved during the two hours of negotiation, but he attributed this to the fact that Mrs. Remus had carefully avoided mentioning Franklin Dodge.

"Did John H. Bruffell offer to give Mrs. Remus $100,000 and a divorce to settle?" Sibbald asked, referring to Conners' Grand Jury testimony.
"I made the offer, but said nothing about a divorce," Conners replied, contradicting what he had said previously. He then claimed that Remus knew nothing about the offer. He admitted that he had made other offers as well, but none had been accepted. When asked about one particular settlement offer of $225,000, he said that he did not know anything about it, and when he was shown his Grand Jury testimony in which he stated that "in the settlement she got about $225,000," he replied that there was an error in the transcript.

Sibbald now began to concentrate on the Remus' divorce case and the frequent postponements of the trial. He challenged Conners about Remus' attempts to have Judge Hoffman removed from the case, and he brought up the State's assertions that Remus had not prepared a defense for use in the trial. Conners admitted that Remus did not have many depositions, in spite of Remus' claims to the contrary, and that he had summoned even fewer witnesses, but he used this testimony to buttress his opinion that Remus was insane at the time. To his way of thinking "any man who tried to handle his own case was insane," and he said that he had tried to persuade Remus to let somebody else handle it for him, but that he had been unsuccessful. Then Sibbald produced a number of divorce depositions which were allegedly to be used in the divorce trial, but Conners could not identify any of them.

Leaving the subject of the divorce trial, Sibbald returned to the State's discredited theory that the killing had been carried out as part of a conspiracy. "Where were you when you heard of the shooting?" he asked.
"I was at home." Conners replied. He admitted that he had seen Remus the night before and that he had asked Klug to pick up the car, but he denied receiving a phone call from Blanche Watson at 8 o'clock the following morning. Sibbald tried hard to find out who told Conners about the killing, but all he got was a number of objections from Elston which were sustained.

"When did you form the opinion Remus was insane?" Sibbald asked, finally changing the subject.
"He became worse and worse," Conners replied and then explained that he had never really thought that Remus was completely insane, but that he

showed signs of insanity when certain subjects were alluded to. "Nothing hurts me more," he said, "than to sit here in Court and say that my friend ever was insane." Sibbald then asked him if he thought Remus was still insane when he saw him at Police Headquarters after the killing. Conners replied that he did not think he was insane, but that he was not normal either.

Conners admitted that he went down to the police station to see Remus to express his sympathy and offered to get him a lawyer, but this offer was turned down. He said that Remus was not quite normal during this conversation and asked a lot of irrational questions, which Conners claimed he could not recall. He testified that he did not spend more than a few minutes with Remus before he was taken into another room to undergo police questioning.

The Grand Jury testimony of Conners was brought up again when Sibbald attempted to show that Remus' rages were simply temper tantrums and not periods of insanity. He read Conners' testimony that Remus "would rave and carry on, but you know that was temper and nothing else." Conners admitted that he had said Remus raved around and pointed out that he had said exactly the same thing on the stand during his direct testimony. The prosecution ended their cross-examination, and Court adjourned for the day.

Assistant Prosecutor Sibbald had tried very hard to discredit Conners by trapping him into contradicting himself. Sibbald was well aware that without a chance to cross-examine Remus, Conners testimony was crucial. But Conners, a cool, quick witted witness, always managed to answer the question put to him just enough to satisfy the Court without incriminating himself or Remus. On the whole, Conners' testimony was unshakeable and a definite asset to the defense.

WEDNESDAY, DECEMBER 7TH

William Hoefft, manager of the Sinton Hotel tobacco stand, testified that he had known Remus for three years and had witnessed a number of his famous "brainstorms" and had concluded that Remus was insane. He recalled being in Remus' room when Remus had just received information that he was going to be killed. He described how Remus then sat with his cheeks in his hands and raved on and on about how he was being persecuted. Hoefft said that he tried in vain to calm him down. However, after about forty-five minutes, Remus calmed down and apologized for his actions. Under cross-examination Hoefft was asked whether there was any chance that Remus had staged the outbursts so that he could be called as a witness to it. He said that he had not even considered this.

Harry Truesdale, a surprise witness, took the stand and testified that Mrs. Remus had offered him $10,000 to kill her husband. Truesdale told his story in a well rehearsed, steady manner, but in such a quiet voice that parts of it had to be re-read to the jury by the court stenographer. Truesdale said that John Marcus pointed Remus out to him at the Springdale Dog Race Track and told him of Mrs. Remus' offer. Four or five days later he went to see Mrs. Remus. She told him she would give him $5,000 once Remus was killed, and that he would receive the other $5,00 from another person, whom she later identified as Franklin Dodge. She gave him $250 for expenses and told him what room Remus occupied at the Sinton Hotel. Truesdale also testified that Mrs. Remus actually said to him that she "wished somebody would beat Remus' brains out." On one occasion, Truesdale tesitifed, Imogene Remus sat with a pistol in her hand and said: "If I see him tonight, I'll kill him myself." "I followed him several times," he said. "Twice I sat in a chair outside his room in the hall." He explained that he had planned to kill Remus in his room but had changed his mind because there was always too many people milling around.

While listening intently to Truesdale's confession, Remus suddenly burst into hysterical sobs; and his daughter Romola, sitting next to him vainly attempted to comfort him. Remus' sister, Mrs. Gabriel Ryerson, in the spectators' area, screamed and wept hysterically when she heard Truesdale say that he intended to kill Remus in his hotel room, Remus remained in his chair for awhile with his face buried in his hands sobbing uncontrollably into handkerchief. His eyes were fixed, his neck swollen and his face purple. Then he looked up and, in a broken voice, asked Judge Shook if he could request a recess. Judge Shook quickly excused the jury. As they filed out of the courtroom all thirteen of them were visibly moved; some had tears in their eyes, and 58 year old Mrs. Anna Ricking was actually weeping.

When they had left the room, Remus turned to the Judge and cried out hysterically, "Your Honor, can we have an adjournment?" A few seconds later "there burst from his throat an eerie yell, a half-strangled wail with a peculiar, hard intonation that swept through the courthouse and elecrtrified the audience, already in a state of emotional suspense." He was led from the courtroom and Romola followed. She was weeping hysterically and at one point fainted. They were ushered into the Judge's ante room. However, their screams and wailing could still be heard inside the Courtroom. Romola Remus was eventually lead away, her screams echoing down the hallways. Her father collapsed on the couch and clutched his knees. He rocked back and forth crying out, "My God, I can't stand it!" The alienists and deputies tried in vain to control him. When Remus continued to scream and moan, the jurors, who were gathered in a nearby room, were removed to a more distant Courtroom.

After raving for about fifteen minutes Remus was taken to his cell in the County jail where his clothes were removed and ice packs applied to his head and hot water bags to his feet, in an attempt to calm him down. He was still lying down in this manner thirty minutes later when the alienists sent a message recommending that Judge Shook call an early midday recess. The Court was adjourned until 2 o'clock. When, at that time, Remus was still twitching uncontrollably and still seemed in a state of nervous tension, Charles Elston and the alienists agreed that Remus was in no condition to return to Court, and they suggested adjournment until the following day.

Judge Shook, amazed by what was happening, decided to pay a visit to Remus' cell himself before making his decision, and after spending half an hour with the defendant, he granted the adjournment. Half an hour later the three alienists issued a signed statement; "We find that Mr. George Remus has recovered from his emotional attack of the morning and at 3 p.m. was resting very comfortably."

If the alienists concluded that Remus was now insane, Judge Shook would have to dismiss the jury and transfer Remus to the Probate Court for a sanity hearing. If he was judged to be insane, he would be committed to the State Hospital for the Insane. He would remain there until he could convince the authorities of his sanity. He could not be tried again on the murder charge for that would be double jeopardy.

There was considerable debate concerning the authenticity of Remus' emotional breakdown. Prosecutor Taft and his staff were convinced that it was staged for the benefit of the alienists and the jury. They pointed out that Remus asked Truesdale to come to Cincinnati to testify and knew beforehand what his testimony would be. In fact, Truesdale himself admitted that he had told the story to Remus on October 5th. Judge Shook even asked him to definitely establish the fact that he had told Remus exactly what he was telling the jury. He was obligated to do so because of the ruling that evidence could only be introduced if it had actually been conveyed to Remus. Truesdale had also signed a statement in front of Remus in which he set forth all the details of his testimony; moreover, it was claimed that Remus had remained calm on that occasion. The prosecution maintained that Romola had also heard the testimony before.

Remus' supporters argued that if Remus staged the outburst to influence the jurors, he would hardly have asked the Judge for a recess, which would cause the jurors to miss most of his performance. It was also argued that Remus, who usually sought publicity, implored a reporter not to take his photograph because he was genuinely distressed and did not want to be photographed in that condition. Elston insisted that Truesdale's testimony was the truth and that Remus' outburst had been spontaneous and genuine. He said that he had checked every aspect of the story and was prepared to put corroborating witnesses on the stand. He also said that Truesdale was keeping to the code of the gangland, which called for a man to tell the truth when the life of another was at stake in a Court of Law.

Feigned or not, Remus' outburst at this stage was a potentially advantageous occurrence. The effect it had on the jury's sympathies was immediately evident. Remus' wailing and moaning would be hard to forget when the jurors were making their decision. Also, very likely, they would remember the testimony that caused his breakdown, testimony which implicated Mrs. Remus and Franklin Dodge in a plot to kill Remus.

Remus' unprecedented hysterical outburst lead to speculation on the possibility that the entire trial would be postponed for a sanity hearing. Earlier Remus had waived his right to a hearing, but it was believed at this stage that one might be held anyway. Judge Shook ended the speculations by announcing that the trial should continue.

THURSDAY, DECEMBER 8TH

Hundreds of people waited outside the Courtroom door hoping to get inside the already packed room. They wished to hear the remainder of the sensational testimony that had caused Remus' breakdown and to see the famous Clarence Darrow in action. Occasionally, Sheriff Anderson and his men had to use their maces to clear a way through the crowd so that the attorneys and witnesses could enter the Courtroom. Eventually Judge Shook ordered that the corridors be cleared because the noise was interfering with the Courtroom proceedings.

Remus was up early in the morning, seeming none the worse for his ordeal of the previous day. After a brief visit from his friend Clarence Darrow, Remus collected his papers and headed to the Courthouse. He arrived ten minutes before Judge Shook entered and started the days's proceedings. When Judge Shook finally entered the Courtroom, Remus immediately stood up and addressed him: "Your Honor I want to apologize to you and the jury for my unmanly conduct of yesterday." Judge Shook simply ignored him.

Harry Truesdale, resuming his testimony, told about going to Mrs. Remus' apartment and being informed by her that "I would have to hurry , as there wouldn't be a long time before the divorce suit came up." After several unsuccessful attempts to get a good shot at Remus, Truesdale spotted him at the Grand Hotel in Hamilton, and Mrs. Remus rushed there to confer with her "hit man." Truesdale became suspicious when he noticed a man standing across the street from them. He was informed that it was Franklin Dodge. He became more and more suspicious when another man joined Dodge and a slow moving limousine started following him. He now decided to see Remus and tell him the whole story. "I told him if his wife would double cross him like that, she might do the same thing to me." Truesdale described Remus' violent reaction to this information and admitted that he was a little afraid of what Remus might do.

Walter Sibbald conducted the cross-examination and immediately attacked the witness by asking him if he was a "man killer?" Truesdale admitted that he was and agreed that his price on this occasion was $10,000. "How many have you killed at $10,000?" Sibbald asked.

"I never killed nobody." Truesdale replied, explaining that this was the first time he had been hired to kill anybody and asserting that he never even carried a gun before. Sibbald continued: "You'd do anything if you got your price, all right?" Truesdale answered: "Yes, I would, if I got enough money for it." Sibbald: "You'd come here and give perjured testimony for it if you got enough money for it?" Truesdale:"No, I didn't give any perjured testimony!" Sibbald: "You'd commit murder for money, but you wouldn't commit perjury for money?" Truesdale: "That's a different thing."

Then Truesdale was forced to admit that he was merely a petty thief whose last arrest had been for stealing a silk shirt from a department store. Sibbald was intent on discrediting Truesdale's testimony by establishing that he was not an experienced gunman. This would lend credence to the prosecution's contention that Truesdale was hired just to catch Remus in the company of another woman. Sibbald called Truesdale"s attention to the midnight meeting with Mrs. Remus outside the Grand Hotel on October 4th. He asked if it was not true that Mrs. Remus had hired him to follow Remus to ascertain whether Remus was seeing another woman, which information she wished to use in her divorce suit, and that he had phoned Mrs Remus that night because he had seen Remus enter the hotel with another woman. Truesdale denied this and insisted that he had told the truth..

Sibbald then showed him a piece of newspaper with a note written on it in pencil, which he claimed Mrs. Remus had written before leaving her hotel room to meet him that night. Truesdale looked at the note but said that he had never seen Mrs. Remus' handwriting so he could not tell if it was hers or not. The note had apparently been written to Franklin Dodge and intimated that she was to meet Truesdale because he had discovered Remus in a compromising position. The note read; "Ruth knows all about this. I'm going up to Hamilton to meet that party. We need this evidence very badly." Sibbald charged that Truesdale had not seen Remus that night but had simply lured Mrs. Remus there with the intention of obtaining money from her. Once again, Truesdale denied the accusation. Truesdale was finally allowed to step down after testifying for two hours, during which time Remus did not once display any of the emotion which had overwhelmed him the previous day.

Many people were surprised to learn that Truesdale could not be prosecuted despite his self-incrminating testimony. He was immune from prosecution because there was no conspiracy statute in Ohio. Moreover, the United States Supreme Court under Chief Justice William H. Taft, had ruled "A mere intention to commit a crime is not punishable unless followed by some overt act. Consequently a party cannot be held for an offense if he voluntarily abandons the plan or scheme to commit that offense before its execution."

Clarence Darrow was sceduled to next take the stand, but Prosecutor Taft argued against his testifying as a witness to Remus' character. He claimed that this testimony would introduce facts having little or no bearing on the case. Remus answered by pointing out that the State had attacked his reputation as a lawyer and he had every right to prove their statements were false.

Remus then launched into a long speech, during which he waved a white handkerchief in the air dramatically. He praised Darrow as a man and as lawyer, even labeling him "the sage of the 20th Century." He asserted that he was extremely proud "that this great humanitarian takes up his time to testify for me." Ignoring the prosecution's objections, Remus simply waved the handkerchief in Taft's face declaring that "surely the Chief Justice's son should appreciate the legality of my argument." Then he told about how he had succeeded Darrow in handling cases for the electrical. plasterers, and steam fitters unions in Chicago. He described some of these cases and explained that on occasion he had even been sent by the unions to assist Darrow in more important cases. He also intimated that he incurred the enmity of the Chicago Bar Association because of his championing organized labor.

Once again the prosecution objected, but Judge Shook allowed Remus to continue since the jury was out of the room. Judge Shook eventually halted Remus' oration and instructed the stenographer to strike it all from the record. He told Remus that everything he had just said could have been introduced as testimony if he had said it himself from the witness stand, but as he had chosen not to testify, it would not be allowed to stand on record.

Judge Shook finally ruled that Darrow might be allowed to testify, and the jury was recalled. Darrow informed the jurors that he had known Remus for thirty to thirty five years. He testified that Remus had a good reputation as a lawyer in Chicago. He described him as a good citizen, and declared: "His reputation as a lawyer-I believe it to be good. It was good. I say it from the fact that I never heared it questioned."

Taft undertook the cross-examination himself. "Don't you know he was known as the weeping, crying Remus?" Taft asked the famous lawyer. "I know he was a very emotional man and somewhat unstable." Darrow replied. He denied knowing anything about any investigation by the grievance Committee of the Chicago Bar Association, and he admitted that he had only found out the previous day that Remus had been disbarred because of his bootlegging activities.

"Don't you know that in 1920 Remus was indicted in Chicago for conspiracy to violate the prohibition law and that the indictment is pending?" Taft asked him, but this drew an objection from Remus, who claimed that the statement was erroneous. Nonetheless, the witness was instructed to answer the question. He said that he had not known about the indictment, but declared:"I would not regard it as relating to peace and quiet."

Then Taft alluded to Remus' bootlegging activities and asked Darrow whether he could still regard Remus as a law abiding citizen. Darrow spent some time looking out the window, obviously thinking about his answer, before turning back to face the County Prosecutor and answering in a low voice, "I know a good many law abiding citizens who buy it."[8]

Thomas Hogan, a Chicago lawyer who said he had known Remus for eight years but had not seen him in as many years, was the first character witness on the stand in the afternoon. He testified to Remus' good character and legal abilities. When asked by Basler if he still held the same opinion when faced with the knowledge of Remus' bootlegging activities, Hogan replied that although he himself did not drink, he did not consider violation of the prohibition laws a moral offense. During Hogan's testimony reference was made to hi-jacking as one of Remus' activities. This accusation infuriated Remus, who denied that there was any evidence that he had hi-jacked any liquor convoys and claimed that the subject had been brought up simply to prejudice the jury. He further defended his activities as a bootlegger, proclaiming proudly that he had "no apologies to make for having sold good liquor since 1919."

Michael Igoe introduced himself as the South Park Commissioner in Chicago and stated that he had been assistant District Attorney and that he had served for six years as the Democratic leader of the Illinois House of Representatives. This impressive witness testified that Remus' reputation as a lawyer was good and that he was always considered a quiet, peaceful person. On cross-examination Assistant Prosecutor Basler asked him if, in view of the fact that Remus had been convicted of bootlegging activities in Cincinnati and been indicted for similar offenses in Chicago and elsewhere, he could still "consider his reputation for peace and quiet, for truth and veracity, as a man

---

[8]Darrow predicted that prohibition would bring "a reign of terror, intimidation, violence, and bigotry unprecedented in the modern world."

and a lawyer, good." Igoe looked straight at Basler and without hesitation replied, "Yes, I consider it good."

During the cross-examination Igoe admitted tha he had represented Remus in the Cincinnati prohibition trial, and Basler enquired about the attorney's fee he received. Remus rose to object, but the witness raised a hand to stop him. "Don't," Igoe said to him. "I'm glad to tell about my fee. I understand Mr Taft has been making some speeches around here about my fee." He then told the Court that he had received $5,000 for his representation of Remus in that trial. Basler's attempt to prove that he had actually received more than this amount was unsuccessful, Igoe exclaiming emphatically that he "never got a dime in cash from George Remus."

FRIDAY, DECEMBER 9TH

The first witness, Joseph La Buy, a former Municipal Judge, testified that he had practiced law in Chicago for twenty-five years and had shared a suite of offices with Remus for fifteen years, during which time he got to know the defendant well. He testified that Remus had visited him at his home two months after being released from the Atlanta Penitentiary, and that during this visit he concluded that Remus was insane. "He wasn't the same man I had known," he told the jury, and explained how Remus rattled on about his estranged wife, and how she was driving him crazy with the divorce, and also how she planned to kill him. He described how he tried to reason with him, but Remus would not even remain seated long enough to listen to him. "He looked wild and would jump up and walk around." La Buy also told the jury how he once found Remus in a dimly lit room: "He was standing there leaning against the wall scratching his head and crying out, 'Oh my God! Mrs. Remus is driving me crazy. She won't talk to me. She is driving me crazy.'" Under cross-examination La Buy admitted that Remus had given him an automobile, but he explained that it was a payment in lieu of money that Remus owed him. La Buy was the final witness for the defense.

At this point several deposition were read. The first was from John Snook, the warden who took over the running of Atlanta Penitentiary when Warden Sartain was arrested. He stated that Mrs. Remus visited her husband two or three days before his release and the two had argued over Mrs. Remus' decision to travel to Atlanta rather than staying in Cincinnati, where she could be reached by her husband. He also asserted that while they were talking, Mrs. Remus suddenly jumped up and for no apparent reason started to shout that Remus had threatened to hit her and that she was afraid of him. According to his deposition, Snook managed to quiet Mrs Remus down and assure her that nothing was going to happen to her. Warden Snook said that there was absolutely no reason for this outburst of hers and that Remus told her that he would not hurt her and had no reason to. The Warden also testified that Remus was indeed called a rat, but only by a certain class of prisoners.

In the second deposition, Russell Moritz, an assistant to John Marshall during the Jack Daniels trial, testified that while they were in

Indianapolis, Remus had pointed out to him two men whom he identified as hired gunmen.

After the depositions were read into the record, Charles Elston rose and announced that the defense rested. A short recess was called, and when the jury returned to the Courtroom Prosecutor Taft rose and announced that the State was ready to present its rebuttal testimony which they expected to take anywhere from five to ten days, but they first requested that Richard Simmons be recalled for cross-examination. This cross-examination focused on activities at the Ohio and Kentucky Distilling company where he held the position as company lawyer. It was intended to prove that Remus was involved in the company after his release from Atlanta, and as a result had money and was obviously sane enough to conduct business. Most of the testimony revolved around liquidation figures and the trust fund that was set up for Romola Remus.

The prosecution now set out to destroy the defense's portrait of George Remus as a devoted, but sinned against, husband driven insane by his wife's infidelity. Its first witness, Mrs. Elizabeth Felix, testified that she attempted in vain to bring about a reconciliation between the estranged couple. She described Imogene Remus as a loving and devoted wife who sought to preserve her marriage. George Remus, as she pictured him, was at times ill tempered, truculent and lacking in affection for his wife.

Mrs. Felix described in detail a violent argument that started when she tried to convince Remus that his wife lived a "blameless life" in Atlanta. She testified: "An argument started, and he got very much upset. He was excited and said she had betrayed him. When I defend her, he becvame violent." She continued:"I told him that he had abused and mistreated her to my certain knowledge, and he said that anything should be forgiven a man in prison." When another flare up occurred later in the day. Mrs. Remus, through her tears, declared that she would die before she would ask him to take her back. Remus sneered and clenched and unclenced his fist as he vowed "he was going to kill Franklin L. Dodge." Mrs. Felix explained that she finally managed to calm things down by flattering Remus.

Taft asked Mrs. Felix about Remus' mood during that visit, and she replied that he seemed a bit depressed at first, but he perked up after swimming in the pool. She attributed his depression to a newspaper article stating there was a warrant for his arrest. She then described how Mrs. Remus would leave the penitentiary crying and how on one occasion she found Mrs. Remus outside the prison after Remus had kicked her out early so he could play ball with some other inmates. "Was the name of Dodge mentioned?"

Taft asked."Yes," Mrs Felix replied, and then related that Dodge's name had come up in their conversation and Remuus declared that he wanted to kill Dodge, despite stating a few minutes earlier that all the money in the world wasn't worth spending one hour in jail. Mrs. Felix re-iterated that when they left, Remus was completely calm and he even kissed his wife goodbye. "Was Mrs. Remus in love with Remus?" Taft asked, and Mrs. Felix replied emphatically that she was.

SATURDAY, DECEMBER 10TH

A rumor that Remus was planning to kill Charles Taft led to the beefing up of the already tight Courtroom security. Chief Justice Taft warned his son and advised him be especially carefull. The Chief Justice had been informed by a man with connections in the St. Louis underworld "that Remus was especially angered at Charlie, and that he was looking for a weapon to use it on Charlie."

Mrs. Felix continued her account of a woman wronged by the husband she loved and left to support herself on hardly any money at all. She told how Mr. Felix managed Mrs. Remus' accounts, and how she would pay her bills to him monthly, but how, on occasion, she would ask for extra time to pay because she was short of money. Remus objected. He declared that she had hundreds of thousands of dollars. Then Mrs. Felix related the details of her first meeting with Dodge in Atlanta when she was giving a deposition for use in the divorce hearing, and she denied that he and Mrs. Remus had shared a hotel suite during that visit. She explained that Mrs. Remus had both her sister and her daughter with her on that occasion. She met Dodge for the second time at the Alms Hotel where Mrs. Remus was in the company her sister. She asserted that at no time did they behave like lovers. According to her, Mrs. Remus only referred to him as Mr. Dodge, never addressing him by his first name or the endearment "daddy," which she used when speaking to Remus. She ended her testimony by stating that Remus "was sane-entirely sane."

In spite of her testimony that Mrs. Remus struggled to survive on the amount of money she had, Mrs. Felix admitted, under cross-examination, that when in Atlanta, Mrs. Remus stayed in the Biltmore Hotel, "one of the finest and most luxurious in the whole South." She also admitted to having witnessed Remus in the grip of one of his "outbursts," but she still insisted that Remus was sane.

The prosecution, intent on establishing that Remus was sane during the two year period prior to the shooting, called to the stand John Theobold, the Deputy United States Marshall who accompanied Remus from Atlanta to Cincinnati after his release. Theobald testified that he had spent time with the defendant on various occasions and was convinced he was sane. Defining a rage as a situation when "a man wants to fight," Theobold said that he never saw Remus like this, and he stated that he never had any problems with him. He admitted that Remus was apt to get excited and talk loudly, but he declared that "if that is insanity we would all be insane."

Under cross-examination Theobald testified that when Remus left Atlanta Penitentiary he did not have any money except the $10 that was routinely given to inmates upon their release, and that he had used this to buy food and milk for one of the inmate's family. During re-direct examination the prosecution attempted to counter his testimony by asking questions about Remus' alleged bribing of prison officials for special services, but Remus' objections were sustained.

William McHugh, also a deputy United States Marshal, refused to say whether he thought Remus was sane or not because he might be wrong. He testified to being in Remus' company often and admitted that he had seen him riled up and excited, but he denied that on one occasion he and Conners had spent an hour walking up and down with him trying to calm him down.

The most exciting event of the day, however, occurred outside the Courtroom when John S. Berger was arrested for perjury only minutes before he was due to catch a train out of Cincinnati. He was immediately taken to police headquarters and then rushed over to the County Courthouse, where he was released on bond. He told the reporters that he had known about the arrest prior to the warrant being served and that he remained in Cincinnati to meet it. He claimed that Franklin Dodge was instrumental in the arrest and he asserted that he would prove his testimony to be true. "I was the star witness for Remus," he declared pompously, "and this is an effort of the prosecution to break down my testimony and to intimidate other witnesses." The indictment, which ran to a thousand words, did not mention Berger's graphic descriptions of Remus' outbursts with which he had enthralled the court spectators, but dealt with his denial on the stand that he did at any time try to blackmail Mrs. Remus into giving him $25,000 for Remus, and that he threatened her with great bodily harm if she did not comply.

It also charged that he had declared, untruthfully, that he was never arrested and convicted for a State offense. He admitted that it was true, but claimed that he was innocent and was never convicted. He said that the arrest occurred in 1909 in Savannah, Ga. where he ran an airplane operation. Airplanes then were in their infancy, he explained, and if the wind wasn't just right they couldn't be flown. Apparently he and his partners had placed an advertisement for some flights in the newspaper which was then sent out to people in the mail, but the flights never took place because of the weather. Consequently Berger was arrested for using the United States mail to defraud.

However, he insised that he was not convicted, explaining that the entire matter had been thrown out of court by a United States Commissioner. As to the perjury charge, he told reporters, "I understand from good authority that the picture of a man half my age was shown to the Grand Jury, and the Grand Jury was told that it was a picture of myself. I wish to ask the Prosecutors to let me go before the Grand Jury and let the Grand jurors compare me, in person, with the picture and see for themselves whether it is my picture or not." Prosecutor Taft refused to give the reporters any details about the arrest, but simply said that the Grand Jury was still conducting its investigations.

MONDAY, DECEMBER 12TH

John Berger's indictment was the very first subject brought up when the trial entered its fifth week. Berger was scheduled to appear for arraignment at 11.30 that morning, but Elston immediately motioned for the indictment to be quashed. Berger himself addressed the court charging that the prosecutors had obtained the indictment through fraud. He then pointed to Taft and declared that he had worked all his life "to establish a reputation and these prosecutors...," but he was interrupted by Taft who rose and objected. Berger then turned on him and accused him and his assistants of plotting against him. "That statement comes with very bad grace," Taft retorted angrily, and then went on to say that Berger had told newspaper reporters that he had exaggerated his testimony to impress the jury. Berger then turned to Taft and calmly said: "That is a mistake Mr. Taft."

Judge Shook ended the argument by denying the motion and setting Berger's arraignment for 9.30 the following morning. Judge Shook then turned to the subject of Vernon Chumbley, who was arrested for perjury on November 28th, but was given time to confer with Elston, who was representing him. He was supposed to have been arraigned before Judge Shook that morning, but Elston intimated that he would be filing a motion to quash in this case too, so the Judge also set his arraignment for the following day and advised Elston that he would hear the motion then.

Remus now filed a motion for a temporary restraining order on Prosecutor Taft and his assistants to stop them from "further unlawful and unethical intimidation and coercion" of defense witnesses and also to prevent him from issuing what he considered uncomplimentary statements to the press about him. The motion charged that Taft was intimidating "the cause of the defendant" by dictating newspaper articles to Ruth Remus which were then published as being statements of fact from her. Judge Shook in refusing to consider the motion stated that "the Court has said repeatedly that the case is being tried without regard to the newspaper. The press is here and it is proper that it is here. It is natural in the course of the trial that the newspapers should take different viewpoints. I have not felt that the newspapers have at all times correctly reported the proceedings."

The prosecution's first rebuttal witness of the day. John L. Fogle, a Chicago attorney in charge of the investigation committee of the Chicago Bar

Association, testified that although Remus was not a member of the association, he had been called before its investigative committee on a number of occasions to answer claims filed against him by his clients. He did not give any details of the claims, and Judge Shook interrupted to indicate that he did not want the details of these claims introduced if they dealt with controversies between capital and labor. Fogle stated that Remus' reputation as a man and a law-abiding citizen was sometimes good and sometimes bad, but his reputation as a lawyer was bad most of the time. He said that he had known Remus and consulted with him frequently between 1913 and 1917, and in his opinion Remus was sane although he "did not restrain his actions fully."

Joseph Thomas, a jailer at the Dayton jail, where Remus was confined for six days after his release from Atlanta, testified that he saw Remus often at the jail and that he seemed normal then. He described how Remus acted as prosecutor at the "kangaroo court" held by inmates where new prisoners would be fined $1 for the joint tobacco fund. Charles Hinds, the Deputy Sheriff at Montgomery, then testified that while he was on duty in the Dayton jail, Remus had assisted another inmate and administered camphor and ammonia to the man who had collapsed in a fit. He asserted that the inmate, Fred Nicholas, was in very bad shape and may have passed into unconsciousness if Remus had not been there. This incident was corroborated by Deputy Sheriff Michael Conover. He and Hinds both testified that in their opinion Remus was sane.

A number of witnesses, including the Chief Jailer at Dayton, testified that they saw Remus on occasion and felt he was sane. Deputy United States Marshall, August Steinbach, testified that he accompanied Remus from Cincinnati to St. Louis after his release from Dayton and claimed that Remus did not return to Cincinnati because the Marshall had information that members of the Egan's Rats gang were intending to kill Remus. He admitted that an extra guard was laid on for the trip because of this rumor, and that when Remus heard about it, he got extremely nervous and excited and sent a telegram to Mabel Willebrandt asking for extra protection in St. Louis. He claimed that he thought Remus was sane despite his reaction to the rumor.

Sergeant George Dooley took the stand after Steinbach and related how he had met Remus at the downtown police headquarters immediately after Remus had turned himself in. He then accompanied Remus to the scene of the crime to search for the gun, which Remus said had been lost in the scuffle, and the car which Remus claimed had been abandoned in the park. "He said he shot his wife," Dooley testified, "and he pointed out where the shooting took place." Dooley then corroborated Conners' testimony that he had visited Remus at the police station and when he offered to have an attorney there in the morning, Remus replied: "No, George Remus will defend himself." Dooley said that a police alienist, Dr. Kendig, was then called to examine Remus, and one of the first things he asked was whether he intended to plead guilty. Dooley quoted Remus as saying, "Not for one moment, no sir." "He then told the doctor how many first degree murder cases he had tried in a year," Dooley continued; "He said that he had tried eighteen and won eighteen, I think." Remus then reportedly named the alienists who had testified for him in a number of these cases and asked Dr Kendig if he knew any of them. Dr. Kendig replied that he knew some but not others. Dooley next testified that Remus referred to his wife as "that decomposed mass of clay," and asserted that he had spent thousands of dollars trying to catch her with Dodge, whom he called a "parasite." When asked about Remus demeanor during this interview, Dooley replied that he was "calm and collected" and that he "talked plainly," saying that he had no regrets, and that he answered every question. "From his behavior I concluded he was sane," he declared. The defense chose not to cross-examine. Instead Elston motioned in vain to have his testimony stricken from the record on the grounds of repetition.

The next witness, Lieutenant Frank Mc Neal, who booked Remus when he gave himself up, testified that Remus walked into the station and said that he wanted to give himself up because he had shot his wife, and then told them what he had done and how he had caught a lift downtown before catching a taxicab over to the station. McNeal told the jury how Remus was then taken upstairs where Detective Chief Emmet Kirgan joined in the questioning. He said that Remus told them very calmly that he had left home at about 6 a.m. and driven to the Alms Hotel, and when Kirgan asked if he had gone there to kill his wife and Dodge, McNeal quoted him as saying, "Yes, if I could get them both together." Prior to McNeal's testimony all other witnesses had sworn that Remus went to the Alms Hotel that morning to simply talk to his wife. This was the first time anybody testified that Remus actually admitted that he had any thoughts of killing her. McNeal continued to relate the story of the killing as told to him by Remus that morning, placing emphasis on the way Remus constantly referred to his wife as "that decomposed mass of clay."

Under cross-examination McNeal admitted that Remus had paced up and down in the front office of the station saying that this was the first bit of peace he had had in a year and a half after being "tortured for two years."

After McNeal left the stand, Taft addressed Judge Shook and requested that he be allowed to introduce, as evidence, all the depositions taken for the divorce hearing, pointing out that Remus had agreed to let the documents be introduced. Elston immediately objected stating that they were involved in a homicide trial not a divorce case, but Remus tried to stop him and the two started arguing. Finally Remus jumped up and, addressing the Court, announced that the depositions should be allowed to be introduced. "Let everything go in that the Taft outfit has," he said, pushing a large pile of papers across the desk towards them."The only thing," he continued, "there's so much of it will keep the jury here for days and days, and this is the fifth week they have been here." Elston still objected, though, stating that they were not there to try the divorce case, and Judge Shook agreed with him and sustained the objection. Basler entered the argument at this stage, declaring that there had not been any objection because Remus had overruled the decision made by his co-counsel, but Judge Shook stated firmly that Elston had made the objection and that the objection was sustained. A few minutes later, though, when another witness was on the stand, Judge Shook interrupted the proceedings to announce that he had been thinking about his decision and had decided to take the matter under advisement and would offer his final ruling at a later stage.

Oscar Fender, a manager at the Lincoln National Bank in Cincinnati, the next witness, provided detailed information about the finances of Imogene and George Remus. He indicated that they occasionally had finacial problems. He also testified that "J.P. Alexander and George Remus were one and the same." Fender then described a number of temper tantrums that he had seen Remus have prior to his incarceration at Atlanta, and said that he believed Remus was perfectly sane.

On cross-examination, Elston attempted to esblish that Fender had been involved with Remus in bootlegging activities. Fender denied this accusation, although he admitted that concerning one whiskey sale, he knew something about it, but that Remus made all the arrangements, and he simply took the money in at the bank.

During the noon recess John Berger, once again grandstanding, had a letter delivered to Taft denying all the charges set forth in the indictment. He stated that it was absolutely false that he had perjured himself. He mentioned that Taft and his assistants had made statements to the press to the effect that these charges were true and he felt that these statements were detrimental to his business interests. He called upon Taft "in accordance with section 11343 of the General Code of Ohio, to publish a full and complete retraction of all charges, in as public a manner as that in which the original publications were made." He gave Taft until 5 o'clock that evening to comply with his request or he would instruct his attorney to file a suit against him for damages. Shortly after 5 o'clock Taft sent a note to Berger simply stating: "Your request therein made is refused." Berger filed a suit the following morning claiming damages of $500,000. When asked to comment on the suit, Taft stated that he would be extremely busy while the murder trial continued and that he did not "intend to be bothered by flea bites" until the trial was over.

That evening Berger granted an interview to a reporter for the St Louis *Post Dispatch* in which he boasted about the way he had spoken to "that fellow Taft" in the courtroom that day and had offered to stand before the Grand Jury and let them compare him with the photograph they had been shown. "I guess you heard me bawl him out to a fare-you-well," he boasted. He called the indictment a "dastardly plot" against him and referred to himself as Remus' star witness and the backbone of the defense, the one who gave the "strongest testimony there was at this trial." "I'm clean as a hounds tooth," he declared. "I've been good all my life. My record speaks for it. No man can blacken my good name and get away with it," he warned. "Before he's through he'll think he has a bear by the tail. I'm sticking with this thing forever and ever."

TUESDAY, DECEMBER 13TH

Court opened with the arraignment of Vernon Chumbley and John S. Berger. Judge Shook postponed the hearing of the plea in the Berger case to give Elston adequate time to prepare, Vernon Chumbley's plea was also postponed, and he was informed that he would be permitted to return to the Leavenworth Penitentiary and that he could not legally be served with the indictment until he returned there.

Remus stood up to address the Court after the ruling on Chumbley, declaring that he was Elston's co-counsel in defending Chumbley. Taft challenged this, and Judge Shook ruled he could legally represent himself, but he could not represent Chumbley. He was allowed to continue speaking, though, when he said that he wished to make a statement and file a motion on his own behalf. He asked that the indictments of both Berger and Chumbley be introduced into the record of his own trial so that the jurors, who at this stage were unaware of the proceedings, might witness what he referred to as intimidation by the "novices in the Prosecutor's office." He pointed out that if this request was not granted, he would once again file a petition with the Supreme Court to have the information included. Judge Shook said that he would not allow the information regarding the indictments to go before the jury because, in his opinion, it would be prejudicial to the cause of the defendant, and it was his intention to give the defendant a fair trial. Remus argued against this, claiming that the jury were not totally ignorant of the events as they were bound to see the newspaper headlines and hear the newspaper boys shouting as they walked to the courthouse every morning. "The jury must be blind not to see these headlines," he declared, and therefore must already be influenced to some extent." By introducing the full story into the record he hoped that they would be able to draw their own conclusions about the matter.

Remus also asserted that everything Berger had said under oath was the truth and that Chumbley, who had been indicted for perjury in a deposition for the divorce trial, was still ready to take the stand as a rebuttal witness. He accused the prosecutors of taking advantage of their legal positions and using the Grand Jurors to "hoodwink and besmirch" the proper course of justice. In conclusion he praised Judge Shook for the fairness with which he had handled the Court proceedings. Judge Shook ruled that the motion be filed, and the Jury was brought in to begin the day's proceedings, which Judge Shook started by ruling that the divorce depositions could not be placed in evidence.

Joseph Breitenstein, the first witness of the day, had represented Mrs. Remus during the Jack Daniels trial, and had been implicated by Congressman La Guardia in certain alleged whiskey dealings with Mrs. Remus and Dodge. He claimed the right to withhold confidential information about his client. Basler explained that he would only be asked about testimony already offered by defense witnesses and therefore it would not really be confidential information. Breitenstein's testimony contradicted Conners' account of the incident in the lobby of the Claypool Hotel. Breitenstein asserted that Dodge had walked calmly to the dining room where he had sat at a table while Remus sat at another table nearby. "One or two tables away?" Basler asked, attempting to establish that the two had occupied tables very close to one another and nothing untoward had happened. "That is my recollection," Breitenstein answered.

Breitenstein later testified that he shared a suite of rooms with Dodge during the Jack Daniels trial, and that the only visitor they had was John Gehrum.

"Were there any highball parties or whiskey parties or carryings on of a scandalous nature in that room in which Mrs. Remus participated?" Basler asked.

"There were no highball parties in that room," Breitenstein replied, adding that as far as he knew, Mrs. Remus never even entered the room. He then testified about the incident in Indianapolis that Paul Anderson had described when Mrs. Remus alleged Remus threatened her. Breitenstein told the jury that he was with Mrs. Remus on that occasion and that Remus was walking behind them. He said that he heard Remus say something but he could not hear what it was. Mrs. Remus heard it, however, and she started to scream and become tremendously emotional.

Then Sheriff Elza Canter testified nervously that he saw Remus on an almost daily basis when he was in Portsmouth jail and that, in his opinion, Remus was sane at that time. He described Remus' activities at the jail, explaining that he was a trusty and helped out with certain tasks such as cooking and insisted that he was considered a very model prisoner. On re-direct examination Basler asked Canter about Remus' privileges, asking if it wasn't true that he had told Assistant Prosecutor Clippinger that Remus had more privileges at Portsmouth than any of the other inmates. Canter replied that "in a way he did - yes." His reluctance to elaborate on the subject caused Basler to ask that the record show his surprise at his witness' attitude, and he was granted permission to treat Canter as a hostile witness.

Elston, during his re-examination, asked if it wasn't true that he was given these extra privileges because he was considered to be an honest and trustworthy man. Basler objected stating that if Elston continued that line of questioning then the prosecution would go even further into the matter, intimating that they had evidence they had not yet revealed. Then Remus entered the proceedings stating that he was willing to have the matter explored, and so Judge Shook overruled the objection commenting that he was eager to hear what there was to hear. Elston continued his questioning and then handed the witness back to Basler who immediately asked about allegations that Remus had eaten many of his meals outside the prison walls, at the Portsmouth Hotel. The Sheriff's reply was a non-committal "I couldn't say," and when Basler tried to press him on the issue, Elston's objection was sustained. Canter was finally allowed to step down, and John Heinlein, a porter at the Washington Hotel in Portsmouth, took his place. He testified to seeing Remus around the hotel often, but when asked whether Remus ate his meals there, he could only say that although he had never seen him eating there, extra room service was normally provided during those visits. He also testified that he considered Remus sane during these visits.

Captain Robert L Dunning, Superintendent of the Cincinnati Police Bureau of Criminal Identification, testified that he was present during the interrogation of Remus by the Court alienist, Dr. W.C. Kendig. He said that Remus was "courteous, intelligent, coherent and without regret for what he had done," and he told how he calmly told Dr. Kendig and the other police officers present that he had been following his wife and Dodge for about a year with the expressed intent of killing them if he caught them together. Remus, in his opinion, was sane during this interview.

Next, one of Remus' jailers at Troy, Henry Bashore, testified that Remus was a good prisoner who conducted himself well and was always kind to him. He also testified that he never saw Remus having one of his "brainstorms," but that Remus became "naturally angry" whenever Franklin Dodge was mentioned. He concluded by stating that he believed that Remus was sane.

Although they listened intently, few of the spectators could hear any of the testimony of the last witness of the day. Mrs. Grace Campbell, a frail, middle-aged widow, sister of the slain woman, spoke in such a low voice that a chair was placed for her near the jury box, and Judge Shook sat in a chair placed next to her. Often with tears in her eyes she related how for two months in the summer of 1926 she had attempted to arrange a settlement of the Remus' marital difficulties. At none of the conferences did she see Remus in a rage. In her opinion, Remus was perfectly sane.

She then told of one visit to Remus when she asked him why "My sister cried and was so unhappy and could not sleep at night after seeing him?" Remus replied "that she did not understand him." She then testified to a number of conferences which she attended in 1926, during which Mrs Remus and her representatives attempted to come to a settlement with Remus and his representatives. The prosecution did not push her to give details about the conferences because of her physical frailty and weak heart, but she stated emphatically that not once, during these conferences, did she see Remus in any kind of rage, although she had seen him angry. "He threatened many times," she admitted, "but he always spoke firmly and was very gentlemanly about it."

Mrs. Campbell was shown a number of documents said to be proposed settlements which she was asked to identify and which contained the signatures of Remus, Blanche Watson and others which she also identified. She said that neither Remus nor his wife were well off before the divorce proceedings and denied the defense claim that Mrs. Remus had stolen his property from him. Sibbald showed her a contract which entitled Blanche Watson to sell some whiskey certificates and for the money to be divided between Remus and his wife to meet expenses incurred during the divorce proceedings. "They always talked about money," she told the jury. "They never seemed to have any when they needed it." She asserted that throughout the proceeding year Remus had assured her that he would do no harm to her sister and that he wanted a peaceful settlement and possibly even a reconciliation.

After a brief cry, she regained her composure and described a meeting to discuss a settlement at which Remus got angry and threatened Mrs. Remus that if a setttlement was not reached, he would follow her all the way to China and would "crack a skull. I'll see that you haven't a dime to your name and not a shred of reputation left," she quoted him as saying. Mrs. Campbell burst into tears again after this statement and once again the Court waited for her to recover. She then testified that Dodge's name was mentioned during the conference and that Remus had called him a horrible name, which she had objected to and which he had toned down for her benefit, but she insisted that he did not rant and rave and did not pull his hair out or do anything remotely like that. In spite of the obvious animosity and the failure to reach a settlement, Mrs. Campbell said that both Remus and his estranged wife parted on good terms after that conference. Even during the conference Remus was polite and courteous, sending Ruth Remus out on occasion to buy her mother flowers and candy.

Mrs. Campbell told of yet another conference which took place at the Price Hill mansion and which Conners had testified to earlier in the trial. She said that she was in an adjoining room when she heard a scream, and when she ran into the conference room to investigate she found Remus sitting on the couch with Mrs. Remus. He seemed to be trying to comfort her, and she looked distressed. She said that she was upset because Conners had grabbed her purse away from her. Conners had testified that he had done this because she had tried to pull out a pistol from it. On another occasion, Mrs. Campbell testified, Remus told her that their marital problems were "a battle royal," and that he felt little for what he might do to Imogene's reputation.

Under cross-examination she confirmed that her husband had worked for Remus for a short time as president of the Rugby Distillery and that they had resided with the Remus family in their Price Hill mansion. When she was asked about Mrs. Remus' finances she declared that after one of the conferences at the Deschler Hotel in Columbus they had put all their money together to pay the bill, but she did admit that Mrs. Remus and her daughter both drove expensive cars and that Mrs. Remus had given one to her mother and she too had access to a small, inexpensive one while Remus was in Atlanta. The defense claimed that this car was a Packard roadster and had subsequently been given to Franklin Dodge as a gift from Mrs. Remus. Court was adjourned at that stage and Mrs. Campbell was allowed to step down, although she would be recalled the following day. Remus was visibly uncomfortable the entire time Mrs. Campbell was on the stand.

John Berger was pleased to learn that it was established that he was not the John Berger who had served time in a Minnesota Penitentiary. That John Berger was reported to have a number of tatoos on his arms, whereas the indicted John Berger had no tattoos, and there was no evidence that any ad been removed.

WEDNESDAY, DECEMBER 14TH

A spectacular war of words raged in court today until Judge Shook ended it by using his ultimate weapon, a contempt citation. Rurh Remus, undergoing cross-examination, was asked by Elston whether or not Franklin Dodge had been at the Price Hill mansion while Remus was in prison. Before she could answer, Remus gave a loud "humph." The prosecution objected, and Remus asked that the jury be excluded because "he wished to be heard."

After he discussed transitory maniacal insanity and praised the Court alienists and Judge Shook, he sneeringly referred to the prosecuting attorneys as "these three novices.™

This brought Sibbald immediately to his feet. He approached the bench, white with anger and shaking his fist as he bellowed:"This has gone far enough. I am not going to stand here anymore and listen to this defendant's attacks and slurs upon the Prosecutior's office!" Remus rushed towards Sibbald. Both men were angry and ready to fight, but deputies quickly grabbed them and kept them apart. By this time most of the spectators, excited by the wild Courtroom melee, were on their feet shouting until the baliffs resored order. Judge Shook now ordered Remus not to continue to harass the prosecutors, and Remus, pretending to be contrite, declared: "I apologize to the Court only, and to no one else." Sibbald tried in vain to get Remus to apologize to the prosecutors.

Judge Shook lectured Remus again, declaring "The Court will listen to sound argument, but not an attack on anybody." Remus disregarding the Judge's admonition, continued to attack the prosecutors, accusing them of intimidating his witnesses. Judge Shook, now furious, commanded Remus to sit down. "I don't want to hear anymore," he sternly declared.

Prosecuting Attorney Taft now entered the fray intent on answering Remus' charge of intimidation. He asserted that he had a deposition signed by Shaw declaring that "Remus and Chumbley tried to make him testify that Mrs. Remus and her daughter, Ruth, himself and Franklin Dodge occupied a hotel room in Florida and indulged in improper relations." Taft further charged that when Shaw refused to perjurer himself, a gun man threatened him "unless he testified as Remus told him."

Elston quickly sought to distance the defense from Shaw. "This man Shaw came to me with his story and I told him I did not believe it." Elston added that later when Shaw, who had fled to Chicago, wired for money to return to Cincinnati, he told him to go to Hell.

Sibbald now arose and declared "John Marcus has been in town all all the time this trial has been going on, and we dare them to put him on the stand." Judge Shook now took command. In a slow, deliberate manner he analyzed the unusual situation. He concluded that: "The prosecution has been conducted properly. I have seen nothing wrong or coercive in the way the prosecution has conducted this case." However, he had nothing but harsh words for George Remus. ""The defendant from the start has repeatedly attacked the Prosecutor in open Court." After again absolving the prosecution of any misconduct, Judge Shook considered his difficult situation. "No one realizes more than this Court the seriousness of the charges against the defendant in this case, and we have tried to be patient under almost unparalleld surroundings. Mr. Elston has been able to cope with the situation. The conduct of Mr. Elston has been exemplary. But we cannot overlook these continued attacks on the Prosecutors. We do not wish to do anything to jeopardize the rights of the defendant to a fair trial. However, he must respect the integrity of this Court. The Court finds the defendant in contempt of the Court."

Remus quickly objected, claiming that he had said nothing to warrant the contempt citation. Judge Shook then replied that he had "no personal feelings either for or against the defendant."

Mrs. Campbell returned to the stand, and Elston tried to get her to admit that Mrs. Remus was not as financially strapped as she claimed, and that she actually had hidden assets of her own. However, sustained objections by the prosecution twarted his attempt. All she could testify to was the sale by Blanche Watson of $20,000 worth of whiskey certificates, which Imogene and George agreed to split to cover legal expenses for the divorce.

Assistant United States Attorney General and Director of Personnel, John Marshall (not the same John Marshall who was prosecutor in the Jack Daniels case) was called in the morning to rebut testimony given by Allen Curry regarding his decision to resign as United States District Attorney in St. Louis. Curry had denied prosecution claims that he had been asked to resign because of personal misconduct. Remus immediately jumped up and asked that the jury might be excused while they argued the matter of Curry's impeachment being introduced into the trial. His request was granted, and the jury was led out of the courtroom.

In arguing the admissibility of the testimony Basler pointed to Curry's denial on the stand that he was asked to resign, and he pointed out that during Curry's examination on November 29th, the prosecution had been told by the Judge that they would incur a very severe penalty if they did not prove their accusations. Elston meanwhile declared the question of Curry's resignation to be collateral matter which had no bearing on his credibility as a witness. Remus then turned to Marshall and began to ask him a number of short, blunt questions. At one stage he picked up a Department of Justice file while he referred to it and this drew a retort from Assistant Prosecutor Basler who demanded that he put the file down. Remus replied angrily that he would "not put it down until the Court orders me to do so," and then turning on the Assistant Prosecutor asked him, "Who are you, Mr. Basler, to give me orders?" Judge Shook chided both Basler and Remus for arguing and then turned to Marshall and asked him why Curry had been asked to resign. He replied that "affidavits were placed with the Department stating that Mr. Curry had been found in a room with a woman without any clothes on." Judge Shook ruled that Marshall could be questioned about Curry's resignation, but not about the reason for it, and the jury was returned to the room.

Assistant Prosecutor Basler immediately asked Marshall if Allen Curry had been asked to resign and he replied that he had, at the request of the Attorney General. He testified that Curry officially resigned in Washington on January 20th 1926. The resignation was produced, and Marshall identified it as such before it was passed to the jury to study. Basler then tried to elicit information from Marshall as to the reason for Curry's impeachment, but Judge Shook interrupted him and sent the jury out while he admonished him for his persistence. Basler then tried to dictate a statement to the court stenographer for entry into the record, but Judge Shook stopped him and had the statement stricken. When Basler objected the Judge reminded him sharply that the stenographer took orders from him and not the prosecution or the defense. Basler continued to argue about having the record show, but he was again interrupted by the Judge, who replied sharply that the record should show "that the prosecutor proceeded to ask an improper question before the jury, notwithstanding the order of the Court, and that he put the question, whereupon the Court excused the jury." He also entered it as matter of record that Basler had been warned about the asking of such questions. Marshall was then handed over to the defense for cross-examination.

Remus himself began conducting the cross-examination, and he obtained from Marshall the assertion that he had travelled to Cincinnati when asked to do so by the Attorney General and Prosecutor Taft. In reply to this Remus made a statement about Taft's father being the Supreme Court

Presiding Justice, but he was interrupted by Judge Shook, who said that he was aware of who Taft's father was and that, in fact "everyone knew it." "Many in jail didn't know it," Remus replied sharply, and then added that they knew it now. Remus then attempted to introduce a number of documents that Marshall had brought with him, but Basler objected and Remus argued that if he could not introduce the papers then why should he even continue to cross-examine the witness. As a result, Marshall was allowed to step down.

Then Ruth Remus was called to the stand to rebut testimony by defense witnesses that relations between Mr. and Mrs. Remus were affectionate right up until the day she served him with divorce papers. Dressed in deep mourning, she entered the Courtroom smiling and even nodded acknowledgement to Remus as she passed him on her way to the witness chair. Ruth then related to the jury the tale of an abused wife who loved her husband and tried to do whatever he wanted, only to be repaid by unkind words and deeds. She described in detail a number of incidents that depicted Remus as an abusive husband.

On one occasion during a card game Remus, angry because he lost, threw the cards across the table. "Mother reprimanded him," she said, "and he picked up a five pound box of candy and threw it at her, but it didn't hit her." She then related how when they were staying at the Hotel Gibson she heard her mother scream. As she ran to her mother's room, Remus passed her, looking very angry. "I went into the room and found mother standing there, very scared, her nose bleeding and her dress stained with blood." Ruth started to cry at this point, and she was given time to recover before continuing. "One summer we were at a camp on the Miami River," she continued. "Mr. Remus and mother were in a canoe which he upset. She swallowed a great deal of water, which was later found to contain poison ivy." She described how her mother became so ill that they thought she was going to die, but she was not allowed to continue the narration on objection of Remus.

Ruth also told the jury how her mother visited Remus in the Atlanta Penitentiary and did everything she could to ease his stay there. "Mother tried to do things for Mr. Remus when he was in prison," she said, "but the things she did, did not please him. He would get angry at her and she would leave the prison in tears." On one occasion he allegedly refused to see her, claiming that he did not have the time and wanted to take part in a ball game. Ruth then asserted that Remus had given the Price Hill house to Mrs. Remus before he went to Atlanta. She said that some of the furniture was sold at the auction already testified to by Oscar Fender, while some was moved to

Atlanta when Mrs. Remus moved there to be with her husband, and the rest was put in storage. She testified that after his release from Portsmouth, in June 1926, Remus offered the house back to her mother again, claiming that it was her home and that he was prepared to move into a hotel. Basler introduced a letter into evidence that was alleged to have been written by Mrs. Remus and sent to her husband in the penitentiary concerning the sale of the furniture from the mansion. It read; "I an selling almost all and when you return we will have a little home somewhere and I know we will be far happier." He insisted that this proved that Remus knew about the stripping of the house and was in full agreement with it. Ruth also denied that Remus had given her mother jewelry valued at $150,000 before he left for Atlanta.

When she was asked about the incident in which Berger allegedly demanded $25,000 from Mrs. Remus. Ruth said that she had heard Berger talking to her mother on this occasion and had specifically heard him demand this money and threaten her if it was not forthcoming. She denied that her mother had attended any cocktail parties during that time in Indianapolis and declared that her mother never left their suite at night. She described a visit that Remus and John Rogers made to their suite at the Alms hotel and quoted Rogers as commenting to Remus that her mother was "not the kind of woman you represented her to be." Elston objected to this testimony, but Remus told him to allow it. "We want the facts to go before the jury if they are facts," he declared.

Ruth then contradicted Harry Truesdale's testimony, admitting that he had been hired by her mother, but that his duties were only to follow Remus and catch him in a hotel with another woman. She said that Truesdale and John Marcus had visited Mrs. Remus at the Alms Hotel where they were staying at the time. She said that she listened from behind the bedroom door and heard Truesdale tell her that he knew Remus was spending time in a Cincinnati hotel with another woman and that he normally went there after attending the dog races. He said that Remus usually reserved a room ahead of time and he could find out when he was going to be there from the clerk. She said that her mother agreed that this was important information that could be used to her advantage in the divorce case, but she refused to give Truesdale or Marcus any money, or enter any agreement with them, until they could bring her evidence. "The next afternoon I saw him again," she said. "He was introduced as Mr. Childs." She related how her mother asked if he had found anything, but she claimed that he avoided answering the question. Mrs. Remus then suggested that Remus may have registered under the name of H. Reimer. A few days later, she said, she and her mother left for Chicago and only returned at the end of September.

She then told the jury that on October 4th, her mother went out at about 10.30 p.m. "I had given her a clipping from a paper about the Remus suit," Ruth explained, " and mother wrote something on the clipping and put it in an envelope." She said that she did not know whom she sent it to. The clipping, which had already made one appearance in the Court room was presented to her for identification. She said that it was the clipping that she had cut out and the note was written in her mother's hand, and then the note was read out to the jury: "Leaving now for Hamilton. John Marcus introduced me to this man. R. made reservations for rooms. Hope we can catch him. Ruth knows all about it. Go to Ruth at once if they hurt me. I am brave and realize the evidence is important." It also gave a recognizable description of Truesdale as the man introduced by Marcus. During the reading of this note, Ruth began to cry again and Sibbald, who was conducting the examination, waited until she had calmed down before asking what time her mother returned that night. She replied that it was approximately 1.30 or 2. a.m. When asked her opinion concerning Remus' sanity, she replied that she thought him sane.

During her cross-examination Ruth was questioned about her previous testimony, when she said that Remus acted "like a crazy man." She explained that she had not meant crazy as insane, but that "he had a mean, angry, vicious look about him." Then Elston asked Ruth if Franklin Dodge was ever at the house. She seemed intent on avoiding the issue, claiming that she could not remember, but she finally admited that he had visited on occasion.

During the day, Remus filed another motion in the Common Pleas Court. This was a result of the ruling handed down by the Supreme Court when he filed a motion to have the Prosecutors temporarily restrained from harassing his witnesses. He had been told on the occasion that the correct procedure was to go through the Common Pleas Court and then if necessary take it to the Supreme Court in error proceedings. The same charges were made in this second motion as were made in the first, with the added charge that Taft was helping Ruth Remus to compile her articles for certain newspapers in his office. He charged that Taft not only had influence over the content of these articles, but that he was keeping her, and a number of other State witnesses, away from all but specifically chosen reporters. In connection with his charges of intimidation he further charged that Franklin Dodge and

Harry Brown (Mrs. Remus' brother) accompanied the attorneys on their trip to Washington to collect depositions without the authority of the Court.

John Berger was back in the news when it was revealed that there was a carnival promoter by the same name who allegedly operated a number of street carnivals at the turn of the century. This man was described as a confidence trickster who swindled his clients and eventually ended up serving a term in a Minnesota prison after complaints from officials in Atlantic City in 1908 and Atlanta in 1912. Berger flatly denied any knowledge of this other John S. Berger and claimed that he was never in Minnesota or Atlantic City or Atlanta. He insisted that he was being framed. On December the 13th the Cincinnati *Post* ran the headline: "Berger Cleared of Allegations." The news story asserted that Police reports had already shown that Berger had never been a carnival operator, although it seemed that Taft had come to an opposite conclusion.

THURSDAY, DECEMBER 15TH

The State presented only two witnesses during the day, before resting their case. The first witness, Charles F. Beach from Atlantic City, the secretary of the Policeman's Benevolent Association of New Jersey, testified that he had not seen Berger since 1908 when he had known him to be a carnival operator of dubious character. He asserted that Berger was a person whom he would not believe even under oath. Remus and Elston objected in vain.

On cross-examination Elston established that Beach had had some trouble with Berger back in 1908, before asking if it was not true that Berger's circus was swept out into the ocean during a storm. He admitted that there had been a storm, but denied that the circus had been swept out to sea. Elston got Beach to admit that he had ill feelings against Berger since that time. On redirect examination, Taft attempted to show that Beach's bad feelings were shared by many, and he called attention to the letters critical of Berger that Beach received after the disastrous circus. Beach said that the letters were from people who claimed that Berger had cheated them.

Mrs. Julia Brown, Mrs. Remus' elderly mother, was called to the stand in the afternoon. It was an ordeal for her to testify, and several times recesses had to called as she seemed about to faint. Like her daughter, Grace Campbell, she found it difficult to talk loud enough for the jury to hear her, and her chair had to be moved closer to the jurors' section, positioning her right across the table from Remus. Most of the questions asked of her were phrased so that she only had to answer "yes" or "no." However, she did elaborate on some of the answers, causing the jurors to strain forward, intent on catching every word. Most of her testimony corroborated that given by Ruth Remus. She too had heard Berger ask Mrs. Remus for $25,000 and threaten her when she refused to pay. She described one incident at the Price Hill mansion when Remus became angry at the mention of Franklin Dodge. "I won't use the words he did for they weren't very pretty words," she notified the jury. In spite of outbursts like this Mrs. Brown declared that in her opinion Remus was sane. Under cross-examination she admitted that Remus had invited her to move into the Price Hill mansion when he was sent to Atlanta, and she had done so.

Mrs. Brown was a strong rebuttal witness against allegations made by John Rogers, the newspaper reporter from the St Louis *Post Dispatch*. Rogers had testified to a visit he paid with Remus to Mrs. Remus' apartment at the Alms Hotel and Mrs. Brown agreed that the meeting took place, but she reputed Rogers' claim that Mrs. Remus had said she was glad to see Remus and that he had pushed her away, and also that Mrs. Remus had claimed that her husband would not hurt her. Mrs. Brown also said that reconciliation was discussed, and she told Rogers that she did not think it was possible if Remus continued to make the sort of charges he was making against her daughter in the newspapers. She said that she told Rogers that she resented these charges and that he replied that he understood the charges weren't true and that Remus would retract them if Mrs. Remus would go back to live with him.

When Mrs. Brown stepped down from the stand, Taft stood up and announced that the State rested. Then Elston announced that the defense also rested, although they had not called even one rebuttal witness of their own. The newspaper reporters and the spectators were surprised that neither side had put Franklin Dodge on the witness stand.

When both sides had announced that they rested, Taft pointed out that the defense was resting without presenting the alienists' report to the jury and without calling any of them to the stand. He stated that the prosecution had rested assuming that Judge Shook would call the alienists to testify if neither the defense nor the prosecution did so. Threrefore, he asked the judge to reopen the case so the alienists could be called to testify. Judge Shook granted his request.

The alienists report was generally complimentary to Remus, describing him as optimistic with "an air of leadership" and a respect for authority and asserted that "his sexual life showed no perversities." His physical appearance was described as "symmetrical in form" with "no evidences of nutritional disturbances." His memory, insight and understanding were rated as good. "No hallucination or compulsive phenomena" became apparent during the examination. The report stated that he was fully cooperative "being alert, friendly and courteous." The report contained a sketch of his life from birth right up until the time he decided to leave Chicago and enter the bootlegging business in Cincinnati. According to the report, he told the alienists that he had gone into bootlegging because he was "feeling the strain of the responsibility of defending criminal cases," and was determined to get into something less strenuous. When the alienists asked if bootlegging wasn't more of a strain than being a criminal lawyer, he replied that "the responsibility was not nearly so great" because the longest term one could serve on a liquor conviction was two years, while as a lawyer he was trying to prevent people from being sent to the electric chair, or spending their entire lives in jail.

Asked when it was that he finally made up his mind to go through with the killing, he replied that it was a couple of days before October 6th. He then gave them an account of that morning explaining that he had been told that Dodge was with Mrs. Remus at the hotel. He was asked whether he felt any sensation at any time which made him think that he might be insane, and he answered that he "felt a halo about his head for 8 or 12 months before the killing," although it was not a permanent sensation. He also said that his sanity had returned about "6,8 or 12 hours after the killing." The report also stated that he was aware that he would have to face the legal ramifications of what he had done. He told them that he did not care "whether or not I go to dust," and that he had killed Mrs. Remus as a matter of principle. As to his defense, he outlined his plea as "transitory maniacal insanity," and told them how he had defended William Ellis on this plea and was able to get him off with a fourteen year sentence rather than the death sentence. Finally he was asked again:"When did you make up your mind to kill Mrs Remus?" and he replied: "When I saw her laughing and joking as she left the Alms Hotel."

However, the alienists were unanimous in rejecting Remus' temporary insanity plea. They explained that there are three basic elements in a diagnosis of "acute transitory mania" or "transitory maniacal insanity," as Remus preferred to call it: excitement, loss of consciousness or memory, and a resultant deep sleep. They claimed that none of these elements were evident in Remus' case and that his outbursts, testified to in Court, did not comply with any recognized classification of insanity. They were simply "expressions of violent hate expressed with the appropriate degree of anger." They also found that he did not conform with any class of paranoia. As a result of these findings they unanimously declared Remus to be sane at the time of the killing.

FRIDAY, DECEMBER 16TH

Judge Shook ruled that only three paragraphs of the sixteen page report of the alienits could be introduced into the Court record. These paragraphs dealt solely with the conclusion that Remus was sane at the time of the shooting. Taft's objection to the ruling was denied, but he was granted permission to introduce more of the report by calling the alienists to testify. Taft began by calling Dr. Wolfstein to the stand. The alienist proceeded to narrate the full story of Remus' life before Taft questioned him concerning Remus' sanity. In spite of vigorous objections from Remus and Elston, Taft was allowed to ask Dr. Wolfstein the three questions which, in the State of Ohio, were used to determine sanity or insanity."Did George Remus know right from wrong when he killed his wife?"
"Was he a free agent in forming the purpose to kill?" and "Did he know the killing was an offense against the laws of God and Man?" Dr. Wolfstein, without hesitation, replied "yes" to each question.

Dr. Wolfstein then testified that on three occasions Remus confessed that he was thinking of killing his wife before the morning of October 6th, which legally constituted intent to kill. He related how Remus admitted to making various threats before actually killing his wife, which he defended as "a matter of principle." He then described Remus' emotional reactions as normal. He asserrted that Remus "expressed indignation when appropriate, showed emotion and expressed sarcasm, uttered jests and displayed facial expressions always "approriate--commensurate" with the situation.

At this point the jurors were informed that Remus had been allowed considerable freedom of action during the trial at the request of the alienists so that they might observe him in various situations, which would help them in determining his mental state.

Next Dr. Wolfstein pointed out that although Remus was supposed to react "in an insane manner" every time Franklin Dodge and Mrs. Remus were mentioned, both names were repeated "at least 100 times" during the course of the trial with no effect on Remus whatsoever. Dr. Wolfstein, in stating that he felt Remus was sane, asserted that Remus had a good mind, which he managed to keep under excellent control.

Despite vigorous objections by the defense, Taft was allowed to have Dr. Wolfstein describe and comment on the three Remus outbursts that occurred while the jury was absent. "In these three episodes in the court room," the alienist testified, "Mr. Remus' face was red, his head was red, his movements accelerated and his remarks indicasted anger. That was, in my judgment, just an indication of normal anger., He concluded:"I got the impression of a clear mentality, general clear expression and general normal conduct, a good mind and for the most part a good mind under excellent control."

When questioned about "transitory maniacal insanity," he replied that this term was no longer used in the medical profession. "What used to be called temporary maniacal insanity," he explained, "now is classified as delirium which sometimes follows such diseases as scarlet fever, pneumonia, smallpox and other blood diseases. During such delirium, acts may be committed resembling the description of temporary maniacal insanity. They are always followed by a deep sleep and utter lsack of memory as to the acts committed during the delirium." Remus' condition after killing his wife obviously did not meet this criteria. "His mind was clear", Dr. Wolfstein said. "He remembered distinctly what had happened . He did not fall into a deep sleep. He talked coherently."

Under cross-examination the doctor admitted that insanity was a subject upon which experts tended to disagree. Elston asked if it was not true that the subject of insanity had its parallels with the subject of law. "There is considerable disagreement isn't there?" he asked. Dr. Wolfstein replied: "I can't qualify as an expert on law, although I think I might after sitting here in this courtroom so long, listening to this trial." This answer brought a chuckle from the spectators, and even Judge Shook smiled. Dr. Wolfstein also admitted that on the day of his most violent and hysterical outburst in Court, Remus had insisted that the session continue, but that the alienists recommended the adjournment. During re-direct examination Taft asked Dr. Wolfstein if he thought Remus might have been putting on an act that day for the benefit of the alienists, but the Doctor replied that he "would hesitate to say that any attack of that kind was a sham. " "I can only say," he continued, "that it was not indicative of any form of insanity."

Dr. Mabel Fernald, Director of the Psychological Laboratory of the Cincinnati Public Schools System, took the stand to testify that, in her capacity as a public school psychologist, she had conducted a series of psychometric tests to determine Remus' mental capacity. She testified that Remus' mental capabilities were that of an average adult and that in some tests he even dropped to that of a ten year old boy, although she did point out that he might do better under more normal circumstances. During her testimony, Remus sat quietly and at times openly grinned at the jurors, many of whom smiled back.

Elston immediatel asked Dr, Fernald:"Didn't Mr. Remus tell you he was charged with murder in the first degree, and that he didn't have time to be bothered with such nonsense?" "Not exacctly in those words," the psychologist answered, "but words to that effect."

Then Elston launched into his cross-examination with the obvious intent of picturing the tests used by Dr. Fernald as ridiculous and being closer to a joke than a scientific examination. He detailed each test, showing what Remus was asked to do and then how well he did on each task. He even had Dr. Fernald take some of the tests. He claimed that as part of one of the tests Remus was asked to draw pictures of some articles which he was shown briefly. Dr. Fernald testified that Remus failed this test, and Elston intimated that perhaps he may have failed it because he had never drawn anything in his life. Dr. Fernald agreed that Remus had told her this at the time and admitted that it was possible for a man to be an artist and not be intelligent or to be intelligent and not be an artist. Elston then launched enthusiastically into a demonstration of one of the tests which had Remus and a number of the spectators in giggling fits and which drew a warning from Sheriff Anderson, who eventually had to ask for order. Even some of the jurors could not refrain from laughing.

Dr. Baber, Superintendent of the Longview State Hospital for the Insane, took the stand to answer much the same questions as were put to Dr Wolfstein. He too answered "yes" to each of the three questions relating to the tests for insanity, and he too testified that Remus was sane at the time he shot his wife. His cross-examination began a few minutes before court was recessed and a feeling of tense excitement shot through the room as Remus stood up to question him. In an ironic situation, a man who was claiming that he was insane up until very recently was cross-examining an expert on the subject of insanity.

Remus began by getting Dr. Baber to admit that doctors often disagreed on the definition of insanity. Remus then asked the doctor to tell the jury what his own definition was. "We must first define what sanity is," Dr. Baber replied. Remus then asked if sanity was not just "the reverse of insanity?" Dr. Baber conceded that this was essentially true, and then he defined insanity as being "any prolonged deviation from the normal method of thinking or action." Remus then asked him if it was not true then that insanity was merely "an abnormal condition of the mind?" When Dr. Baber replied that this was not necessarily true, Remus asked him to cite one example, if he could, of a situation where "an abnormal condition of the mind was not insanity." The doctor was considering his answer to this when Judge Shook interrupted and stated that he would have to answer the question the following morning as it was time to adjourn for the day.

However, before Judge Shook could adjourn the Court, Remus offered a 109 page (33,000 word) hypothetical question that he wished to ask the alienists the following day, and he requested permission to give copies to the jurors, the Judge and the prosecuting attorneys so that they could familiarize themselves with the contents. He also requested that he be given approximately three hours in Court the following morning to devote to the question. Judge Shook pointed out that it would be up to him to decide whether the question could be introduced and said that he would consider it that evening and give his ruling the following morning.

SATURDAY, DECEMBER 17TH

When Dr. Baber returned to the witness stand in the morning, Remus tried to get him to recognize Kraft-Ebbing and Caesar Lombroso as experts in the field of mental disorders . Dr. Baber refused to do so and pointed out that their books were published many years ago, (the most recent was published in 1905) and medical opinion had changed since then. Remus asserted that he was simply attempting to show just how wide the gap of medical opinion was when it came to the subject of insanity, and he succeeded when Dr. Baber admitted that he had read approximately twenty-five different texts all written by so-called authorities on the subject of insanity, and which gave as many different definitions of insanity. Dr. Baber also claimed that he did not like to use the terms "insanity" or "lunacy" because they were too vague. He stated that instead of using one umbrella term, it was becoming more a sign of good practice to use specific terms for different areas of mental illness.

Pressed to tell what his opinion of insanity was, Dr. Baber launched into a twenty minute speech during which he described various types of mental disturbances, including "mania," a condition Remus claimed to be suffering from when he shot his wife and which the doctor described as "depressive maniacal psychoses." Remus asked him at one stage if he did not recognize "irresistible impulses" as being a condition of insanity, but the doctor replied that there was no way of determining whether an impulse was irresistible or not, and he claimed that because of this he did not recognize the term at all. Eventually Judge Shook interrupted this section of the examination and requested that Remus keep the interrogation within a reasonable time framework.

The third and final alienist, Dr. Charles Kiely, Assistant Professor of Neurology at the University of Cincinnati and Neurologist at the Cincinnati General Hospital, took the stand after Dr. Baber and he too asserted that Remus was sane at that moment and was sane when he shot his wife. He was also questioned about the Remus' outburst in Court while Harry Truesdale was testifying, and he asserted that there was no evidence of insanity in that or the other outbursts. He claimed that they were simply a "combination of fear and rage."

Dr. Kiely's examination took the court till noon when he was allowed to step down, and Taft rose and announced once again that the State rested its case. Elston followed suit for the defense. Elston and Taft then addressed the Court concerning the charges which Judge Shook would present to the jurors before sending them out to deliberate. In a murder case, the Judge could charge the jury to come out with one of a number of verdicts: First Degree murder without mercy, which carried a death sentence; First Degree murder with mercy, which carried a life sentence with no recourse to a pardon; Second Degree Murder, which also carried a life sentence, but which offered a chance of a pardon; Manslaughter, which carried a more flexible jail sentence which could run from anywhere between one year to twenty years. Finally, there would be a "Not guilty" option. The prosecution insisted that since Remus had admitted that he killed his wife, this option could not be presented. If it were, it would be synonymous with a verdict of justifiable homicide, which was not recognized by the State of Ohio.

The defense noted that the United States Supreme Court had ruled that no Judge had the jurisdiction to charge a jury to find a defendant guilty of any crime, and that by not giving the option of a straight acquittal the Judge would be violating this ruling. He would essentially be usurping the authority of the jury. The only other option open to Judge Shook would be to include a charge of "not guilty on sole grounds of insanity." If the jury reached this verdict, Remus would be bound over for an insanity hearing. If found insane, he would be sent to a hospital for the insane until it could be proven that he was sane enough to re-enter society. If he was found to be sane, he would walk free, and three alienists had just sworn under oath that Remus was sane.

Taft argued for the exclusion of the "Not guilty" verdict, reminding the Court that Remus had admitted his guilt, and that should the jury somehow find him not guilty, he would escape any punishment. Taft gave, as precedents, two Ohio murder cases where the not guilty verdict was omitted and the decision was upheld both times by the upper Courts. Then Elston charged that the jurors should not be obligated to make a decision about Remus' sanity on the testimony of the alienists, but should be allowed to consider all the testimony provided. He also charged that Remus should be acquitted if the prosecution could not prove, beyond a reasonable doubt, that a murder had been committed, and he pointed out that it was the burden of the State to prove that Remus was guilty and not the burden of the defense to prove that he was innocent. Remus had previously declared that leaving out the not guilty option was an infringement of his constitutional rights as incorporated in our bill of rights by our forefathers, which permits men charged with crime to have a fair trial. Remus' answer to Taft's argument was the suggestion that he return to law school.

Judge Shook agreed to take these points into consideration when he charged the jury, but made it clear that once he made his mind up, he would not accept any further arguments on the subject. Each side now had four hours in which to present their closing arguments, but with only two and a half hours left to the day's session, it was decided that they would split the time in half, and each present their introduction. Judge Shook then ruled that neither side should refer to the subject of a direct acquittal until he had decided whether or not to include this in the charges.

Taft opened the State's final argument by insisting that Remus had committed "the most atrocious murder in the history of Cincinnati" when he killed his wife to stop her from revealing the extent of his assets during the divorce hearing set for that fatal morning. Remus saw it was finally coming to a showdown," he told the jury. "Conners said the Government was asking Remus for $10,000,000 in taxes. We know they were after at least $150,000. The government was looking for the property and Imogene knew too much, and she was going to talk. Remus knew that and he shut her mouth in the only way he knew how. He shot her. The whole course of his history in Cincinnati was leading up to that day."

Then Taft described Remus as an arrogant man with a "swelled head," who enjoyed seeing his face in the newspapers and who on purpose courted the press. "Remus was a fine publicity hound," he said. "You saw him here turning around and talking to the newspaper reporters." He also depicted him as a crooked coward, a"squealer" and a "rat," pointing out that he had turned against the men he had bribed in Atlanta and the men he had dealt with in St. Louis during the Jack Daniels operation. He alluded to the defense claims that Remus was afraid that Dodge and Mrs. Remus would attempt to kill him in St. Louis during the Jack Daniels case. "Remus wasn't afraid of that," he proclaimed, stating that Remus was actually afraid of the Egan's Rats gang who had been involved in the Jack Daniels conspiracy. "Those were tough babies, and Remus had snitched on their associates. Of course Remus was afraid." Taft also claimed that Remus was afraid to take the witness stand because "he knew what we would have done to him." Then he implored the jurors not to be influenced by Remus' theatrics. He predicted that when Remus would address the jury , he "will throw a fit in front of you, go down on his knees, maybe throw himself into a faint. He certainly will weep, but he wouldn't let the State cross-examine him, for he knew it would hang him."

Taft then characterized Imogene Remus as just the opposite of her husband, as a "little woman" who was cheated by the man she loved, but who stood up for herself when threatened by him, a woman who "knew too much" and died because of it. Taft charged that "on October 6 George Remus was facing a showdown, and rather than face it, he killed her."

Taft then referred to Franklin Dodge as the "most famous co-respondent in the United States, perhaps in the world." He claimed that Remus had purposely set out to sully his name by repeatedly accusing him of seducing Mrs. Remus and conspiring with her to steal his property and deport him. "Is there a better story than the wife of the King of Bootleggers linked up with the ace of the Prohibition department?" Taft claimed that Dodge had been greatly wronged and pointed out that he could not even be put on the stand to defend himself because the evidence against him was purely hearsay. "There's only one statement of fact in evidence about misconduct between Dodge and Mrs. Remus," Taft pointed out, "only one to which Dodge could have come on stand to deny, and that was from John S. Berger, and you know that was denied by others."

Then Taft insisted that there was only one verdict possible in this case and that was murder in the first degree with a sentence of death by electrocution. "There never was a case where the defendant was so clearly guilty of cold-blooded, calaculated, ruthless murder than this. You can only find him guilty of first degree murder and you can show him no mercy." He urged the jury not to find Remus not guilty by means of insanity. In closing he explained that he was asking for the death penalty because "There will be just one time when the people of the State of Ohio will be safe from George Remus and that is when he is dead."

When Elston had the floor, he attacked the prosecution's theory that Remus had killed his wife because she knew too much, arguing that this was a theory that they had latched onto after their "conspiracy" theory fell apart. "What was she going to tell that he was afraid of?" he asked, charging that the entire theory that she was going to tell of his hidden assets was simply a case of the prosecution clutching at a straw as they drowned. He implied that this "showdown" theory was just as flimsy as the previous one. "Blanche Watson, who had no stain on her name, has been branded a murderess," he declared, stating that George Conners and George Klug were also not murderers, even though they spent some time in Atlanta on prohibition related charges. "Where is one solitary, scintilla of evidence in the case to brand them as murderers?" he asked. "I don't think there was ever made in this courtroom or in any other Court any accusation that was less justified than that one." He claimed that the prosecution had conceived the conspiracy theory because they did not have a case without it. "If they had as a strong a case as they said they had, there would have been no necessity for bringing in all these people."

Elston then depicted Remus as a kind and generous husband who not only attempted a reconciliation with his wife, but who also was always courteous to her at their various settlement conferences, even though he knew the truth about her and Franklin Dodge. Elston described Mrs. Remus as a conniving, vicious woman who used her husband and then left him while he was still in prison. "When Remus came to Cincinnati to engage in the bootlegging business, his wife came with him," Elston pointed out. "He made money, and she knew how he made it. She enjoyed it luxuriously. She never said 'George Remus, I don't want that money - you made it bootlegging'." He then attacked Mrs. Remus' family for condemning Remus when they had also lived off his money in full knowledge of where it came from. He noted that Remus trusted his wife implicitly and pointed to the fact that he had given her power of attorney over his property while he was in Atlanta, a privilege which she had openly abused. "They said she had no money. She couldn't be travelling all over the United States, taking Ruth Remus, Mrs. Campbell and Mrs. Brown along on nothing."

Continuing to attack the prosecution's image of Mrs. Remus, he declared: "They say she was not a publicity hound. If she was doing all the things the people said she was doing, I don't wonder that she shunned publicity." Then he challenged Taft's statement that Dodge had not been called as a witness because there was nothing substantial for him to deny by holding up a contract that had been introduced as evidence during the trial. He maintained that it showed Dodge's signature on an agreement to sell whiskey certificates, and this was far from hearsay. "They try to make Franklin L. Dodge Jr. look like an eminent gentleman," he declared, "but I tell you that if it had not been for Franklin Dodge, George Remus would not be here charged with murder and you would not be here."

Elston then noted that it was the County Prosecutor who first thought that Remus might be insane. It was he who sent a Probate Court alienist to the police station on October 6th to examine Remus. He pointed out that Dr. Kendig, who conducted the examination, was not called to the stand by the prosecution, the only logical deduction for that being that he considered Remus to be insane. Basler interrupted Elston at this junction to announce that they would introduce Dr. Kendig's report now if they wished. "You had your opportunity - don't pull that stuff now," Elston replied.

Throughout his closing argument, Elston spoke eloquently, presenting his arguments logically and forcefully. On a number of occasions his comments drew murmurs of approval from the spectators, and Judge Shook threatened to clear the spectators' gallery if order was not maintained.

When Court was adjourned, both sides still had over two hours left in which to present their statements to the jury. After watching Remus' antics throughout the five weeks of the trial, the spectators were convinced that his final plea to the jury would be a memorable occasion.

That weekend reporters tried in vain to elicit from Remus his plans for conducting his final argument. He merely told them that it would be one of the finest closing arguments of his career, and discussed with them the similarity of his case with that of William Ellis whom he had represented in Chicago under a plea of "temporary insanity." The marked difference between that case and this one, he pointed out, was that "the Ellis case involved an atrocious killing." He concluded his interview with the reporters with the question: "Fancy yourself in prison, locked behind the bars and for months and months knowing that the woman to whom you had given everything in life, your very soul, was in the arms of another man. Wouldn't it drive you to madness? Wouldn't it?"

Over the week-end Franklin Dodge issued the following statement to the press: "I have been under subpoena for over nineteen days, waiting to be called to testify in the case of the State versus Remus. The subpoena was issued by the defense. Why they have failed to call me, in view of all their repeated assertions regarding my conduct, about which they knew I would have no hesitancy in speaking the truth to anyone, anywhere and at any time, I fail utterly to understand. Why the State has not used me is very easy to understand, since in all the testimony produced by the defense there has not been a single syllable of direct testimony of any kind against me. On the contrary, whenever my name was mentioned it has been in the vaguest sort of hearsay and round-about-testimony."

Referring to Remus' constant reference to him in the press and in the Courtroom, Dodge stated further that "the widespread publicity which Remus has been able to get to disseminate this gossip, hearsay and third-hand testimony has made many people unthinkingly believe that it was true. Thinking people do not stoop to gossip, and now Remus has had a chance to prove his statements, he has failed utterly." In conclusion, the statement read; "It is a disappointment to me not to have been called so that the truth of the situation might have been known," and then went on to condemn Remus as violently as Remus had condemned him.

Ruth Remus left Cincinnati over the weekend to attend the funeral of her blood father in Milwaukee, Wisconsin, but before she left she announced that she would be initiating proceedings to have her adoption by Remus legally abolished and would be changing her surname back to Holmes. She declared that she wouldn't want to bear the name of Remus any longer.

MONDAY, DECEMBER 19TH

The largest crowd of spectators since the Remus trial began jammed the corridors of the Courthouse, and only a few managed to get into the "standing room only" Courtroom. They were an unruly and noisy crowd, and Judge Shook eventually ordered that the corridors be cleared and that no more spectators would be allowed into the Courtroom, even if someone left.

Charles Elston opened the morning session with a scathing attack on Franklin Dodge. Referring to him, in true Remus-like fashion, as "the dirty rotten skunk" and "that filthy louse," Elston claimed that he did not take the stand "because he didn't dare testify. There were too many things for him to deny." Elston then mentioned the accusations that had been made against Dodge that he failed to deny. These included the incident in the lobby at the Claypool Hotel and Dodge's hiding behind his car at the Remus' mansion to not be recognized by Mueller, the caretaker. "Why did he hide? Would any of you jurors hide up in the prosecutors office like Dodge has been doing all during the course of the trial and not take the stand and deny all these accusations? No red-blooded American would stand by and have his character besmirched like that without taking the stand on his own behalf. Only a reprobate like Dodge would stand for a thing like that."

Then Elston explained that Remus did not testify because there was nothing he could add to the testimony already given. "Remus' testimony would only have been cumulative," he declared, adding that if he had taken the stand his testimony on the Jack Daniels case alone would have kept them there until New Years Eve. Pointing out that their defense was insanity, he declared that he did not know of one case where a defendant who pleaded insanity was put on the stand.

Elston then defended Remus' character. He insisted that Remus had never been unfaithful to his wife as she had been to him, and he challenged the prosecution to show proof of "one iota of infidelity." He charged that if there was any such evidence in the divorce depositions, which the prosecution had intimated there was, they would have "shouted it from the housetops." That they had not even pushed strongly for the introduction of the depositions was proof enough that they contained nothing of importance.

"They call Remus a publicity hound,"" Elston he declared. "I haven't seen the prosecutors shrink from publicity. They answered every question very kindly that was put to them by newspaper men." He further asserted that the claim that Remus sought publicity was an attempt by them to create prejudice against the defendant. He then attacked the alienists' report, declaring that it was only based on scientific experimentation which was often wrong, and he referred to the psychometric tests as "rot and foolishness." "You jurors do not need alienists to make up your minds," he insisted. As to the prosecution's theory that Remus shot his wife because it had come down to a "showdown," he charged that there was no evidence whatsoever to support this claim, and if the prosecution really believed in it so strongly, they would have presented it at the beginning of the trial, instead of proceeding with the almost farcical conspiracy theory. He argued that there was no "showdown" because the government had already questioned Mrs. Remus when she had visited the Internal Revenue offices shortly before October 6th, and Remus was aware of this.

Next Elston boldly asserted that there was indeed a motive for the killing, It was Remus' insanity, brought on by his wife's infidelity. Elston described how Imogene Remus and Dodge had conspired to keep Remus in jail while they stole his property and planned his deportation. "They even went so far as to take him from the great land of the free and the home of the brave and send him back to Germany "with nothing but a little bundle over his back." In contrast Elston depicted Remus as the wronged man sitting in jail receiving affectionate letters from his wife while she was running around with another man, and even when he learned the truth, he hoped for a reconciliation."Never in history or fiction will there be found another Imogene Remus, and never in the world will there be found another sewer rat like Franklin Dodge." "Was there ever a woman who had less reason for doing it than Imogene Remus? And yet they say he was in a normal state of mind on October 6th when he had the faith of a little child." Referring to Taft's statement to the jury that "there never was a clearer first degree murder case than this one," Elston smiled and then informed the jurors that he had come against the County prosecutor in many cases "and he says the same thing every time."

Elston then informed the jury that the prosecution wanted them to convict Remus ""on the nasty, dirty insinuations that have been made." This brought an objection from Taft. Judge Shook replied that the defense was prone to using "somewhat vigorous" language, and he instructed the jury that they should not consider these kinds of statements made during the closing arguments as factual evidence. They should see them for the emotional appeals that they were. Finally, standing in front of the jury Elston made his appeal for clemency. "Turn him loose for Christmas, that time when there's peace on earth and good will to men. Bring a peace of mind to the man who has suffered the tortures of hell for more than two years. Let George Remus be judged in the spirit of peace on earth and good will to men. I know then you will have righted the greatest wrong that has ever been done to any man."

When Elston finished, Remus stood up; dressed in a light grey suit with sprig of holly in his label, clutching an armful of papers and a number of law books, he slowly approached the jurors enclosure. Remus addressed the jury in a slow, deliberate voice which emphasized the key words in each sentence. "Here before you stands Remus, the lawyer. In the chair there," he continued, motioning to the chair he had recently occupied, "sits Remus, the defendant, charged with murder. The eyes of the whole civilized world have been turned on this case and on George Remus, the murderer of his wife." Remus then turned to Judge Shook and, holding himself in an almost military fashion, thanked him for the fairness with which he had conducted the trial, and turning to the jurors, he thanked them too for the time they had given away from their families.

After these formalities he launched into a summary of Dr. Baber's testimony, concentrating on the admission that there were a number of different definitions and opinions on the subject of insanity. "Apply your common sense reasoning"" he declared. "When emotions register in the cranium or brain cells, if they cause an emotion - that's what insanity is. It is nothing more than an abnormal condition of the mind. When a crime, under these circumstances is committed, there is an abnormal condition of the mind."

Remus then launched into a laudatory speech about George Conners, his closest friend and right hand man, whom he referred to as "so noble and beautiful a character." In contrast, he denounced Franklin Dodge, his personal nemesis, referring to him as:"That ace among dry agents, that deuce among his fellow men," and called him a "moral leper" and "human parasite.". This last comment drew a strong objection from Assistant Prosecutor Basler, and Remus was warned about using such phraseology. In response, Remus turned to the jury and agreed that at times he did get a little emotional and a little excited. "But," he exhorted, "who wouldn't in my place?" He declared that he had been in nine jails since 1922 and then re-iterated his declaration that "not for all the money in the universe" would he do anything that might result in him spending any more time in jail. After this statement Court was adjourned for the noon recess.

In the afternoon, Remus still had an hour in which to finish his statement. Gesticulating madly with his arms to convey his meaning, he walked up and down in front of the jury, sometimes raising his voice to make a point and sometimes whispering for effect, but there was no fainting and no weeping as Taft had predicted and which the spectators had hoped to see. Remus continued as he had begun, rambling from one subject to another, some only remotely connected to the immediate trial, and hardly even mentioning the shooting for which he was on trial.

On more than one occasion Judge Shook had to warn him to stay within the subject matter. The prosecutors also voiced objections, most of which were sustained, and most of which brought angry retorts or denunciations from Remus, who would leap towards the prosecution desk to deliver his salvos. This brought a reprimand from Judge Shook, who pointed out, as he had done before, that the prosecutors were not the ones on trial.

Undetered, Remus now attacked Taft, who had asked the jury whether they would want Remus as a neighbor, implying that he was an unsavory character, not fit to live in decent society. "This defendant," he declared, "started in life at $5 a month, and he may have contaminated his neighbors. I would gladly lay down my life today for one drop of the blood which flows in the veins of your prosecutor, son of that noble statesman, the Chief Justice of the United States, and a former President, but ladies and men of the jury, we could not all be born with a golden spoon in our mouths like Charles P. Taft the second." When the Prosecutor objected to this kind of comment, Remus launched into a speech on how he had given his full support to Taft's father when he ran for President, before rambling off on the subject of prohibition.

Remus denounced the Volstead Act, calling it "one of the greatest criminal and legal abortions of all time." He repeated his claim that he never sold bad liquor, something which he considered to be an honorable deed in a business run by so many criminal bootleggers who cheated their customers. "This prohibition law," he declared, "is making hypocrites out of our Judges, our prosecutors and our citizens as well." Judge Shook warned him about straying into the area of prohibition, but Remus simply insisted that if it wasn't for the prohibition laws he would not be there on trial for murder. This statement was stricken from the record, however, after an objection from the prosecution. But Remus insisted on returning to the subject again, and referred to himself as a martyr to the drinking cause, and this time Judge Shook stopped him and warned him that the Volstead Act and the prohibition laws were not part of the trial and he should refrain from discussing them.

Next, Remus defended his decision not to take the witness stand in own defense by informing the jury that if he had testified they would have been kept in the Courtroom for at least another ten days, " and the names of 200 to 400 respectable men and women would have been dragged inevitably into the Remus case.".

Franklin Dodge was Remus next target. Pacing up and down in front of the jury Remus declaimed: "Oh1 That social leper, that contemptible mass of human nothingness that was kicked out of the Department of Justice, who used his badge as an agent of the United States Government to enter my home and debauch my wife." When Taft objected to Remus' violent denunciation of Dodge, Remus quickly retorted: "Are you protecting that character, Mr. Taft?" Basler quickly objected, asserting that Remus knew that Dodge resigned, and he seemed intent on arguing the point until Judge Shook put a stop to it by telling Remus that the time allocated to him had run out, but that he was prepared to give him another half an hour because of all the time wasted with objections and Court rulings.

Remus chose not to waste his time by continuing the argument with Basler, and he was about to change the subject when Judge Shook suddenly got up and left the Courtroom with his hands pressed against his chest, gesturing the alienists to follow him. He had not been feeling well, and it was feared that he might be having a heart attack. The bailiffs quickly ushered the jury out of the courtroom, and everyone waited to learn what had happened. Fifteen minutes later Judge Shook returned to the Courtroom and announced that he had simply suffered an attack of indigestion. The jury was returned, and Remus continued his closing argument.

Once again Remus attacked Franklin Dodge, describing how he and Imogene Remus had taken everything he owned. As proof ,he pulled back the sleeves to his coat to reveal his shirt sleeves and the cuffs adorned with "penny cuff buttons." Then he discussed the conspiracy theory that the prosecution had proposed at the outset of the trial, but which they had failed to prove. He admitted that he shot his wife, but he pointed out that he did it in broad daylight during the morning rush hour traffic and argued that this could hardly have been the actions of a man who had sat down with a group of people and planned his wife's killing. He argued that any person who would kill another person while a crowd watched him had to be crazy.

Then, standing in front of the thirteen men and woman who had listened to his every word, his hands visibly shaking, his face red from his physical exertions and his voice hoarse, he exclaimed: "I have suffered tortures of living hell for two years. I am not asking for mercy, but justice."

Remus' closed his address to the jury in a characteristic, dramatic fashion: "The defendant does not desire any sympathy or compassion in any shape or form whatsoever. If you, who have a higher power than the President of the United States in this case feel that the defendant should go to the electric chair, do not flinch. The defendant will not flinch. The defendant stands before you in defense of his honor and the sanctity of his home.The defendant is on trial for that. If that is a crime, punish him. As you ponder on your duty bear in mind that which is most sacred is your home and your family." Remus paused for a few seconds and in a voice just above a whisper said: "I thank you. Merry Christmas to you."

The prosecution split their time equally between Basler and Sibbald. Basler, who opened, immediately attacked Remus for not taking the witness stand. "Did Remus take the stand - the coward?" he asked.,Then he accused Remus of being a "snitch," a man who purposely turned on his criminal friends and associates. He taunted Elston by offering to introduce Dr. Kendig's report, which Elston had mentioned on the previous Saturday, but Elston simply pointed out that he could not introduce it now as it constituted new evidence, and Dr. Kendig could not be put on the stand to be cross-examined. Judge Shook agreed.

Basler then set out to impeach Conners as a witness by agreeing with Remus' assertion that Conners was loyal to him. He pointed out that when Remus was adamant that he was not insane, Conners agreed with him, and when Remus changed his mind and decided to plead insanity, Conners also agreed with him. "That's loyalty, isn't it?" he asked. To back up this accusation, Basler read a portion of Conners' Grand Jury testimony in which he insisted that Remus was sane. This brought an objection from a very hoarse Remus, who charged that if Basler was going to read part of the testimony, then he should read all of it, but Judge Shook interrupted the objection and informed him that Ohio law did not necessitate the reading of the entire transcript. Basler then continued his reading, but Remus again protested, and Basler turned on Remus and asked him to stop interrupting. In marked contrast to his normal behavior, Remus apologized and sat back in his chair as if resolved not to move from it again.

John Berger was Basler's next target. The Assistant Prosecutor referred to the man as a "wretch." Remus immediately jumped up and objected to this description of his witness, but Judge Shook was not sympathetic. "Both sides have indulged in some epithets that have been shocking to the Court and no doubt to the jury," he stated, but Basler changed his description to that of "miserable." He launched an all-out attack on the testimony of the man who had claimed to be the star witness, but who the prosecution felt was the star perjurer. Referring to Berger's statements about seeing Mrs. Remus and Franklin Dodge in the Claypool Hotel in Indianapolis in a state of almost total nudity, Basler sarcastically commented that Mrs. Remus must have removed all her clothing and just waited for Berger to enter the room.

Basler then called attention to the fact that Remus was still in business as was evidenced by his maintaining a suite at the Sinton hotel, which he used as offices, and his constant references to Blanche Watson and George Conners as his secretaries, but that no one knew just what his business was,. a very strange set of affairs. Basler was still addressing the jury when Judge Shook adjourned Court for the day. He would be given time to finish in the morning before handing over to Walter Sibbald for the close.

TUESDAY, DECEMBER 20TH

Assistant Prosecutor Basler summarized the arguments presented by the defense and then asked the jurors to see beyond them and concentrate on the facts. "What's this all about? Why it's about a cold blooded murder: the murder of Mrs. Remus and how he lay in wait for her.The issue in this case is murder, and don't forget it. He grabbed that warm, pulsating, human being and shot her down in cold blood." Basler insisted that the shooting was the only issue at stake, and it was a case of cold-blooded murder and nothing else, and the prosecution had proven this beyond a doubt.

Then to undermine Remus' popularity in Cincinnati, Basler read an excerpt from a letter Remus wrote to his daughter in which he referred to Cincinnati as being an overgrown village and referred to its citizens as very bigoted and so selfish that they did not know where justice lays.

Next Basler attacked the defense's plea of insanity, declaring that just because the defendant claimed that he was insane, be should not escape punishment. "If your place was robbed Mr. Trautman," he asked one of the jurors, "would you rush into the prosecutor's office and say, 'oh, don't prosecute, that man's insane'?" He appealed to the jury to look beyond the insanity plea, claiming that it was "just an excuse to get before this jury the unwritten-law defense, which the law of Ohio does not recognize." "The issue in this case is murder," he insisted, "and don't forget it." Basler also mentioned the evidence that had been given through people like Conners to the way Remus threw fits and flew into rages which the defense interpreted as periods of insanity, but which the prosecution asserted was simply a case of temper tantrums. "Remus was the little boy who had to have his own way or he got mad and red in the head," he said.

Basler then described Remus' fit in the Courtroom on December 7th when Harry Truesdale was testifying. Although the jury had been excluded from the Courtroom for most of the outburst, they had learned about it through the testimony of the alienists. Basler declared that the fit was nothing but an act. "Ever see an insane person apologize to the Court and announce beforehand that he was going to throw a fit?" he asked. "I brand that fit a fake, an absolute fake, but no more a fake than the entire defense has been." Referring to the fact that Remus was claiming to be insane at the time of the murder but to be perfectly sane at the present time, Basler stated it was impossible. "There is no short cure for insanity," he asserted.

The Assistant Prosecutor then referred to Remus' prior criminal activities and maintained that the entire trial had been a struggle between the criminal elements and decent society. He depicted Remus' three main witnesses, Conners, Berger and Rogers as "three horsemen who galloped in to tell dirty stories to Remus just to see him get red and rave," and he pictured Remus' fall from decent society , remarking: "Remus deliberately stepped into this filth."

Next Basler declared that the defense's accusations against Mrs. Remus and Franklin Dodge were unfounded. He insisted that Remus had never found them together in any kind of compromising situation and that all the information presented was hearsay. Basler argued that "even if she were wrong he had no right to shoot down a defenseless person." In closing, Basler implored the jury: "If you want to do right by your fellow citizens and churchgoers, you will come back after you have deliberated and say: 'He is guilty--he must die.'"

Assistant Prosecutor Walter Sibbald started his closing argument by reading to the jury excerpts from a letter which had been introduced into the Congressional Record and which indicated that Remus' complaints against Franklin Dodge had been looked into by the Justice Department, but that no evidence could be found to substantiate his claims. Remus interrupted his reading, however, to exclaim that "every statement is a lie." Sibbald objected to the interruption, and Remus apologized, but Sibbald, still angry, insisted that "nobody is going to sit here and say that I lie." Elston then came to the support of his co-counsel and explained that Remus had been speaking about the statements contained in the letter, not about statements made by Sibbald. Sibbald looked as though he was about to continue the argument, but Judge Shook called for order and instructed him to continue with his closing argument.

Once again Sibbald charged that Remus had deliberately used the press to sully Mrs. Remus' name prior to the shooting and throughout the trial. He admitted that she might not have been an angel . "She couldn't be George Remus' wife and be that," he said. "She was Queen of the Bootleggers, and anything she did, like anything Remus did, was news, and the newspapers ate it up. They had the King of the Bootleggers, the Queen of the Bootleggers and the ace of the prohibition forces." He contended that Remus could have fed them any bit of gossip about his wife and Dodge and they would have pounced on it as the truth. As to Remus' claim that he was a model husband who was never unfaithful and never deserved the treatment he got from his wife, Sibbald pointed out that his first wife had divorced him on grounds of cruelty, and that there was plenty of evidence that he treated his second wife even more cruelly. He then referred to the testimony given by a number of State witnesses who said that Mrs. Remus would leave the penitentiary crying after visiting her husband, and that, on at least one occasion, the these tears were result of the physical abuse that she had received from her husband, who struck her and falsely accused her.

Sibbald then launched an attack on the testimony of Harry Truesdale. He asked whether Mrs. Remus would have offered a person $10,000 to kill her husband and then gone out to Hamilton herself to kill him? He also pointed out that Truesdale's testimony was inconsistent with other testimony about what happened the night before the shooting. Truesdale testified that he went to the Sinton Hotel at about 4 or 4.30 pm to tell Remus about the plot to kill him, but August Bruck testified that he was with Remus at the hotel between 4.pm and 8 pm, when he left to catch his train. Yet he did not see Truesdale. Neither did he see George Conners or George Klug there, but Klug testified that he met Remus and Conners at the hotel soon after 5.pm. to pick up the keys to the car. He also called attention to the defense's failure to present witnesses to prove that Remus was ready for his Divorce Court hearing.This added weight to the prosecution's claim that he intended to kill his wife before the hearing. He ended with an impassioned plea to the jury to find Remus guilty of first degree murder.

All that remained now was for Judge Shook to present the charges to the jury and then send them out for their deliberations. He gave the jury five possible verdicts: First Degree Murder without mercy; First Degree Murder with mercy; Second Degree Murder; Manslaughter; and Not Guilty on the grounds of insanity. He also released a six page statement regarding his decision not to give the option of a straight acquittal verdict. This statement was not seen by the jurors.

In this statement Judge Shook gave six conditions for a killing to be legally justified: Self defense; accidental death; Insanity; legal execution of a criminal by officers of the law; death at the hands of military personal acting under proper command; death at the hands of a policeman in the course of duty. He then pointed out that both Remus and Elston had gone on record to admit that Remus had killed his wife and further testimony showed that he had intended to kill Franklin Dodge at the same time. He also stated that, according to the testimony, Remus had told officers that he had killed his wife as a matter of principle. The Judge then took cognizance of the arguments made by both sides for special charges and he took account of the fact that the defense had entered a plea of insanity. He further pointed out that if Remus felt that he was in some sort of "unfortunate position," it was through "reason of his own conduct." As a result of two days of deliberation he finally stated that "the Court, upon careful consideration, is brought to the inevitable conclusion that the defendant is entitled to a verdict of not guilty solely on the grounds of insanity."

In presenting the charges to the jury he mentioned the alienists report on Remus' insanity and instructed them to consider it along with the rest of the testimony if they felt that they could not accept the results enclosed solely in the report. He outlined the various legal rules and tests which were recognized as constituting a state of insanity and instructed the jurors that if they "should find that the defendant has proved by a preponderance of the evidence that he was insane at the time he shot and killed his wife," then it would be their duty to find him not guilty on the grounds of insanity. He explained to them that he had allowed a lot of evidence into the trial that dealt with relations between Mrs. Remus and Franklin Dodge, reminding the jurors that some of the stories told may have been false and that he had only allowed this to show how the stories affected Remus' mind. He instructed them to take note of this when making their decision. He explained that the stories told presented no evidence for any case of justification, pointing out that the law did not recognize the right of one person to take the life of another "because the latter may be of bad moral character." Judge Shook then dismissed the unneeded thirteenth juror.

In conclusion, he had a short conference with the attorneys from both sides during which they discussed the exceptions to the charges and had them dictated to the stenographer for entry in the Court record. At 1 p.m. Judge Shook sent the jury to the deliberation room with the instruction that if they had not reached a decision within fifteen minutes, they should return to the Courtroom so that the noon adjournment could be called. When the fifteen minutes were up, the jurors returned to the Courtroom and announced that they had not reached a decision. They were then given one and a half hours for lunch, after which they were instructed to return to the deliberation room.

At five minutes to three the jurors knocked on the door of the jury room to signal that they had reached a decision. Since the jurors had one and a half hours for lunch, this left under half an hour in which to deliberate upon the verdict. One juror later claimed that they had reached their verdict in ten minutes. Since the jury took such a short time to reach their decision, it took over an hour for the bailiffs to find all the attorneys and Court officials before the verdict could be read.

When the jury returned to the Courtroom, they were wearing sprigs of holly and some of them were openly smiling. Remus sat at his desk, white faced and taut, sucking nervously on one arm of his horn-rimmed glasses. Deputy Sheriff Stagnaro then read the jurors roll, and each juror answered to his or her name. Then Judge Shook leaned forward at his desk and instructed the foreman to give the verdict to the Clerk of the Court. Harry G. Byrd rose and handed over the sealed envelope which contained the crucial decision. Turning to the hushed courtroom, Sherman Palmer, the Clerk, opened the envelope and drew out the piece of paper on which was written:

> "We the jury, on the issue joined, find the defendant not guilty of murder, as he stands charged in the indictment, on the sole ground of insanity."

Remus, who had been peering over Elston's shoulder while the verdict was read out, collapsed in his chair and let out his breath in a sigh of relief, while the color slowly returned to his face. The courtroom remained silent for a few minutes while the verdict sunk in, and then the spectators started cheering, shouting and screaming as the baliffs sought in vain to restore order. Remus, now in tears, cried out "thank you, thank you." As the Sherrif's deputies led him out of the Courtroom, Remus cried out:"I wanted American justice and I thank you for it."

As Remus left the Courtroom, many of his friends and family hurried into the small side corridor through which they knew he would have to pass on way to the elevator which would take him back to his cell two floors up. They cheered him with enthusiasm. As he entered the elevator and the steel gates began to close, he gripped the bars and shouted out: "I was prevented this morning from saying what I thought about the judge not including a verdict of straight acquittal, but now I can say it. That was the first time such a charge ever was made in an American court of law. But for that I am sure right now I would be a free man."

The crowd of people gathered in the main corridor were informed of the verdict by a reporter. They started chanting: "Not guilty-hurray! Not guilty-hurray!" Back in the Courtroom Judge Shook vainly tried to restore order. Finally, he saw to it that the jury was led out, and then he left the Courtroom. En masse the spectators jumped up, cheering and pushing their way forward trying to reach Elston to congratulate him. They gathered round him pumping his hand while a young girl flung her arms around him and kissed him. Mrs. Ryerson, Remus' sister, rushed to Elston's side and burst into tears as she shook his hand and expressed her gratitude. Meanwhile, in the jury room John T. Rogers, the St. Louis reporter, was being congratulated by the jurors on his testimony.

While Elston fought off enthusiastic spectators, Remus was being beseiged by people who wanted to congratulate the man whose very life had been in jeopardy just a few minutes earlier. Some of the jurors rushed up to Remus' cell as soon as they finished congratulating Rogers. "You know what we said in the jury room?" Robert Hosford questioned the eelebrating well-wishers. "We said let's go out and give him his Christmas present. Let's make him happy this Christmas. He wasn't last Christmas." He then told how they had voted on the verdict and come to a unanimous decision within ten minutes.

Asked why they had not then returned their verdict when they returned to the Courtroom for recess adjournment, Hosford replied that a number of the jurors were worried that if they returned the verdict then, there would be so much activity that they would not get a chance to eat. "I wanted to go back then and relieve this man of his suspense," he continued, "but we decided finally to wait until after lunch." He told how before they left for lunch, Byrd, put the insanity form in his pocket and threw the others down on the table. When they returned from lunch, they held another vote and then filled out the form before signaling their readiness. Asked which testimony had the most impact on the jurors, Hosford replied, with affirmation from the other jurors present, that it was that given by John Rogers and George Conners. "The way the Prosecutors hounded and browbeat Conners," he stated, "he stood up under it for two days without changing his testimony in three words, and when a man can do that, he's telling the truth."

Before leaving the courtroom, Elston had repeated Remus' claim to reporters that the suddenness with which the verdict was returned indicated that, had the jury been offered a straight acquittal option, they would have chosen that, and Hosford backed this up. "If we could have acquitted him clean we surely would have done so. We decided that the man had been persecuted long enough." While Hosford was relating his story, Elston entered the room, having finally managed to escape from the throng in the courtroom. Remus immediately seized his co-counsel's hand and complimented him on the way he had handled the case. Elston modestly replied that he had the benefit of "a most able associate." "No sir," answered Remus, "I was a most unruly client."

Remus then gave a statement to the press: "Thank God for a verdict that lifts the greatest burden man must ever stand." He then thanked the jury, the Court and the sheriffs, even managing to say thank you to the prosecutors whom he had harangued for over five weeks. "God alone knows the thing that is in my heart at this moment,"he continued. "The rest of my life I will dedicate to stifle the insult that is upon our statutes known as the national prohibition act. Had there been no prohibition law to fill the coffers of a class that seeks only and practices only venality there could have been no act for which a jury of my peers would have to acquit me."

After making this statement, Remus posed for the photographers. Many of the photographs taken showed him in conversation with and shaking hands with a number of the jurors, as well as his daughter Romola and his co-counsel, Charles Elston. One of these jurors, twenty two year old Ruth Cross, told him:that the jurors were with him from the start. She explained that as the trial went on and more evidence was introduced she began to pity Remus and hate the prosecutors. "I thought Remus must have been insane when he killed her,"she said, adding that even if he wasn't insane, she still believed he was justified in doing what he did.

While this celebration was going on in the jail, a smaller more subdued group were gathering in the prosecutor's office. Harry Brown and Grace Campbell, Mrs. Remus' brother and sister, refused to answer reporters' questions, but Taft issued the following statement: "To characterize the verdict as a gross miscarriage of justice is to us a trite expression and is utterly inadequate to express half the truth of so nauseating a situation." Off the record he said that it was "all in a day's work.and we take our lickings as they come."

Back in Chicago Remus' first wife was also being besieged by reporters. She was pleased when she received the news, and she told the reporters that she had been confident throughout the trial that her ex-husband would be exonerated. "He was incited to do those things by the actions of his wife and Dodge," she said, "and I am delighted that the jury saw the true state of affairs."

Although Remus had been acquitted on a charge of murder, he now had to face an insanity hearing in the Probate Court to determine whether he was insane at the time of the trial. Within thirty minutes of the verdict being passed in Judge Shook's Courtroom, the papers for the insanity hearing were already being filed with Judge William Lueders, but he claimed that he would not even look at them until the following day. Remus also faced a hearing on the Contempt of Court charge, and this, along with the fact that Ohio Law did not permit bail to persons awaiting sanity hearings meant that Remus had to remain in jail at least until the sanity hearing. When asked how long the sanity hearing was likely to take, Judge Lueders told reporters that the last one had lasted thirty three days. This was an intimation that Remus could expect to spend both Christmas and New Year's Eve in jail. But on the 20th of December 1927 those were the least of Remus' worries. He had escaped the electric chair, and he was ecstatic. All evening he ran around shaking hands and slapping his friends on the back, shouting: "They did it on the first ballot and it was unanimous. Think of that!"

An out-of-town newspaper correspondent who had covered important trials throughout the country described the Remus trial as the "damndest thing I ever saw," and he asked: "Is that the way they always do things down here?"

WEDNESDAY, DECEMBER 21ST

With Remus still in jail and eager to get out, Elston wasted no time in appealing to Judge Lueders of the Probate Court for an immediate insanity hearing. After discussing Elston's plea with the attorneys from another case due to be heard in the Probate Court, Judge Lueders scheduled the Remus hearing for December 28th, and he appointed three alienists, Dr. H.D. Mc Intyre, Dr. Thomas Battliff, and Dr. Herman Hoppe, to examine Remus. This meant that Remus would have to spend Christmas in jail as Judge Lueders also denied an appeal for bail.

The following day the Remus trial jurors presented a petition to Judge Lueders asking him to release Remus on bond or to grant him an immediate hearing. The petition stated that when the jury returned their verdict they did so "after a careful consideration of the facts," and they sought "to have the defendant returned to his mother and family by Christmas." However, Judge Lueders would not change his mind.

A couple of days later the former jurors presented another petition, this time on behalf of John Berger. Addressed to Judge Shook, it stated that they had "fully believed" the testimony given by John Berger and had based their acquittal upon it. Therefore they requested that the perjury charges against Berger be dropped forthwith. The petition enraged Judge Shook, who immediately declared Berger to be in contempt of Court. He charged Berger and the former jurors to appear before him on December 27th, at which time Berger was fined $250 and sentenced to ten days in jail on the contempt charge and released on $1000 bail.

Judge Shook was furious, and he strongly reprimanded the jurors. He declared: "The petition is an insult to the Court and a palpable attempt to influence and sway the Court. The Remus jury had no right to act in this case. This assails not only the integrity of this Court, but it flaunts common decency and is based upon a lack of respect for the Courts." The jurors, one by one, humbly apologized. Berger denied having anything to do with the petition, but he still apologized to the Court.

THE TRIAL - THE WRAP UP

On December 28th, 1927, Remus appeared before Judge Lueders in the Probate Court where he was compelled to take the stand. Remus explained that if he had intended to shoot someone that morning in October he would have organized a better getaway by hiring a driver who would not leave him at the site. He pointed out that the only time he had ever run afoul of the law, before the shooting, was on bootlegging charges, and he took pains to point out that the government was his partner when he was selling liquor, taking $2.20 in taxes for each gallon he sold.

When asked if he had ever referred to himself as being greater than Napoleon, he replied that that was ridiculous. He did mention, though, that when he was in Chicago some lawyers nicknamed him the "Napoleon of the Bar," but he declared that he was not responsible for what other people might call him. He then denied that he had demanded to be taken to the White House for an audience with President Coolidge, although he did acknowledge that he was the subject of discussions between Senator Reed of Missouri and the President.

In an ironic twist, Dr. David Wolfstein was called as a witness for the defense. In fact, the entire hearing seemed unprecedented. In the murder trial Remus fought to prove that he was insane, and when the Court alienists stated that he was sane, he fought them, attacking their professional opinions at every stage. On the other hand, Prosecutor Taft and his assistants, tried to show that Remus was sane, and they upheld the views of the Court alienists. Now the tables were turned. Remus was put in the position of arguing that he was sane, and his best evidence was the alienists' report which he had so strongly attacked only days earlier. Taft, on the other hand, wanted to establish that Remus was insane and should be sent to the state mental asylum at Lima for as long as possible.

Dr. Wolfstein testified that he still considered Remus to be sane. He pointed out that Remus had conducted his own defense during the murder trial and displayed considerable legal knowledge and mental capability. He declared that although he had at no time considered Remus to be "a psychopathic personality," be believed that Remus "could be vile" and was a dangerous man. He characterized Remus as "ruthless, reckless, selfish, eccentric; the kind of man who takes the law into his own hands; a man of irregular tendencies, with a leaning toward the criminal side."

Dr. Charles Kiely also testified that he thought Remus was dangerous; while Dr. Baber refused to give his opinion on that subject. He claimed that he had agreed to testify to the fact that Remus was sane and that is what he would testify to.

Remus' mother, dressed in black and speaking in her native tongue, German, insisted that her son was a good man ,"worth gold," and had never hit her or any other member of his family. She obviously did not think that he was dangerous.

The three Probate Court alienists appointed by Judge Lueders to study Remus reported that although they found Remus to be sane, they did find him to be a "psychopath and therefore a dangerous individual to be at large." They described him as "unmoral, lacking a sense of ethics, emotionally unstable, being subject to unrestrained outbursts of temper and rage and egocentric to a pathological degree."

On December 30th, Judge Lueders found Remus "insane and a dangerous person to be at large." He committed him to the Lima State Hospital for the Criminal Insane until such time as he was judged to be sane and no longer a threat to society. Judge Lueders obviously realized that he would be attacked for practically ignoring the findings of the six alienists who, although finding Remus dangerous, declared him sane, and he defended his decision by accepting full responsibility for it. "The law rests with me," he announced. "It directs the Court to call in medical witnesses, but in the last analysis it is up to the Probate Court to decide from all the evidence in the case whether Remus is sane."

Remus told the reporters that the decision would be appealed. "It's the most humorous decision I've ever known in my whole life, a humorous joke, a farce," he said. Then turning to the testimony of the alienists who had testified to his being dangerous, he told the reporters that they "had better have their minds examined. This shows that they are self confessed perjurers. They say something in one Court and a few days later they come into another Court and say something different." In conclusion, he declared that the Judge's decision was simply ludicrous. "It strikes me as being one of the nine wonders of the world."

Even as Remus was talking to reporters, Charles Elston was busy preparing his appeal. His immediate course of action was to file a writ of habeas corpus in the Common Pleas Court, stating that there was no law that entitled a Judge to confine a person simply because he was dangerous and that therefore Remus was being unlawfully restrained of his liberty. He also filed a motion with the Probate Court the following day in which he requested a new sanity hearing and the release of his client on bail. Judge Lueders refused the request for bail and declared that he would hear the motion on the following Tuesday.

On January 6th, exactly three months after he shot and killed his wife in Eden Park, Remus entered Lima State Hospital. He and Charles Elston had left Cincinnati in the company of two Deputy Sheriffs immediately after Common Pleas Judge Charles Bell dismissed their petition for writ of habeas corpus. Judge Bell pointed out that, according to Ohio law, when Remus was acquitted on the sole grounds of insanity this decision became the "prima facie evidence of the insanity of the person named," and "in the absence of any evidence to the contrary, the Probate Court would be warranted in immediately committing the person so acquitted to the Lima State Hospital." He pointed out that it had not even been necessary for Judge Lueders to appoint Probate Court alienists to study Remus before he made a ruling. He stated that he did not have before him the evidence placed before Judge Lueders because a writ of habeas corpus was not the same as a writ of errors, but it was obvious "from the opinion and order of the Probate Court that Remus failed to prove to the satisfaction of that Court that he was sane at the time of the hearing."

Remus and Elston decided to go directly to Lima, where they expected to get a fairer hearing, and file amother writ of habeus corpus.At Lima Remus was assigned to a ward at the hospital where he would remain under observation by the hospital physicians as well as three private doctors hired by Remus.

Remus finally went before the Allen County District Court of Appeals on February 1st and applied for a writ of habeas corpus claiming that "He was unlawfully restrained of his liberties by detention in the Lima State Hospital." The State argued that only Dr. W. H. Vorbau, Superintendant of Lima State Hospital for the Insane was authorized to release Remus. They cited Section 1998 of the Ohio code which authorized the Superintendant to keep an inmate in the hospital "until such time when he shall be restored to reason, or until otherwise discharged by due process of law." Remus' lawyers cited the State constitution (article 1:8) "the privilege of the writ of habeas corpus shall not be suspended, unless in case of rebellion or invasion, the public safety requires it."

On March 1st, after listening to two weeks of testimony, the three Judges of the Court of Appeals announced that they would take the petition under advisement and would announce their decision within another couple of weeks. On March 20, the court found that the petitioner was not insane and ordered his discharge from the Lima State Hospital. Remus was elated; Taft wasn't. He announced: "I am very much disappointed, but the fight to keep Remus behind bars will go on." And it did. E.M. Botkin, Allen County Prosecutor asked for a stay of judgment on the grounds that the Court of Appeals was without jurisdiction.

On March 30th, Remus was granted a writ of habeas corpus which meant that he could look forward to freedom within a couple of days, pending the results of an appeal by the State attorneys. The County Prosecutor, E.M. Botkin announced that he would defiantly ask for a stay of judgement or a new trial. or failing that he would appeal to the Ohio Supreme Court on the grounds that the Court of Appeals in Lima did not have jurisdiction over the case. Charles Taft declared his dissatisfaction with the result and made a plea to the Lima authorities to not allow him out on bail."The fight to keep Remus behind bars will go on" he declared. Two of the three Appeal Judges defended their decision stating that Remus was obviously sane but they harshly attacked the initial trial verdict which had ultimately led to this final "showdown". "It may be," they announced, "that the verdict in the trial at Cincinnati, which verdict acquitted the petitioner on the sole ground of insanity at the time he committed the homicide, was a miscarriage of justice. We frankly say that if his mental condition was, at the time he committed the homicide, as it was shown to be at the time of the trial before us, the verdict was a most flagrant and reprehensible outrage of judicial administration, which cannot be too strongly condemned."

Finally, on June 20, 1928, almost six months since he entered Lima Hospital for the Insane, won his freedom. The Ohio Supreme Court by a four to three vote confirmed the decision of the Court of Appeals and ordered his release, and Attorney General Taylor announed that he would not appeal the case to the United States Supreme Court.

"It's wonderful. It's wonderful. I'm going back to Cincinnati and make my home there," a jubilant Remus told the reporters.

So ended the clash between two American gladiators in the home of the brave and the land of the free.

The jury's verdict on December 20th may have delighted Remus' friends and supporters, but many people who had followed the course of the trial declared it a travesty of justice. Even Judge Shook was critical of the verdict. He doubted if the jurors could "in nineteen minutes go through all the evidence in the case." He told the jurors: "This verdict you rendered was not supported by the evidence." The managing editor of the Cincinnati *Times-Star* also was critical of the jury, charging that "They tried the Volstead Act, Dodge, Mrs. Remus--in fact anything non-pertinent , but did not seem to know that they were trying the defendant."

Most of the newspaper editors deplored the decision in their editorials. The Cleveland *Plain Dealer* asserted: "Justice flew out of the window when the Remus jury at Cincinnati retired to vote its verdict. The evidence counted for little. Jurymen were sorry for the ex-bootlegger who shot his wife and decided to make him a Christmas present." The Chicago *Daily Tribune* ended its editorial: "Nevertheless the moral of the case lies in the words the judge used in summing it up. 'The law does not justify one person taking the life of another because the latter may be of bad moral character.'"

The Indianapolis *Star* declared that the verdict gave Cincinnati justice "a black eye." It argued that "the average jury was just much too willing to accept the emotional testimony and plea rather then the dry professional evidence provided by the experts. The jury ignored justice and reason and based its findings on maudlin and mistaken sympathy." The Cincinnati *Times-Star* declared that this sort of "mawkish sentimentality" was not only a problem in Cincinnati but was a problem inherent throughout the United States and was something that urgently needed to be addressed. The Cincinnati *Enquirer* asked "Why is expert testimony called for in the judicial proceedings if it is to receive no more attention than the jury gives to the conjectures of lay witnesses who may imagine a person to be insane because of his overt actions and without experience with or study of the mental actions of that person , and without training or ability to make such study."

In reaction to the Remus verdict the National Crime Commission, headed by Newton D. Baker, appointed a special committee to study the subject of juries and the insanity plea. Mrs. Richard Derby, daughter of ex-President Theodore Roosevelt, headed the committee, which reported : "The utter absurdity of entrusting the difficult determination of the mental responsibility of an accused person for his acts to twelve laymen, admittedly unable to pass on the question from their own knowledge or training has been made so manifest in the recent trial of George Remus in Cincinnati as to lead this committee to make this special report." They recommended the "removing of the determination of the sanity of the accused from the jury and placing it in the hands of disinterested qualified experts in the study of mental diseases."

Also the Cincinnati Bar Association called a special meeting and appointed a committee to seek a better means of selecting veniremen. and The Cincinnatius Association lauched an investigation of rumors to the effect that it was customary to call only a certain group and that many juries were composed of repeaters.

Taft stated years later: "I would record one most desirable result of the Remus verdict. The outcry against the system that could produce such a jury was so loud that the Common Pleas judges revised the system completely and called in two well-known business men to draw the names that went into the wheel for the sheriff to pull out. Ever since that day our juries in both civil and criminal matters have been of high average ability and integrity, and the system of handling them is most economical and satisfactory." The procedure to be followed in pleas of not guilty by reason of insanity were repealed and currently "If a defendant enters a plea of not guilty by reason of insanity. The court may order one or more, but not more than three, evaluations of the defendant's mental condition at the time of the commission of the offense." (Section 2945.39 Ohio Revised Code)

After his release from Lima, Remus began a new phase of his life, that of a relatively respectable citizen. The contempt charges that were brought against him during his trial were dropped on July 5th, 1928, and the deportation proceedings against him were dormant. However, the District Attorney, Haveth Mau, continued to dog him on unpaid income taxes. On December 14, 1928 Remus was sued for $158,235.03 and costs for unpaid taxes of 1918 and 1921. On January 25, 1929 Remus compromised his tax assesments withthe government and was discharged of all tax liens against him which totaled $374,175. The District Attorney did not give up that easily, though, and in April 1930 he issued a writ against "the goods and chattels" of the former bootlegger, claiming that the fine was imposed on him during sentencing in the 1922 Prohibition trial. He had been trying to obtain this money since before the murder trial, but he was repeatedly unsuccessful in this attempt.

Whether Remus continued bootlegging or not is debatable. He certainly did not amass a fortune like he had in his heyday, but reports filtered into the Justice Department about him beginning his operation again with Johnnie Gehrum as his partner.

He spent the final years of his life in Covington, Kentucky, with his former secretary, Blanche Watson still by his side, only this time, as his wife. Here he formed the Washington Construction Company, which was set up mainly to redevelop the ten acres of land on which his mansion stood in Price Hill. The mansion was torn down and the land subdivided into smaller units. The swimming pool remained as a public pool for many years.

Remus and his third wife spent a quiet life in their modest house on Greenup street in Covington, with Remus spending his time between his office, the Cincinnati Gymnasium where he worked out every morning, and the various racetracks in Cincinnati, Cleveland and Baltimore. Occasionally he was mentioned in the newspapers, normally in connection with money that he felt was owed to him by people he had been associated with during his bootlegging days. One of these was a claim filed against the estate of Edward J. O'Hare, one of his partners in the Jack Daniels scam, who was shot dead in Chicago in 1939 and whom Remus claimed had tricked him out of his rightful share of the Jack Daniels profits. None of these attempts succeeded.

In August, 1950, Remus suffered a severe heart attack at his home in Kentucky, and five months later he slipped into a coma from which he never recovered. He died on January 20th, 1952, with his wife and daughter, Romola, by his side. The funeral service was held at the Immanuel Baptist church in Covington and as the Reverend Morris Coers, delivered the sermon, stressing the biblical passage "He that is without sin among you, let him cast a stone." Remus' body lay in an expensive, silver and gold plated casket, lined with rich blue velvet and surrounded by two whole carloads of flowers. The funeral was attended by thirty mourners, most of them past associates of the man who had once been the King of the Bootleggers.

Charles P. Taft II tried to make the best of the situation.. He sent a telegram to his father claiming only that Remus had been "declared insane," perhaps hoping that this would give an impression of victory, when it was actually the best decision the defense could legally obtain.

In his report about his term in office, he stressed the percentage of cases he had won, neglecting to mention the loss of the one that was possibly the most important of his career - The Remus Murder Trial. He wrote a catharsis motivated article entitled "So This is Justice!" in which he placed some of the blame on the public's favoring the unwritten law, and he made an unwise political move by attributing some blame for the Remus verdict on German American citizens of Cincinnati, claiming that "they have in their hearts a resentment aginst prohibition that is a condition not a theory," and that "For this group Remus appears as a genial individual of their own race, who generously supplied them with good whiskey." Seeking to be optimistic, Taft expressed the hope "that the case is bound to produce some good if the lessons taught by it are thoroughly absorbed by the public and by our lawmakers."

He was soundly defeated in his bid for nomination for a second term by the regular Republican candidate, Nelson Schwab. For the next ten years he did not enter the political arena, but then he was elected to the Cincinnati City Council, on which he served: 1938-42, 48-51, and 55-77. From 1955 to 1957 he was the Mayor of Cincinnati. In 1952 he was the Republican Party's candidate for the governship of Ohio, but he lost to the incumbent, Frank Lauche.

During World War II he resided in to Washington D.C. where he served as Assistant Director of Health, Education, and Welfare, and was a member of the President's War Relief Board, In 1942 he moved to the State Department as Director of the Wartime Economic Affairs Agency. He also was instrumental in getting the Reciprocal Trade Agreement passed.

Deeply interest in religon, Charlie Taft served as the first and only lay president of the Federal Council of Churches and was a delegate representing the Episcopal Church at the First Assembly of the World Council of Churches. He was also very active in the international YMCA movement. During his long career of public service, he served as chairman, fund-raiser or legal counsel for every cause he considered worthwhile, and there were many of them. He died on June 24, 1983.

It is futile, but interesting, to speculate on what his political career might have been if he had succeeded in convicting Remus.

SOURCES

Abbreviations: CA *Chicago American*, CE *Cincinnati Enquirer*, CT *Chicago Tribune,* CP *Cincinnati Post,* CTS *Cincinnati Times-Star,* CCT *Cincinnati Commercial Tribune,* CPD *Cleveland Plain Dealer,* CDN *Chicago Daily News,* IN *Indianapolis News,* IS *Indianapolis Star,* LCJ *Louisville Courier Journal,* SLPD *St. Louis Post Dispatch,* NYT *New York Times,* Senate Investigation *Senate Investigation of Hon. Harry M. Daugherty, Former Attorney General of the United States*, C.T. Charles Phelps Taft 2nd , W.H.T. William Howard Taft

Book One: THE GLADIATORS

Chapter One: **Napoleon of the Chicago Bar**

1 Remus' biography is based primarily on the official report of the alienists at his murder trial. Other sources include the documents in the Remus file (No. 55438/947) in the Department of Labor, Bureau of Immigration, Thirteenth Census, City Directories of Cincinnati and Chicago, and Remus' testimony at the Senate Investigation of former Attorney General Harry M. Daugherty.

3 "the most he ever earned" Remus File-Department of Labor-No. 742/13 Dec. 15, 1926

4 "the weeping, crying Remus" CE Dec 9 1927
"There has been a lot" NYT December 19, 1927
"I want to say" CDN October 17, 1913

5 "We will prove that" CA June 26, 1914
"A condition in which" Ibid
"May God forgive me" CDN October 17, 1913
"I'll kill you!" CA February 28, 1914
"Was a good woman" Ibid
Commenting on the verdict, the State's Attorney, Stephen Malato, sarcastically remarked:"It's too bad John Wilkes Booth and Guy Fawkes didn't have time to avail themselves of the distinguished services of the medical experts of their time. Why hang when the woods are full of psychic specialists and medical experts who can find ready excuses for any murderer?" CA May 4, 1914

6 "Napoleon of the Chicago Bar" NYT December 28, 1927

7 "Hasn't supported me" CDN Feb. 5, 1919 At this time the Remus household included a Swedish maid, Clara Young, *13th Census of the United States*
"On that Holmes woman" CE Jan. 22, 1952
"he doesn't drink but" CDN Feb. 5, 1922

Chapter Two: **King of the Bootleggers**

8 "John Barleycorn Born Almost" CT January 17, 1920

9 "for medicinal purposes" Ibid
"The force of prohibition" Willebrant, Mabel *Inside Prohibition* p.301
"that there were scores" Ibid

10 "I went into it" CCT-Dec. 13, 1925

"the two jews" SLPD January 3, 1926
"If I want to" CMTR May 25, 1922
11 The party was eventually described in various papers. e.g. CT October 7, 1927; CP May 7, 1979] CE January 22, 1952 CP January 2, 1932 Newspaper clipping in Cincinnati Historical Society files-gift of Elizabeth Kellog, May 12, 1952 In a letter written just four days after the party, William Harrison asked Attorney General Daugherty:"Is this man bold to the extent of absolute defiance of the laws and the flouting of your Department? The daily newspapers of January 2nd,-1922 contain accounts of Remus' dedication of a swimming pool here, said to have cost upward of $100,000,00, at which hundreds were present and during which bacchanalian revels, unheard of heretofore in these parts and seasoned by unlimited flow of 'good liquor' were hilariously referred to. The cost of all this, in 'refreshments', decorations and imported nymphs is said to have exceeded five figures. And where were the law guardians during this modern saturnalia? Honestly, don't you think it about time to get busy?" (National Archives, file no. 23-1707-8)
13 "the big leak" Willebrant, Chapter 3, p.41 ff.
"greatest single source of" Ibid
16 "If reports are true" CCT May 24, 1922
17 "Go back to New York" *Saturday Evening Post* Sept 10, 1949, p.57
"very, very active" CE September 8, 1949
18 "may seem a large" Senate Investigation p. 2410
"I now felt that" SLPD Jan. 8, 1928
"there go the whiskey" Ibid
"tear the heart out" On January 24, 1922 Prohibition Commissioner Haynes in a letter marked "Personal and Confidential" to Assistant Attorney General Mabel Willebrant quoted from a letter he received from William Nimo, the general agent assigned to assist Prosecutor Clark in the Remus case. Nimo interviewed former associates of Remus who informed him that "Remus has been moving large quantities of whiskey without proper permits, due to the fact that he has been able to bribe certain Federal Agents. Mr. Remus brags a great deal, about his connections, both in the National and the State Capital, and has boasted that he would tear the heart out of Washington if he was crowded too far." Treasury Department Office of Federal Prohibition Commissioner (National Archives Wash. D.C.)
"enough money in the" SLPD Jan 3, 1926
"why not at all" SLPD Sunday Magazine Jan 8, 1928

Chapter Three: **The Raid**
20 "I am tired of" CE Aug. 3, 1921
"why is it that" Ibid
"if there is any" Ibid
21 "realized for the first" CP October 23, 1921
"separates the sheep from" Ibid October 26, 1921
22 "all good citizens" Ibid
"draw the net tight" Ibid October 23, 1921
23 "All about that big" Ibid October October 26, 1921

"no stone will be" Ibid October 23, 1921

24 "Mr. James Clarke, the former" Senate Investigation p. 2418

Chapter Four: **The "Dry Laws" Trials**

26 "I only wish that" CE November 1, 1921

"That amount is excessive" Ibid

27 "It is inconceivable that" Letter to Attorney General Daugherty from Wm Morrow January 5, 1922 (National Archives)

"affadavit, naming or describing" Search Warrant Section 10496 1/4c

29 "But we expect the" Quoted in District Court of U.S. vs. George Remus et al. (no.2142) p.3 (National Archives-Great Lakes District.) Assignment of Error.

29 "a great many men here" CCT May 12, 1922

"came to the farm" Ibid

31 "five or six times" CCT May 17, 1922

"didn't mean anything without" CCT May 14, 1922

32 "didn't know it was" CCT. CCT May 16, 1922

33 "All you saw, you" CCT May 17, 1922

33 "I wonder what percent" CCT May 19, 1922

"whatever you might think" Ibid

34 "We have just scratched" Ibid

†This is not a" Quoted in Assignment of Error, no. 2142 p.11U.S. District Court, Cincinnati

"They did not bring" CCT May 17, 1922

"I say that our" Ibid

"the financial head of" CCT May 17, 1922

35 "but I say to" Ibid

"I have been engaged" CCT May 17, 1922

36 "a little dryer" Ibid

"the way of the transgressor" Ibid

35 "These men were getting" CCT May 14, 1922

37 "The conviction is there" Senate Investigation p. 2421

"there is no likelihood" Ibid

38 "Remus had been improperly" Ibid p. 3233

Chapter Five: **The Federal Penitentiary**

39 "is being treated like" Atlanta *Constitution* March 13, 1926

41 "Remus further told me" (Letter of Franklin Dodge to J. Edgar Hoover) Deparment of Justice files)

Chapter Six: **The Senate Investigation**

42 "Jesse Smith knew so much" CT December 21, 1926; Although most people did not believe Smith was murdered, few people believed that he took his own life because of ill health. "After the Senate investigation a rather widespread opinion prevailed that he was confronted with exposure of his alleged grafting operations and committed suicide either to escape possible punishment or to avoid the mental anguish and ignominy of being cast off by his friends." NYT December 19, 1926

43 "in the best mental" Senate Investigation p.2394
"the grestest comedy" Ibid p. 2400
"scruple of liquor ever" Ibid p. 2400
"we do not feel" NYT May 15,1926
44 "pass whiskey saloon every" NYT May 15, 1926
"Prohibition is a football" NYT June 18, 1926
"glorified personal servant" Senate Investigation p. 3295
45 "craved liberty and caught" Affadavit by George Remus August1984
"the assertion that either" CT Aug 30, 1924
"I am ready to stand" CCT Sept. 3, 1925
48 "Damn'em $5,000 won't work" Letter from John G. Marsahll to Mabel Willebrant-Dept. of Justice Sept. 2, 1925 (National Archives)
"you told me to" SLS Nov. 16, 1927
"Never have such matters" Ibid
49 "he will, if not" CE June 22, 1952
""My wife must have"CCT Sept. 2, 1925
"Crime does not pay" CCT Sept. 3, 1925
"like a bolt from" SLS Nov. 16, 1927
"the best and most"η Ibid

Chapter Seven: **"Milking" the Jack Daniels Distillery**
53 ""after it is all" SLPD Dec. 14, 1925

Chapter Eight: **The Case of Jack Daniels**
58 "You don't know George" SLPD Dec. 15, 1927
59 "the most worried man" Ibid
60 "We feel that there" IN Dec. 16,1925
"thrill and excitement" SLPD Dec. 16, 1925
"In your opinion is it" IN Dec. 16,1925
61 "We are called upon" U.S. District Court Indianapolis, Indiana CRH 2878 (National Archives-Great Lakes District)
62 "put whiskey on the market" Dec. 17,1925
"one of the biggest" SLPD Dec. 31, 1925
"This doesn't look like" Ibid

Chapter Nine: **Marital Strife**
63 "thrashed out in a divorce" IN Dec. 18,1925
"I would not be" *Congressional Record: 69th Congresss 1st Session. (1926)p.6174*
"Their conduct in the" Ibid
"travelling around the country" Ibid
65 "The charges are absolutely" Letter from Franklin Dodge to Congressman La Guardia (April 8, 1926)
66 "George Remus is an atheist" Ibid
"The files of the Bureau" Memoradum from J. Edgar Hoover to Attorney General Daugherty. April 24, 1926
67 "a small cell where" LCJ Dec. 19, 1927
"I set out to make" Asssociated Press Release # 2009

68 "My husband, George Remus" Remus File (55438/947) Dept. of Labor Dec. 22,1926

Chapter Ten: **In his Father's Footsteps**

70 "He had big, dark eyes" Taft, Mrs. William Howard, *Recollections of Full Years* p. 37
"he is so full" Mrs. Taft to W.H.T. Feb. 3, 1904
"he behaves pretty well" Ibid Feb. ? 1904
"he insists on running" W.H.T. to C.T. Jan. 7, 1903
71 "As to Charles, he" W.H.T. to Mrs. Taft Feb. 7, 1904
"Bob who came in" Ibid Sept. 14, 1906
"We call him the" *Esquire* Nov. 30, 1986
72 "just as notional" Quoted in Ross, Ishabel *An American Family: The Tafts–1678 to 1964* p. 131
"I am the Governor" C.T., *Democracy in Politics and Economics* p.40
74 "He rushed around the ship" Mrs. Taft *Recollections* p. 156

Chapter Eleven: **The White House Gang**

76 "remarkable for his calmness" Looker, Earle *The White House Gang* p.13.
"to confound all rules" Ibid
"It's all very sporting" Ibid p.17-19

Chapter Twelve; **Around the World**

78 "Compliments to Hon. W.H.T." Murray, Robert H. *Around the World with Taft* p.40.
"servants in imperial livery" Ibid p. 71

Chapter Thirteen: **Prep School Days**

82 "To give the boys" *Taft School Catalogue*
"In scholaship I am" Quoted in Ross, p. 275
83 "feel such interest and" Quoted in Patterson, James T. *Mr. Republican: A Biography of Robert Taft* p. 30
"all the class honors" NYT Dec. 17, 1911

Chapter Fourteen: **The President's Son**

84 "If Charlie Taft the" NYT July 4, 1908
85 "Our children were already" Taft, Mrs. W.W. *Recollections* p. 330
"go sailing and play tennis" Barker, Charles E. *With President Taft in the White House.* p.32
"no place for kids" Ibid
86 "If there is any" NYT April 4, 1909
"I was committing hari-kari" Manning, Helen Taft "My Brother Robert Taft" *American Magazine* p. 104
87 "I'd just grab hold" CE June 4, 1978
"Let them have a" Butt, Archie, *Taft and Roosevelt* p. 173
"Charlie is never quiet" Ibid

Chapter Fifteen: **Coming of Age**

91 "I would regret it" W.H.T. to C.T. May 30, 1917
"I am not ambitious" W.H.T. to Newton Baker August 31, 1917
92 "And now Charlie dear" W.H.T to C.T. April 9, 1918
"where shell holes overlapped" C.T. to his mother April 6, 1918
"It is quite a feeking" C.T. to his wife April 4, 1918
93 "Our prayers go with you" W.H.T. to C.T. March 24, 1918
"I suppose one ought" C.T. to his wife April 4, 1918
"That tall, attractive young"" Gen Harbord to W.H.T May 2, 1918
"Your namesake Charlie is" W.H.T to Charles P. Taft Sept. 16. 1918
94 "I was somewhat disappointed" W.H.T to C.T. May 7, 1918
"Staff job in GHQ." C.T. to Helen Taft April 1, 1918
"In spite of the hopes" C.T. to his mother Oct. 8, 1918

Chapter Sixteen: **A Young Lawyer**

96 Cincincatus See *Cincinnati's Citizens Crusade A History of the Cincinatus Association* by Louis Leonard Youer
97 "There is no Republican" CP June 25, 1983
"The sheriff and Prosecutors" Abstract of an address of Charles P. Taft 2nd Candidate for County Attorney at Avondale School, July 14, 1926 (Cincinatti Historical Society Archives) p.1
"if the Citizen's Ticket" Ibid
"the fairest way" CE June 4, 1978
98 "has become an attorney" Looker, Earle, *The White House Gang,* p.64
"wiser than most in" Archie Butt *op cit* p. 326
"If we had been" Manning, Helen Taft, *op cit* p.105
"it is very full of humor" W.H.T. to Mrs. Taft Oct. 5, 1904
99 "a career of great promise" *Remarks of Judge Stanley Strube at the Initiation into Office of Charles P. Taft 2nd as Prosecuting Attorney of Hamilton County, Ohio Jan. 3, 1927* (Historical Society of Cincinnati Archives)
"Taft family ought to" Ibid
"No person convicted of" NYT March 13, 1922

Book Two: THE GLADIATORS

Chapter Two: **Pre-Trial Preparations**

108 "If she had a safety" NYT Oct. 12, 1927
109 "You know I love you" NYT Oct. 9, 1927
"travelling around together" Ibid
"Remus' idea of a defense" W.H.T to C.T
110 "This case must be tried" Letter from Judge Shook to the press (filed in Hamilton County County Clerk's office)
112 "We expect to prove" CPD Nov. 13, 1927
"anyone who thinks I'm insane" SLPD Oct. 8, 1927

Chapter Three: **Jury Selection**

"the method of selection ought" CPD Nov. 4, 1927

"Women jurors will first ask" NYT Oct. 13, 1927
115 "Remus the lawyer is fighting" CE Nov. 14, 1927
"In the Court room I'm" CTS Nov. 19, 1927
"I've been in the same" CE Nov. 14, 1927
"Remus, unscrupulous as the devil" W.H.T to C.T. Oct. 23, 1927
116 "I hope your next birthday" CPD Nov. 14, 1927
"this man Conners, called Remus' lieutenant" SLS Nov. 16, 1927
"It is ridiculous to think that" CPD Nov. 15, 1927
"The claim of the defense" CE Nov. 16, 1927
117 "If these alienists conclude" SLS Nov. 16, 1927
"that every law-abiding person" CPD Nov. 15, 1927
"moral turpitude is not affected" SLPD Nov. 15, 1927
118 "Was the accused a free agent" CPD Nov. 15, 1927
119 "There never was a case" SLS Nov. 15, 1927
"The press is here" CE Nov. 15, 1927
"So far as I know" Ibid
"A nice statement to be made" NYT Nov. 15, 1927
"It has been the pleasure" Ibid
"five hundred judges and lawyers" NYT Nov. 19,1927
"Man, if I had you" CE Nov. 19, 1927
"Get back on your side" NYT Nov. 19, 1927
"When you were on the" Ibid
"not for the benefit" CE Nov. 19, 1927
121 "Did I make an impression?" Ibid
"They may bind Remus" NYT Nov. 20, 1927
122 "a bullet in there for" Ibid
"I have lived with" SLPD Nov. 21, 1927

Chapter Four: **November 21st**

123 "Each side will be limited" Judge Shook's insructions filed by County Clerk, Hamilton County, Ohio.
"Your Honor, I have" NYT
"The State's evidence will show" CE Nov. 21, 1927
"approached his wife, who" Ibid
"It was deliberate and premeditated" CE Nov. 22, 1927
124 "We will introduce evidence" SLPD Nov. 21, 1927
"that the killing was with" Ibid
"at the time of the" Ibid
125 "He learned the truth" CE Nov. 21, 1927
"We expect to show" Ibid
"For God's sake don't" SLPD Nov. 22, 1927
126 "crouching, not just kneeling" Ibid
"stood perfectly still until" Ibid

Chapter Five: **November 22nd**

127 "something in his hand" SLPD Nov. 22, 1927
30 "Not any I know of" (Klug's interrogation is reported in the CE Nov. 22, 1927)

"Didn't we tell you" SLPD Nov. 22, 1927
129 "Do I understand your mind" CPD Nov. 22, 1927
"We have got nothing" Ibid
131 "Any witness in this case" Ibid
"On the contrary it will" Ibid

Chapter Six: **November 23rd**
132 "We gave Klug a long" SLPD Nov. 24, 1927
133 "it will be shown that" SLPD Nov. 24, 1927
"must show first there was" CPD Nov. 24, 1927
134 "Thankful! Yes a million times" CE Nov. 24, 1927

Chapter Seven: **November 24th**
135 "These books have saved" SLPD Nov. 25, 1927
"It cost me several hundred" SLPD Dec. 13, 1927
"my inclination will be" CPD Nov.25, 1927

Chapter Eight: **November 25th**
"Mother opened the taxicab door" CT Nov. 26, 1927 (Ruth's testimony is quoted in CT, CPD and CE)
138 "Well, He had men" CT Nov. 26, 1927
"They had three cars" Ibid

Chapter Nine: **November 26th**
139 "Basing our conclusion upon" SLPD Nov. 27, 1927
140 "I have just done some" NYT Nov. 27, 1927
141 "Remus would become much worked" CE Nov. 27, 1927
142 "He talked incoherently and" CPD Nov. 27, 1927
"just as though he" NYT Nov. 27, 1927

Chapter Ten: **November 28th**
143 "There must be independent evidence" SLPD Nov. 29, 1927
"That beautiful little daughter" CPD Nov. 29, 1927
"beat his clenched fists" NYT Nov. 29, 1927

Chapter Eleven: **November 29th**
145 "Did you ever see"; SLPD Nov. 30, 1927
"Yes sir, I did"; Ibid
"facts, whether proved true"; SLPD Nov. 30, 1927
146 "Did you see her"; CE Nov. 30, 1927
"Yes, she left with"; Ibid
"Mr. Remus will never" CPD Nov. 30, 1927
"wringing his hands, uttering:" NYT Nov. 30, 1927
"We would be talking" CPD Nov. 30, 1927
"raved, and raved, amd raved" Ibid
147 "That man Dodge has taken" NYT Nov. 30, 1927
"His muscles were contorted" Ibid

"He left my office" Ibid

Chapter Twelve: **November 30th**

149 "Don't you know the furniture" SLPD Dec. 1, 1927
"How many truckloads did" Ibid
150 "if Marshall formed any opinion" Ibid
"If those things would not" Ibid
151 "My God, could it be?"CPD Dec, 1, 1927
"He was in an agitated" Ibid
"from that time on" Ibid
152 "he was more than" CPD Dec. 1, 1927

Chapter Thirteen: **December 1st**

153 "Remus at once flew" SLPD Dec. 2, 1927
"His strugtgles were so violent" Ibid
"I promised to use my influence" Ibid
"I urged the parole" Ibid
154 "Everytime I told him something":SLPD Dec. 2, 1927
"his eyes bulged out" Ibid
155 "We all had private" CE Dec. 2, 1927
"little bundle of sweetness" CPD Dec. 2, 1927
"You are known as" SLPD Dec. 2, 1927
156 "Not until I got up here" Ibid
"Remus would often bluff" Ibid
"Who ate the cheese?" CPD Dec. 2, 1927
"There wasn't a man down" Ibid
"You're the man who drank" NYT Dec. 2, 1927
157 "a promoter of high class" SLPD Dec. 2, 1927
"lay bare some very" Ibid
"she wouldn't even take" NYT Dec. 2, 1927
"Remus was absolutely insane" SLPD Dec. 2, 1927
"Your wife and her heavy lover" CPD Dec. 2, 1927
"I told Remus his wife" NYT Dec. 2, 1927
158 "I thought Mr. Remus" Ibid
"His manner was dramatic" CPD Dec. 2, 1927

Chapter Fourteen: **December 2nd**

159 "Is it your opinion" SLPD Dec. 3, 1927
"He was insane up" Ibid
"If the prosecution gets cute" Ibid
"I figured they would discount" Ibid
"Now, Mr. Taft I'm talking" Ibid
"Isn't it true that" Ibid
160 "Did you control him?" Ibid
"Is Remus sane now?" SLPD Dec. 3, 1927
"Then shooting his wife" Ibid
"I would think so" Ibid

"Even though Mr. Dodge" Ibid
"In my opinion he" Ibid
"Remus can bear comparison" SLPD Jan. 3, 1926
161 "On that subject" SLPD Dec. 3, 1927
"Oh Daddy don't kill" Ibid
"I ran and he followed" Ibid
"That's what I get" Ibid
"His neck swelled up" Ibid
"It's driving me mad" Ibid
162 "One minute Remus would" Ibid
"I formed the opinion" CPD Dec. 3, 1927
"His memory was very clear" SLPD Dec. 3, 1927
"It was sufficient to convict" Ibid
"I wasn't on the jury" Ibid
"raved and threw his" Ibid
163 "she was only fit" Ibid
"I base it principally" Ibid
"I'm gone! I'm gone!" Ibid
"What did he mean" Ibid
"I told him he was going" Ibid
164 "Dodge fairly skated across" NYT Dec. 3, 1927

Chapter Fifteen: **December 3rd**
165 "Remus flew into a rage" SLPD Dec. 4, 1927
"If I get hold of her" CPD Dec. 4, 1927
"stroked his face and broke" SLPD Dec. 4, 1927
166 "anything that was brought" Ibid
"He was ill for" Ibid
"I prevented myself from" Ibid
167 "I'll settle things right" CT Dec. 4, 1927
"She is in the legitimate" Ibid
"make it very thorough" NYT Dec. 4, 1927
168 "My mother had not" CT Dec. 4, 1927
"as if they had forgotten" Ibid
"He has long believed" Ibid

Chapter Sixteen: **December 5th**
169 "The entire civilized world" CE Dec. 6, 1927
"issued a stream of publicity" Ibid
"if any contempt was committed" Ibid
"Remus does not dare" Ibid
"Remus is not taking" Ibid
"I heard Remus prompting" SLPD Dec. 6, 1927
"The press has indulged" CE Dec. 6, 1927
170 "It kept Remus, myself" Ibid
"If we are going into" SLPD Dec. 6, 1927
"Don't you know that" Ibid

171 "Didn't George Remus tell" Ibid
"Knowing conditions at Atlanta" Ibid
"unless they were given" CE Dec. 6, 1927
172 "He did tell me that" Ibid
"Remus is a man who" CE Dec. 6, 1927
"We will bring Judge" NYT Dec. 6, 1927

Chapter Seventeen: **December 6th**
173 "Practicall all off my grand" Dec. 7, 1927
174 "With the St. Louis crowd" CPD Dec. 7, 1927
"It wasn't a St. Louis" Ibid
"there is a way to do it" CE Dec. 7, 1927
"propound and couch and objection" Ibid
"My life is at stake" Ibid
"trying to administer justice" Ibid
"would take from her every shred" Ibid
175 "Did John H. Bruffell offer" Ibid
"I made an offer" Ibid
"In the settlement she got" Ibid
"I think any lawyer who" Ibid
"Where were you when" Ibid
"When did you form" Ibid
"He became worse and worse" Ibid
176 "Nothing hurts me more" Ibid
"would rave and carry on" Ibid

Chapter Eighteen: **December 7th**
177 "wished somebody would beat" SLPD Dec. 8, 1927
"If I see him tonight" CE Dec. 8, 1927
"I followed him several times" SLPD Dec. 8, 1927
178 "Your Honor, can we have" Ibid
"there burst from his throat" CE Dec. 8, 1927
"My God I can't" CPD Dec. 8, 1927
"We find that Mr. George Remus":SLPD Dec. 8, 1927

Chapter Nineteen: **December 8th**
180 "Your Honor, I want to apologize" CE Dec. 9, 1927
"I would have to hurry" CPD Dec. 9, 1927
"I told him if his wife" Ibid
"How many have you killed" (Truesdale's questioning is recorded in the CE Dec. 9, 1927)
181 "A mere intention to commit" CE Dec. 9, 1927
182 "the sage of the" NYT Dec. 9, 1927
"that this great humanitarian" Ibid
"surely the Chief Justice's son" Ibid
"His reputation as a lawyer" CPD Dec. 9, 1927
"Don't you know he" SLPD Dec. 9, 1927

"I know he was a" Ibid
"I would not regard" CT Dec. 9, 1927
183 "Don't you know that" Ibid
"I would not regard it" Ibid
"I know a good many" CP Dec. 9, 1927.
"no apologies to make" NYT Dec. 9, 1927
"consider his reputation for peace" CT Dec. 9, 1927
184 "Yes, I consider it good" Ibid
"Don't, I'm glad to tell" Ibid
"never got a dime" Ibid

Chapter Twenty: **December 9th**
"He wasn't the same" SLPD Dec. 10, 1927
"He looked wild and" Ibid
"He was standing there" Ibid In a letter by (name blocked out) he charged "Remus shortly after the National Prohibition act became operative, went into the bootlegging business with an Italian named (blocked out) and he was subsequently indicted in Chicago for conspiracy to violate the national prohibition act, this case never went to trial, as it was fixed by Judge Joe Le Buy for a large sum of money, and the files in the possession of the government were stolen from the District Attorney's office in Chicago." Letter from Savannah, Georgia, Nov. 24, 1926 to Immigration Inspector, Cincinnati. (file no. 435/947 Reference to this allegation was also made by Senator Burton Wheeler in the Investigation of Harry Daugherty. " the information that comes to us is to the effect that Remus paid two checks of $60,000 dollars each for the purpose of squashing a case against him in Chicago."p.3232
186 "An argument started and" CPD Dec. 10, 1927
"he was going to kill" CE Dec. 10, 1927
"Was the name of Dodge" Ibid
187 "All the money in" Ibid Ibid
"Was Mrs. Remus in love" CT Dec. 10, 1927

Chapter Twenty One: **December 10th**
188 "that Remus was especially" W. H.T. to
"was sane-entirely sane" CE Dec. 11, 1927
"one of the finest and" Ibid
"a man wants to fight" CE Dec. 11, 1927
189 "if that is insanity" Ibid
"I was the star" SLPD Dec. 11, 1927
190 "I understand from good" CE Dec. 11, 1927

Chapter Twenty Two: **December 12th**
191 "to establish a reputation" CPD Dec. 13, 1927
"That statement comes with" Ibid
"That is a mistake" CE Dec. 13, 1927
"the Court has said" Ibid
192 "did not restrain his" Ibid

"He said he shot" Ibid
193 "No, George Remus will" Ibid
"Not for one moment":Ibid
"From his behavior I" Ibid
"Yes, if I could get" NYT Dec. 13, 1927
"that decomposed mass of clay" CE Dec. 13, 1927
"tortured for two years" NYT Dec. 13, 1927
194 "Let everything go in" Ibid
"J.P.Alexander and George Remus" CE Dec. 13, 1927
"in accordance with section" NYT Dec. 13, 1927
"I guess you heard me" Ibid
195 "Your request herein made" Ibid
"intended to be bothered" Ibid

Chapter Twenty Three: **December 13th**
196 "novices in the Prosecutor's office" CE Dec. 14, 1927
"The jury must be blind" Ibid
197 "One or two tables" Ibid
"That is my recollection" Ibid
"Were ther any highball" Ibid
"There were no highball" Ibid
"in a way he did" Ibid
198 "I couldn't say" Ibid
"courteous, intelligent, coherent and" Ibid
199 "My sister cried and" CPD Dec. 14, 1927
"that she did not" NYT Dec. 14, 1927
"He threatened many times " Ibid
"They always talked about" Ibid
"crack a skull. I'll see" Ibid

Chapter Twenty Four: **December 14th**
201 "these three novices" CPD Dec.15, 1927
"This has gone far" Ibid
"I apologize to the Court" Ibid
"The Court will listen" CE Dec. 15, 1927
"I don't want to hear" CPD Dec. 15, 1927
"unless he testified as" SLPD Dec. 15, 1927
"This man Shaw came" Ibid
202 "John Marcus has been" CE Dec.15, 1927
"The prosecution has been conducted" SLPD Dec. 15, 1927
"The defendant from the start" CPD Dec. 15, 1927
"No one realizes more" NYT Dec. 15, 1927
"no personal feelings either" CPD Dec. 15, 1927
203 "not put it down" SLPD Dec. 15, 1927
"affidavidts were placed with" Ibid
"that the prosecutor proceeded" CE Dec. 15, 1927
204 "Many in jail didn't" CE Dec. 15, 1927

"Mother reprimanded him" CE Dec. 15, 1927
"I went into the room" Ibid
"One summer we were" Ibid
"Mother tried to do things" SLPD Dec. 15, 1927
205 "I am selling almost all" CE Dec. 15, 1927
"and not the kind of woman" Ibid
"We want the facts to go" Ibid
"The next afternoon I saw" Ibid
206 "I had given her a" Ibid
"Leaving now for Hamilton" Ibid
"He had a mean, angry" SLPD Dec. 15, 1927

Chapter Twenty Five: **December 15th**
208 "I won't use the words" CE Dec. 16, 1927
209 "an air of leadership" CE Dec. 16, 1927(The entire 4, 500 word report of the alienists was published in the CE and is also filed with the Clerk of Court, Hamilton County, Ohio.)
"feeling the strain of the" Ibid
"the responsibility was not" Ibid
210 "felt a halo about" NYT Dec. 16, 1927
"whether or not I go" Ibid
"When did you make" CE Dec.16, 1927
"When I saw her" Ibid
"expressions of violent hate" NYT Dec. 16, 1927

Chapter Twenty Six: **December 16th**
211 "Did George Remus know" CE Dec. l7, 1927
"in an insane manner" Ibid
"at least 100 times" Ibid
212 "In these three episodes" CPD Dec. 17, 1927
"What used to be called" SLPD Dec. 17, 1927
"There is considerable disagreement" CE Dec. 17, 1927
"I can't qualify as" Ibid
"would hesitate to say" NYT Dec. 17, 1927
213 "Didn't Mr. Remus tell you" Ibid
"Not exactly in those" Ibid
"We must first define" NYT Dec. 17, 1927
"just the reverse of" CE Dec. 17, 1927
"any prolonged deviation from" Ibid
214 "an abnormal condition of the mind" Ibid

Chapter Twenty Seven: **December 17th**
215 "depressive maniacal psychoses" CE Dec. 18, 1927
"combination of fear and rage" Ibid
216 "not guilty on sole" CT Dec. 18, 1927
217 "the most atrocious murder" CPD Dec.18,1927
"Conners said the Government" CE Dec. 18, 1927

"Remus was a fine publicity" CT Dec. 18, 1927
"Remus wasn't afraid of that" SLPD Dec. 18, 1927
"Those were tough babies" Ibid
"he knew what we" Ibid
"he will throw a fit" CPD Dec. 18, 1927
218 "on Oct. 6 George Remus"CT Dec. 18, 1927
"most famous co-respondent in" LCJ Dec. 18, 1927
"Is there a better" Ibid
"There is only one statement" CE Dec. 18, 1927
"Never was a murder more" Ibid
"It's either a case of" CPD Dec. 18, 1927
"there will be just one" CT Dec. 18, 1927
"What was she going" CE Dec. 18, 1927
"Blanche Watson, who had" Ibid
"Where is one solitary" Ibid
219 "If they had as": Ibid
"When Remus came to Cincinnati" CE Dec. 18, 1927
"They say she had" Ibid
"They say she was" Ibid
"They try to make Franklin" NYT Dec. 18, 1927
220 "You had your opportunity" CE Dec. 18, 1927
"the Ellis case involved" CPD Dec. 18, 1927
"Fancy yourself in prison" Ibid
"I have been under subpoena" CPD Dec. 18, 1927

Chapter Twenty Eight: **December 19th**
222 "the dirty rotten skunk" SLPD Dec. 20., 1927
"because he didn't dare" CE Dec. 20, 1927
"Why did he hide?" Ibid
"Remus' testimony would only" Ibid
"They call Remus a publicity" CPD Dec. 20, 1927
223 "you jurors do not need" Ibid
"with nothing but a little" SLPD Dec. 20, 1927
"Never in history or fiction" LCJ Dec. 20, 1927
"there never was a clearer" CE Dec. 20, 1927
"on the nasty, dirty" CT Dec. 20, 1927
224 "Make this a good Christmas" CE Dec. 20, 1927
"Here before you stands" SLPD Dec.20. 1927
"apply your common sense" CE Dec. 20, 1927
"so noble and beautiful" SLPD Dec. 20, 1927
"that ace among dry" CT Dec. 20, 1927
"But who wouldn't in my" CE Dec. 20, 1927
"not for all the money" LCJ Dec. 20, 1927
225 "This defendant started life" NYT Dec. 20, 1927
"one of the greatest" CE Dec. 20, 1927
"The prohibition law is making" NYT Dec. 20, 1927
226 "and the names of 200" CT Dec. 20, 1927

"Oh! That social leper" LCJ Dec. 20, 1927
"Are you protecting that" CE Dec. 20, 1927
"penny cuff buttons" Ibid
"I have suffered the torture" LCJ Dec. 20, 1927
227 "The defendant does not desire" NYT Dec. 20, 1927
"Did Remus take the stand" CPD Dec. 20, 1927
"That's loyalty, isn't it" Ibid
"Both sides have indulged" Ibid

Chapter Twenty Nine: **December 20th**
229 "What's this all about" CTS Dec, 21, 1927
"If your place was robbed" Ibid
"just an excuse to get" Ibid
"The issue in this case" Ibid
"Remus was the little boy" CE Dec. 21, 1927
"Ever see an insane" CTS Dec. 21, 1927
230 "There is no short" Ibid
"three horsemen who galloped" CTS Dec. 21, 1927
"Remus deliberately stepped into" Ibid
"even if she were wrong" Ibid
"If you want to do right" Ibid
"She couldn't be George Remus'" CTS Dec. 21, 1927
"She was Queen of the Bootleggers" Ibid
232 "The Court, upon careful consideration" NYT Dec. 21, 1927
"should find that the defendant" Ibid
"because the latter may be" CT Dec. 21, 1927
233 "We the jury, on": CE Dec. 21, 1927
"I wanted American justice" NYT Dec. 21, 1927
"I was prevented this morning" CPD Dec. 21, 1927
"Not guilty-hurray!" CE Dec. 21, 1927
234 "You know what we said" SLPD Dec. 21, 1927
"I wanted to go back" CE Dec. 21, 1927
"The way the Prosecutors" Ibid
"If we could have" Ibid
235 "a most noble associate": Ibid
"Thank God for a verdict" CT Dec. 21, 1927
"God alone knows the thing" CE Dec. 21, 1927
"That was the first" Ibid
"I was with you" SLPD Dec. 21, 1927
"I thought Remus must" CT Dec. 21, 1927
"To say that this was" CT Dec. 21, 1927
"all in a day's work" CE Dec. 21, 1927
"He was incited to do" CT Dec. 21, 1927
236 "They did it on the first" CE Dec. 21, 1927
"Damnest thing I ever" Ibid

Chapter Thirty: **December 21st**

237 "after a careful consideration" CTS Dec. 22, 1927
"to have the defendant" Ibid
"The petition is an insult" NYT Dec. 22, 1927

Chapter Thirty One: **The Wrap-Up**

239 "Napoleon of the Bar" CT Dec. 29, 1927
"a psychopathic personality" NYT Dec. 29, 1927
240 "ruthless, reckless, selfish, eccentric" Ibid
239 "psychopath and therefore dangerous" Ibid
"insane and a dangerous" Ibid
"The law rests with me" CT Dec. 29, 1927
"It's the most humorous" NYT Dec. 31, 1927
"had better have their minds" Ibid
"It strikes me as being" Ibid
241 "prima facie evidence of the insanity" SLPD Jan.6, 1928
"from the opinion and order"
"He was unlawfully restrained" NYT Dec. 31, 1927
242 "that the petitioner was not"
"I am very much disappointed" NYT March 30, 1928
"The fight to keep Remus" NYT March 30, 1928
"It may be that the verdict" Ibid
"It's wonderful-it's wonderful" NYT June 20. 1928
243 "in nineteen minutes go through" NYT Jan. 28, 1928
"The verdict you rendered" Ibid
"They tried the Volstead" Hubert Taft to W.H.T. Dec. 22, 1927
"Justice flew out of the window" CPD Dec. 22, 1927
"The law does not justify": CT Dec. 22, 1927
"the average jury was"
"Why is expert testimony" CE Dec. 21, 1927
"The utter absurdity of entrusting" *The Literary Digest* "How to Avoid Remus Verdicts" (June 27, 1928 p.14)
"removing the determination of" Ibid
244 "I would record one most desirable" Taft, *City Management* p. 169
"If the defendant enters a plea" Ibid
245 "they have in their hearts" Taft, Charles P. 2nd, "So this is Justice" *World Work* May, 1928 pp. 96-97
"that the case is bound" Ibid

Bibliography

Asbury, Herbert, *The Great Illusion: An Informal History of Prohibition* Doubleday & Co. Garden City, New York, 1950

Barker, Charles E. *With President Taft in the White House* A. Krock and Sons, Chicago. Illinois 1947

Beatty, Jerone "The Other Taft" *American Magazine*, July 1947

Butt, Archie, *Taft and Roosevelt: The Intimate Letters of Archie Butt, Military Aide* 2 volsa. Doubleday, Doran and Co. New York, 1936

"Charlie Taft's Big Chance", *Fortune,* August, 1947

Duffy, Herbert Smith *William Howard Taft* Minton, Balch New York 1930

Green, Ben A. *Jack Daniel's Legacy* Shellbyville, Tennessee 1967

Haynes, Roy A. *Prohibition Inside Out*, Doubleday New York 1923
Hearings before the Senate Committee on Investigation of the Attorney General Washington D.C. 1924

Hess, Stephen *American Political Dynasties From Adams to Kennedy* Doubleday & Co Garden City, New York, 1966

Investigation of Hon. Harry M. Daugherty, Formerly Attorney General of the United States, Washington D.C.: Governement Printing Office

Kraft-Ebing Dr. R Von *Text Book of Insanity Based on Clinical Observations For the Practitioners and Students of Medicine* Philadelphia, Penna. F.A. Davis Co. 1904

Literary Digest "How to Stop Remus Verdicts" June 23, 1928

Locker, Earle *The White House Gang*, Revell, New York, 1929

Manning, Helen Taft, "My Brother Robert Taft" *American Magazine* January, 1952

Mellin, William J."I was a Wire Tapper" *Saturday Evening Post* September 10, 1949

Morison, Elting E (ed.) *The Letters of Theodore Roosevelt* 8 vols. Cambridge University Press & Harvard University Press, Oxford University Press, Cambridge, Mass. and London, England

Murray, Robert H. *Around the World with Taft,* F. B. Dickerson Co. Detroit, Michigan, 1909

North Eastern Reporter Comprising all the Current Decisions of the Supreme Courts of Ohio, Illinois, Indiana West Pubklishing Co. St Paul, Minnesota, 1928

Pringle, Henry F. *The Life and Times of William Howard Taft* Farrar & Rinehart, New York, 1939

Ross, Isabel *An American Family: The Tafts--1678 to 1964* The World Publishing Company, Cleveland, Ohio, 1964

Taft, Charles P. 2nd *City Management: The Cincinnati Experiment*, New York: Farrar & Rinehart Inc. 1933

---------------- *Democracy in Politics and Economics*, New York: Farrar, Straus, and Young Inc., 1950

---------------- *Why I am for the Church*, New York: Farrar, Straus and Co. Inc., 1947

---------------- *You and I---and Roosevelt*, New York: Farrar & Rinehart, Inc. 1936

Taft, Horace Dutton, *Memories and Opinions*, New York: The Macmillan Company, 1942

Taft, Mrs. William H. *Recollections of Full Years*, New York: Dodd, Mead, and Co. Inc. 1914

Tierney, Thomas Y. *Darrow:A Biography* Thomas Y Crowell, New York 1979

Willebrant, Mabel *The Inside of Prohibition* The Bobb-Merrill Co. Indianapolis, Indiana 1929

Index

N

O

P

Q

R

V

W

Z